Praise for

The War That Made America

"A tale with many facets . . . Anderson writes with intelligence and vigor. He has given us a rich, cautionary tale about the unpredictability of war." —*The New York Times Book Review*

"Well-written, well-organized and well-illustrated . . . All this makes for a great story. . . . Anderson's admirable project is a reminder that if the long ago conflict he so ably depicts had gone another way, the newspaper you're reading now would likely be written in French."
—*The Wall Street Journal*

"Short does not mean simplistic. Skillful . . . Compelling . . . This is history at its finest." —*The Star Telegraph*

"*The War That Made America* is an important introduction to a forgotten war, and a fascinating chapter in the life of a Founding Father long before he became a dad." —*The Albany Time Union*

"A smartly written history of the Seven Years' War in America. . . . Lucid and swift-moving . . . Anderson's book will awaken interest in a critically important period in colonial history." —*Kirkus Reviews*

"The author of the award-winning, scholarly account *Crucible of War* offers a scaled-down, popular version of that history in this companion volume to the PBS documentary. . . . An excellent introduction to a conflict that most Americans know little about. . . . Like the best popular historians, Anderson combines exhaustive research and an accessible prose style in a volume that should help rescue the French and Indian War from historical obscurity." —*Publishers Weekly*

"An outstanding account of a frequently misunderstood war."
—*Booklist*

"This vibrant, sweeping history . . . deserves a place on the bookshelf of every American."
—Gary B. Nash, author of *The Unknown American Revolution*

ABOUT THE AUTHOR

Fred Anderson is a professor of history at the University of Colorado, Boulder. He is the author of *A People's Army: Massachusetts Soldiers and Society in the Seven Years' War*, winner of the 1982 Jamestown Prize; *Crucible of War: The Seven Years' War and the Fate of Empire in British North America, 1754–1766*, which won the Francis Parkman and Mark Lynton prizes in 2001; and, most recently (with Andrew Cayton), *The Dominion of War: Empire and Liberty in North America*.

THE WAR THAT MADE AMERICA

A Short History of the French and Indian War

FRED ANDERSON

Illustrations chosen and captioned by

R. Scott Stephenson

PENGUIN BOOKS

PENGUIN BOOKS

Published by the Penguin Group
Penguin Group (USA) Inc., 375 Hudson Street, New York, New York 10014, U.S.A.
Penguin Group (Canada), 90 Eglinton Avenue East, Suite 700, Toronto,
Ontario, Canada M4P 2Y3 (a division of Pearson Penguin Canada Inc.)
Penguin Books Ltd, 80 Strand, London WC2R 0RL, England
Penguin Ireland, 25 St Stephen's Green, Dublin 2, Ireland (a division of Penguin Books Ltd)
Penguin Group (Australia), 250 Camberwell Road, Camberwell,
Victoria 3124, Australia (a division of Pearson Australia Group Pty Ltd)
Penguin Books India Pvt Ltd, 11 Community Centre,
Panchsheel Park, New Delhi – 110 017, India
Penguin Group (NZ), cnr Airborne and Rosedale Roads, Albany,
Auckland 1310, New Zealand (a division of Pearson New Zealand Ltd)
Penguin Books (South Africa) (Pty) Ltd, 24 Sturdee Avenue,
Rosebank, Johannesburg 2196, South Africa

Penguin Books Ltd, Registered Offices:
80 Strand, London WC2R 0RL, England

First published in the United States of America by Viking Penguin,
a member of Penguin Group (USA) Inc. 2005
Published in Penguin Books 2006

Copyright © War That Made America Productions LLC
and French and Indian War 250, Inc., 2005
All rights reserved

THE LIBRARY OF CONGRESS HAS CATALOGED THE HARDCOVER EDITION AS FOLLOWS:
Anderson, Fred
The war that made America : a short history of the French and Indian War /
Fred Anderson.
p. cm.
Includes index.
ISBN 0-670-03454-1 (hc.)
ISBN 0 14 30.3804 4 (pbk.)
1. United States—History—French and Indian War, 1755–1763. I. Title.
E199.A595 2005
973.2'6—dc22 2005050397

Printed in the United States of America
Maps by Jeffrey L. Ward

Except in the United States of America, this book is sold subject to the condition
that it shall not, by way of trade or otherwise, be lent, resold, hired out, or otherwise
circulated without the publisher's prior consent in any form of binding or cover
other than that in which it is published and without a similar condition
including this condition being imposed on the subsequent purchaser.

The scanning, uploading and distribution of this book via the Internet or via any other means
without the permission of the publisher is illegal and punishable by law. Please purchase only
authorized electronic editions, and do not participate in or encourage electronic piracy
of copyrighted materials. Your support of the author's rights is appreciated.

To some gaffers in Fort Collins

Preface

Today, two hundred and fifty years after the French and Indian War, most Americans are no more familiar with its events and significance than they are with those of the Peloponnesian War. Few know that George Washington struck the first spark of a war that set the British North American frontier ablaze from the Carolinas to Nova Scotia, then spread to Europe, Canada, the Caribbean, West Africa, India, and, finally, the Philippines. Historians call this immense conflict the Seven Years' War; with great justice and characteristic vigor, Winston Churchill described it as "the first world war." It overthrew what had been stable balances of power in both Europe and North America and helped to foster a secessionist rebellion in Britain's North American colonies. That the man who triggered the war by trying to project British power into the heart of the continent should have gone on to lead an American revolutionary army and then to serve as the first president of the United States is surely one of the greater ironies in a national history that abounds in them.

This book, and the television series it accompanies, tells the tale of the little-known war that helped to shape George Washington into a man capable of playing the role he ultimately did in American history. But Washington is only a part of the story. In bringing to an end the French empire in North America, the French and Indian War undermined, and ultimately destroyed, the ability of native peoples to resist the expansion of Anglo-American settlement. The war's violence and brutality, moreover, encouraged whites—particularly those on the frontier—to hate Indians with undiscriminating fury. In the prewar world of competing empires, Indian-hating had of course been far from unknown. Yet it had never been so indiscriminate, if only because backwoods settlers knew that their survival could easily hinge upon making accurate distinctions between friendly and hostile groups. The widespread Indian-hating that the French and Indian War engendered would be reinforced by the War of Independence and contribute to the formation of American cultural identity, sanctioning the removal or annihilation of native peoples as necessary to the advance of civilization.

In that sense the story that this book tells is not merely of the French and Indian War as a prelude to the American Revolution with which we are familiar—the struggle for liberty against oppression, rights against power, independence against subjugation. It is a darker story than that: one in which imperial ambitions produce unpredictable, violent results; in which victory breeds unanticipated disasters for the victor; in which the evidently benign growth of a population of peaceable farmers leads to the wholesale destruction of native peoples. This one is as much a part of American history as the brighter, more familiar, more comfortable story of rights defended and liberty maintained, which is the usual way we think of the birth of our Republic. That both stories meet in the person of George Washington is a fact worth remembering as we seek to understand the causes, character, and consequences of a war no one wanted, but which nonetheless transformed the colonists' world forever. It is not too much to call it the war that made America.

Contents

Illustrations and Maps

ILLUSTRATIONS IN THE TEXT

COLOR INSERT

page

Prologue: New York, July 1776

Worse times lay ahead—far worse—but George Washington did not know that on July 20, 1776, when he finally found time to answer the letter his old comrade Adam Stephen had written more than two weeks earlier. Ordinarily the general, a punctual correspondent, would have replied more quickly to the man who had once been his second-in-command of the Virginia Regiment, and who was now a colonel in the Continental Army. But the last few months, and the last few weeks in particular, had been a time that tried Washington's soul as severely as any since the war began. Lately he had barely had time to perform his official duties, much less attend to his private correspondence.

Washington had arrived in New York on April 13 as a hero—the most famous man in North America, and perhaps in the English-speaking world. In the summer of 1775 he had taken command of the Continental Army and directed its first great sustained operation against the British, the Siege of Boston, to a successful conclusion. Impatient of the celebrations and ceremonies that followed, he had lingered only a week after the British abandoned the city in March, before moving his headquarters to New York. There, as he knew only too well, a magnificent harbor, central location, and water access to the interior via the Hudson River would give his adversary, General William Howe, an ideal base of operations. Since no one knew when the enemy might appear, Washington had set to work immediately to prepare New York's defenses.

George Washington, **by Charles Willson Peale, 1776.** *John Hancock commissioned this portrait during Washington's brief visit to Philadelphia in May 1776 to confer with Congress regarding the defense of New York. Peale, who four years earlier had commemorated Washington's French and Indian War service in another portrait, now included in the background an image of Boston, recently evacuated by the British army.* (Brooklyn Museum)

Nothing had gone smoothly or well. The complex topography of river, harbor, and islands made the area around the city of New York hard to defend, and the thousands of men whom Washington needed to build fortifications had been slow to arrive. As usual, discipline had been a problem, especially among the militiamen on whom he had to rely for much of his manpower. He had been plagued, as always, by shortages of arms and supplies. With the ceaseless application of energy and effort, matters had gradually improved through May and June. But on June 22, just as things were looking up, a nest of Loyalist conspirators had been uncovered. The organization, which allegedly included (among others) the mayor of New York City and eight Continental soldiers, had been passing large quantities of counterfeit currency, provided by British agents who hoped to undercut public confidence in the Continental Congress's paper money. Two of the suspected soldiers, in jail, were overheard to speak of a plot to assassinate Washington and raise an insurrection at the moment British invasion forces arrived. Both men were members of Washington's personal guard.

Washington ordered one of the men, Thomas Hickey, to be tried by court-martial on the twenty-sixth. The court found him guilty and condemned him to die. Perhaps twenty thousand soldiers and civilians turned out on June 28 to watch Hickey swing from the gallows on Bowery Lane. The next day they watched an even more dramatic spectacle unfold as more than a hundred Royal Navy warships and transports sailed into the lower harbor and anchored off Sandy Hook.

As Washington's men worked feverishly to complete their fortifications, dispatches arrived from Canada reporting that the Continental expeditionary force (which had seized Montreal the previous year but had suffered heavily from desertion and smallpox) had been defeated with heavy losses. Abandoning the Saint Lawrence Valley, the Continentals were in retreat toward Lake Champlain, where they hoped to regroup at Crown Point in time to resist an expected invasion. Washington sent a trusted subordinate north to prevent the collapse of the army, but in reality he could do even less in that distant quarter than he could in Manhattan. On July 3 he watched helplessly as thousands of redcoats disembarked on Staten Island, which they fortified to receive the reinforcements who were soon to follow. By the twelfth another 150 sail of naval vessels and transports had arrived, bearing fifteen thousand more troops. This brought Howe's strength up to about twenty-five thousand men, almost twice the number under Washington's command. No one needed to tell him that they were also far better trained, equipped, and supplied than his own raw troops.

In the midst of it all, copies of the Declaration of Independence arrived from Congress at Philadelphia. Washington had ordered the whole army to parade on July 9 and directed that his officers read the document to each regiment, to cement among his men the sense that they were fighting not merely to force Britain to recognize their rights, but to create a nation

A View of the Narrows between Long Island and Staten Island, with Our Fleet at Anchor and Lord Howe Coming In, 1776. *A British military artist sketched the British fleet lying off Staten Island as the Howe brothers—General William and Vice Admiral Richard—prepared to launch their assault on New York.* (Spencer Collection, The New York Public Library, Astor, Lenox, and Tilden Foundations)

of their own. Morale did, in fact, improve. That evening a mob of soldiers and townsmen celebrated Independence by pulling down the equestrian statue of George III that had stood on Bowling Green. But whatever rise in spirits the Declaration occasioned was soon undone, for Washington, at least, by his army's first brush with the enemy. On the twelfth the British almost offhandedly ran two frigates, an armed schooner, and a pair of tenders past the American batteries and sailed them up the Hudson as far as the Tappan Zee. There they had anchored, with God knew what mischief in mind, severing Washington's communication by water with Albany and the northern army. Half his cannoneers had not reached their positions until the ships were out of range. Those who did had fired in a frenzy, showering nearly two hundred rounds on the passing vessels without inflicting appreciable damage. Except, that is, to themselves: several half-trained crews, forgetting to sponge the bores of their guns between firings, suffered deaths and maiming wounds when the charges exploded prematurely.

We know that these forbidding developments preoccupied Washington as he replied to Colonel Stephen's letter, for he described them in detail. One might assume that Independence was on his mind, too, yet he made no mention of it. Instead, surprisingly, he concluded with this:

> I did not let the Anniversary of the 3d or 9th of this Inst[an]t [month] pass of[f] with out a grateful remembrance of the escape we had at the Meadows and on the Banks of Monongahela. [T]he same Provedence that protected us upon those occasions will, I hope, continue his Mercies, & make us happy Instruments in restoring Peace & liberty to this once favour[e]d, but now distressed Country. Give my Complim[en]ts to the Several of y[ou]r Corps of my acquaintances and believe me to be D[ea]r Sir
>
> Y[ou]r Most Obe[dien]t Ser[van]t,
> Go: Washington

With responsibility for preserving the independence that Congress had just declared pressing more directly on him than on anyone else in America, in other words, the commander in chief of the Continental Army was thinking less about the future of the United States than about his personal history. The specific experiences that came to mind were those that he and Stephen had shared more than twenty years before: defeat at the Battle of Fort Necessity on July 3, 1754, and defeat when under the command of General Edward Braddock at the Battle of the Monongahela, on July 9, 1755.

It may not seem obvious why Washington, under enormous stress and facing the most daunting challenges of his life, should have paused to make "grateful remembrance" of the twin disasters that began his military career. Yet for Washington, as for many other middle-aged Americans in 1776, the benchmarks of meaning by which present circumstances could be measured had been fixed by experiences in the Seven Years' War—the conflict that British colonists called "the late French war," and which would come to be known as the French and Indian War. The central public event of his life, as for a whole generation of his contemporaries, had been Britain's destruction of New France and its seizure of the eastern half

New York July 20th 1776.

Dear Sir

Your Letter of the 4th Inst. came duly to hand — I thank you for yr kind congratulations on the discovery of the vile Machinations of such vile Ministerial agents. — I hope the untimely fruit of their Intentions will in the end recoil upon their own heads — all the Measures heretofore projected, has done so I think; except in Canada, where an unaccountable kind of fatality seems to have attended all our movements since the death of poor Montgomery. —

We have a powerful Fleet under the Command of Lord Howe in full view of us distant about 8 Miles from this City — the Troops (from the best Acct. amounting to about Eight or nine thousand Men) are upon Staten Island, fortifying themselves and waiting the Re-inforcement from England, which every fair wind is expected to bring. — this Reinforcement from different Acct. will be from Fifteen to 20,000 Men. — Our Strength greatly inferior

George Washington to Adam Stephen, July 20, 1776. *Washington penned this letter to Colonel Adam Stephen, his comrade in the French and Indian War, amid frenzied preparations for an attack. "We have a powerful Fleet under the Command of*

unless the New Levies come in much
faster than they have done, which I hope
will be the case as harvest will soon be
over and that Plea, at an end.—

Two Ships on the 12th, to wit the
Phoenix of 44. Guns & Rose of 20, exhibited
a proof of the incompetency of Batteries
to stop a Ships passage with a brisk
wind & strong tide where there are no
obstructions in the water to impede their
motion — the above Ships pass'd through
an incessant Fire from our Batteries
without receiving much damage — they
were each hulled several times & their
Rigging a little damaged but not so as
to retard their way up the River to
what is called the Tappan bay a wide
part of the River out of reach of Cannon
shot from either shore. — here they now
are, having cut of the Water Communica
tion with Albany, & our Army on the
Lakes, entirely.—

I did not let the Anniversary
of the 3d or 9th of this Instt. pass of with
out a grateful remembrance of the
escape we had at the Meadows and on

Lord Howe in full view of us," Washington noted before recalling shared wartime experiences twenty years before. (Emmet Collection, Miriam and Ira D. Wallach Division of Art, Prints and Photographs, The New York Public Library, Astor, Lenox, and Tilden Foundations)

the Banks of Monongahela.—the same Providence that protected us upon those occasions will, I hope, continue his Mercies, & make us happy Instruments in restoring Peace & liberty to this once favourd, but now distressed Country.— Give my Complim.ts to the Several of y.r Corps of my acquaintances and believe me to be D.r Sir

Y.r Most Obed.t Serv.t

Go: Washington

[illegible] Emmet Collection, Manuscripts and [illegible] Division of Art, Prints and Photographs, The New York Public Library, Astor, Lenox and Tilden Foundations of North America. That stunning victory—by which, Britons on both sides of the Atlantic believed, their nation gained the most glorious empire since Rome's—had changed their world forever, shaping the convictions of colonists no less than those of their countrymen across the sea. And in ways that no one quite understood, that very victory had also created the conditions of the empire's demise, in only a little more than twelve years' time.

Because Washington the Revolutionary hero is so familiar to us, we sometimes find it hard to imagine how he grew into that role. Yet long before he became a revolutionary, George Washington had been a soldier of the British empire, seeking to extend the authority of his king into the heart of the continent. Frontier warfare and the martial values of British imperialism had shaped his views and actions as a young man, while his survival in battles that had left hundreds of men dead and wounded convinced him that "Providence" (a term he tended to prefer to "God") had spared his life to a purpose connected, somehow, to the mission he pursued. Precisely how he would achieve that destiny might be hidden from him, as it obviously was in the summer of 1776, but he never doubted that it was real. Nor did he ever doubt that if he were to succeed, he could not forgo the tests of courage, steadfastness, and virtue that alone could make his life a means worthy of achieving the ends Providence ordained.

The coming of the Seven Years' War in America (that is, the French and Indian War, 1754–1760) is a story often told in terms of the struggle of two great, fundamentally different empires for preeminence on the continent. In this telling, New France, a Catholic empire based on trade and Indian alliances that stretched in a great arc from the Gulf of Saint Lawrence to the Great Lakes, the Mississippi Valley, and the Gulf of Mexico, is wholly opposite to the British colonies of eastern North America—a Protestant empire based on farming settlement and transatlantic commerce, vigorous and growing but still confined to the area east of the Appalachian Mountains. The contrasting colonial populations alone were enough to symbolize the differences between the two: whereas in the mid-eighteenth century the whole French population of North America amounted to about fifty-five thousand, the white colonists of the British mainland provinces numbered at least 1.1 million, and owned an additional quarter-million enslaved African Americans. With a numerical advantage of twenty to one over their rival and a rate of growth sufficient to double their population every twenty-six years, two things seemed inevitably true of the British colonies. First, they were destined to expand westward beyond the mountains, into the interior of the continent; second, by sheer force of numbers, if nothing else, they would overwhelm the French who claimed that territory. According to this version of the story, the war itself, while colorful and dramatic, changed little. Anglo-American mastery in North America was effectively determined before the first shot was fired.

By reducing the number of contending parties to two, this telling of the tale vastly oversimplifies the story of the war and makes it impossible to grasp its real significance. In fact three, not two, powers competed in northeastern North America—French, British, and Iroquois Confederacy. If we find it difficult at first to see the Six Nations as a third independent actor in the great imperial drama, that is probably a result of two misconceptions. First is our tendency to assume that empires are necessarily large institutional structures, organized by states, in which a metropolitan nerve center makes policy and projects power to a distant periphery in order to achieve its goals. Second is the old habit of imagining that Indians were fated to vanish from the American scene once Europeans had arrived. Like the counterpart image of Indians as noble savages, this erroneous and pernicious notion has persistently prevented Americans from seeing the crucial roles that native peoples played in shaping the development of the continent.

But it is possible to conceive of empire in a broader way, as the extension of dominion, or control, by one group over others. This creates a more historically inclusive idea of empire (one that embraces among others the Mongols, the Vikings, and the first Arab Muslims, all of whom extended the dominion of their groups before they were fully organized as states) and helps us to see that the Iroquois League had been practicing its own brand of imperialism for more than a century before the Seven Years' War began. Imperialism, indeed, was a strategy by which the Iroquois League survived—indeed, prospered—in the intensely competitive world of eighteenth-century North America.

Because it was other native people over whom the Iroquois sought to exercise dominion, understanding the Seven Years' War as the product of not two but several groups pursuing their interests and struggling for survival creates not only a more inclusive, but also a more surprising, complex, and morally ambiguous story. It is a story whose outcomes were anything but predetermined; a story in which consequences of huge importance for European states and American colonists hinged on decisions made by Indian people who assessed their potential to realize advantage and then acted with the same kind of calculation and skill as the subtlest of Europe's diplomats. Above all, it is a tragic tale, for it depicts the passing of an era in which native people determined the most important historical outcomes on the North American continent, and describes the beginning of a new age in which Indians find themselves shouldered aside, marginalized, and largely written out of the American story.

To begin, then, we must understand the origins, nature, objects, and limitations of Iroquois power in the northeastern quarter of North America in the middle of the eighteenth century. Only then will it become clear that the greatest war of the eighteenth century was above all the product, as well as the progenitor, of a struggle for independence. That the people striving to liberate themselves were a collection of perhaps three thousand Indians living near the site of modern Pittsburgh, and that the group whose control they were fighting to escape was made up of other Indians, is only the first of many surprises in the tale. That the result of their struggle was to create the circumstances that made the American Revolution possible is perhaps the greatest.

PART ONE

THE END OF A LONG PEACE

CHAPTER ONE

A Delicate Balance

By the middle of the eighteenth century, European colonists had lived in North America for nearly a century and a half. They had dealt with native peoples through that whole time—as indeed their predecessors had for the century that preceded the founding of permanent settlements, when European mariners had fished in American waters and coasted along the eastern seaboard in search of wealth and trade—in ways that were by turns peaceful and violent. Those complex interactions between natives and newcomers had both enabled colonization to succeed and limited its success, yielding results that ultimately depended on the decisions and acts of the Indians themselves. Inasmuch as the different European nations competed with one another for influence and power on both sides of the Atlantic, they needed Indians as trading partners, military allies, sources of labor, and sources of land. Insofar as the Indian groups competed with one another, they also understood the Europeans as valuable trading partners, allies, and providers of the weapons and other manufactured goods they needed to survive (and indeed to prosper) in what had become a dangerous and uncertain new world.

Contact with the strangers from beyond the seas had altered native life in almost unfathomable ways. For perhaps a hundred centuries before regular transatlantic contact began at the end of the fifteenth century, the human populations of the New World and the Old had been isolated from each other, and hence unable to exchange pathogens; as a result, infectious

THE
AMERICAN MAGAZINE,

PRÆVALEBIT ÆQUIOR.

AND
MONTHLY CHRONICLE for the *BRITISH* Colonies.
Vol. I. N°. VI. FOR *MARCH* 1758.

CONTAINING.

I. DEBATES in MARYLAND.
II. PHILOSOPHICAL MISCELLANY.
III. MONTHLY ESSAYS.
IV. POETICAL ESSAYS.
V. HISTORY of the WAR in *NORTH AMERICA*.
VI. MONTHLY CHRONICLE.

To be continued (Price *One* Shilling *Pennsylvania* Currency each Month)

By a SOCIETY of Gentlemen.

Veritatis cultores, Fraudis inimici.

PHILADELPHIA.

Printed and Sold by WILLIAM BRADFORD, at the Corner-House in *Front* and *Market-Streets*.

***American Magazine* cover.** *This 1758 woodcut from a Philadelphia periodical includes emblematic British, French, and American Indian figures. Despite its obvious biases, the image shows the Indian in a position of strength as he chooses between the Bible and bolt of cloth offered by the Briton and the purse of money and tomahawk presented by the Frenchman, as representatives of competing European empires.* (Library of Congress, Rare Book and Special Collections)

microbes in the Americas had evolved along different paths from those in Eurasia and Africa. When native peoples in the Americas confronted the epidemic diseases that arrived from Europe along with the colonists, therefore, they lacked the immune defenses of colonizers who had been exposed in childhood to viral epidemic diseases like measles that operate on adult victims with calamitous intensity. The establishment of permanent settlement beachheads at Jamestown (1607), Quebec (1608), Plymouth (1620), and Fort Orange (on the site of modern Albany, 1624) brought close, continuous contact between native and European populations that permitted not only measles, but also chicken pox, smallpox, diphtheria, influenza, and other infections to enter the neighboring Indian communities and then to spread along lines of trade among local native groups, into the surrounding regions.

The effects of the resulting "virgin soil" epidemics beggar description. Ultimately they destroyed as much as 90 percent of the native population of North America. One estimate holds that an indigenous population east of the Mississippi numbering more than 2 million in 1600 shrank to less than a quarter-million by 1750. This decline did not occur simultaneously everywhere on the continent, however, but piecemeal, always striking those native populations in continuous contact with Europeans first. The groups that suffered the initial damage therefore needed to limit their losses if they were to remain viable cultural, social, economic, and military entities.

Overwhelmingly their response was war. There were, of course, shamans in Indian communities who performed healing rituals and treated the sick with traditional remedies. But such palliatives did little to forestall the wholesale destruction of life that occurred with each epidemic episode. As much as half the population of any given village or band died within days or weeks of an epidemic's appearance; those lucky enough to survive remained vulnerable to the appearance of other viral diseases to which they also had no immune defenses. The only way to maintain population levels in the face of such devastation was for the survivors to undertake raiding expeditions against other groups in "mourning wars." The goal of mourning warfare, which ethnologists understand as a response to bereavement, was less to kill one's enemies than to take women and children from enemy groups as captives. They in turn could be adopted into the raiders' families as replacements for lost members, or, alternatively, enslaved as substitutes for missing workers. As warriors, enemy adult males were all but impossible to assimilate, and hence rarely adopted. Captured warriors were typically tortured to death in rituals that allowed their captors to appropriate the victims' spiritual power. The victims in return had whatever consolation came with a chance to die a warrior's death, demonstrating their courage and fortitude in the face of indescribable pain.

1666 Paris document (detail). *This detail from a French copy of Iroquois (probably Seneca) pictographic writing illustrates warriors returning from a campaign with scalps and a bound prisoner. Iroquois and other northeastern American Indian women produced highly decorated captive halters and ties for use in securing captives obtained through "mourning wars."* (Centre des Archives d'Outre-Mer, Aix-en-Provence. Archives Nationales, France [Col. C. 11 A2 Fol. 263.269]. Tous droits réservés.)

Sustaining populations was the principal goal of mourning wars, but not all Indian nations were equally adept at achieving it. Those who had access to European weapons—particularly steel-edged weapons and firearms—tended to be the most successful. To obtain these, warriors needed commodities, above all beaver pelts and other valuable animal skins, to trade to their European suppliers. As a result, the taking of booty, an ancillary activity before the arrival of the Europeans, became as central to Indian warmaking as the vital business of captive-taking. In a complex, unintended way epidemic diseases promoted wars among Indian groups that greatly magnified their demographic losses, even as these wars evolved into a commercial enterprise in which European merchants provided guns and ammunition in return for plundered pelts and hides. Inevitably raids became ever more deadly as wars intensified, creating a seemingly unbreakable cycle of violence, death, and retribution.

Among the most successful Indian practitioners of this new, commercialized war were the Five Nations of the Iroquois, a religious and ceremonial league made up of the Mohawk, Oneida, Onondaga, Cayuga, and Seneca peoples of what is now upstate New York. Their close ties with the Dutch traders of Fort Orange yielded the guns and ammunition that made warriors of the Five Nations the most feared and effective raiders in the northeastern quarter of North America. By the late seventeenth century they had eliminated whole peoples from the Ohio River Valley and the lower Great Lakes Basin, conducting expeditions that ranged from modern Wisconsin to northern New England, and from the Arctic shield of Ontario to South Carolina.

The very success of the Iroquois in pursuing these "beaver wars" created its own limits, for two reasons. First, external behavior and even language were more easily altered than deep-seated values, and the adoption of large numbers of captives inevitably diluted the cultural coherence of the captors' communities. Adoptees who had previously been converted to Catholicism posed a particular threat to the ability of the Five Nations to carry on their warfare against the French and their native allies. These converts formed the nuclei of Francophile factions within each of the Five Nations. Pro-French groups began to become influential in Iroquois policy just at the time that the second factor—the growing ability of the French and their allies to fight back—came to the fore.

Beginning in the late 1650s and 1660s, French officials, missionary priests, and traders established themselves among the refugees who sought shelter from Iroquois attacks in the area west of Lake Michigan and south of Lake Superior, in what is now Wisconsin and the upper peninsula of Michigan. Many of these groups had been enemies before the Iroquois had attacked them, and having a common enemy did nothing to make them friends; mutual suspicion and hostility, indeed, embroiled them in internecine conflicts that made it all the more difficult for them to stave off raiders from the Five Nations. The French who lived and worked among them took advantage of this disorder by taking on the metaphorical role of Father: a mediator of disputes and a source of trade goods. These manufactures, particularly arms and ammunition, were given as gifts to local leaders who could in turn redistribute them as gifts to their own followers, building up coteries friendly to the French. Meanwhile

French Indian traders provided an eager market for the Indians' beaver pelts and other furs, and supplied the ammunition, brandy, and other goods the Indians needed. All this activity created a framework for a non-coercive alliance system, what has been called a cultural "Middle Ground." As the French armed, supplied, evangelized among, and traded with them, the peoples of the Middle Ground became increasingly capable of defending themselves, and slowly moved to reoccupy areas, such as the Wabash and Illinois river valleys, from which the Iroquois raiders had driven them.

Eventually, at the urging of the French and in cooperation with French troops sent in the mid-1660s as part of Louis XIV's strategic plan to dominate North America militarily, the Indian allies of New France grew strong

Calumet (pipe stem), c. 1780–1830. *Early French and Canadian visitors to the Mississippi Valley and Great Lakes region observed the widespread ritual use of smoking pipes with highly decorated stems dubbed "calumets." Traditionally associated with peace and alliance, the calumet ritual was an important component in diplomatic exchanges between New France and American Indian allies.* (Peabody Museum, Harvard University, Photo 99-12-10/53099.2 T2997)

enough to strike back against the Iroquois. With the English takeover of the Dutch colony of New Netherland in 1664, the Iroquois lost their main arms supplier and thus the ability to carry on offensive warfare in search of captives and wealth; soon they found it impossible to defend Iroquoia against invasion. The Five Nations sought to replace the Dutch with the English, and succeeded in forging an alliance—the so-called Covenant Chain—with New York in the 1670s. Unfortunately for the hopes of the Five Nations' leaders, the English proved poor substitutes for the Dutch, and utterly inadequate allies in time of danger. Over the last third of the seventeenth century, the Five Nations suffered devastating losses and grew ever more factionalized internally. By the beginning of the eighteenth century, the Iroquois had lost perhaps a quarter of their population at the hands of their enemies and had little choice but to make peace with New France and its native allies.

The result was the Grand Settlement of 1701, a set of treaties concluded simultaneously with the French at Montreal and the English at Albany, by which the Five Nations stepped back from the brink of destruction. At Montreal diplomats representing the League pledged to remain neutral in all future wars between the French and the English. In return for this great concession the French agreed that the Iroquois could hunt on lands north of the Great Lakes and trade at France's newly established commercial emporium, Fort Detroit, between Lake Erie and Lake Huron. At Albany, meanwhile, the League's representatives ceded to the English crown all Iroquois claims to the country north of the Great Lakes—a largely fictitious claim based on the Iroquois "conquest" of the region in the Beaver Wars. Because this was a region that the English had no capacity to occupy, the cession's main effect was to reaffirm the Covenant Chain alliance with the English, and to place the Iroquois theoretically under the protection of the English king, as Father. The English knew nothing of the Iroquois promise to New France that they would remain neutral in future Anglo-French wars; the French knew nothing of the Iroquois reaffirmation of the Covenant Chain binding them to the English colonies, and nothing of the Iroquois cession to England of lands that lay (so far as Louis XIV and his ministers were concerned) wholly within the bounds of New France.

The Grand Settlement enabled the Iroquois to carve out a position of neutrality between the increasingly competitive empires of France and England. When the two powers went to war in Europe, their colonists in the New World attempted to attack one another as well; indeed, it had been the first of those Anglo-French conflicts, the War of the League of Augsburg (1689–1697), that prompted the French and their allied peoples to attack the Iroquois homeland with such terrible effect. Having gained little but destruction and loss as England's ally and France's enemy, the Iroquois now discovered that their new position of neutrality gave them considerable leverage against both powers because it made Iroquoia—an area that was itself a buffer between the French and English colonies—the fulcrum on which Iroquois diplomats could counterpoise the empires against each other. With this dawning realization came the birth of a new balance-of-power diplomatic system in eastern North America, which was largely responsible for rendering Anglo-French imperial competition indecisive for a full half-century.

When conflict next erupted between France and England—as it did soon after the Grand Settlement in the War of the Spanish Succession (or, as it was known in the English colonies, Queen Anne's War, 1702–1713)—the Iroquois exploited their supposed military alliance with the English by gaining information about planned attacks on New France and passing it along to the French. Meanwhile, the Five Nations reaped rewards from the renewed Covenant Chain in the form of English subsidies—diplomatic gifts of trade goods, arms, ammunition, and other supplies. When the English finally moved to invade Canada by way of Lake Champlain in 1709 and 1711, several hundred Iroquois warriors joined the expeditions and then did their best to sabotage them by delay and by passing along intelligence to the enemy. The result, an indecisive war that weakened both empires and enriched the Iroquois League, demonstrated beyond doubt the utility of avoiding an exclusive alliance with either European power. Neutrality had served the interests of the Five Nations admirably.

The cessation of hostilities, however, served them even better. During the Long Peace—the thirty years between the Treaty of Utrecht in 1713 and the outbreak of the next Anglo-French war in 1744—the Five Nations became increasingly adept at maintaining the delicate balance between empires to their own advantage. Now they found themselves not only in a position to continue controlling the flow of information between New France and New York but also to act as middlemen in the smuggling trade that went on between the two colonies via Lake Champlain and the Richelieu River. The admission of the Tuscaroras to the League as a sixth nation in 1726 greatly enhanced Iroquois military power and enabled them to expand their raids against a variety of southern Indian groups, notably the Cherokees and the Catawbas. This limited form of mourning war enabled the Iroquois to continue rebuilding their population and spiritual power without the risk of French retaliation, for these enemies were either allied with the British of the Carolinas or with the Spanish in Florida.

The era of Iroquois neutrality furnished another opportunity for the League to regain power and wealth, as well, in building a mutually beneficial relationship with the new British province of Pennsylvania. This colony, founded in 1681 as an experiment in pacifism and religious liberty by the aristocratic English Quaker William Penn, was one of the greatest anomalies of its day: an English colony that forswore the use of force against native peoples, but rather promised them peace and traded with them on fair and open terms. Penn's willingness to trade freely with the local Indians—at first mainly Lenni Lenape (or Delawares), who lived in the eastern part of the province in the Delaware River Valley—extended to providing them with firearms and ammunition. In the absence of a militia or any organized form of self-defense among the colonists, easy access to arms offered the Indians what amounted to an ironclad guarantee that they had nothing to fear from Penn and his colonists.

As word spread among native groups (especially those that had been living farther south) that Pennsylvania offered a refuge from the wars that afflicted them, Penn's colony became a haven for Indians as much as it was for European immigrants. Ensconced in the upper Delaware Valley and the Susquehanna watershed farther west, selling lands at a pace that suited them to a proprietor who paid well, and secure in their trading relationship with the merchants of Philadelphia, the Delawares and other Indian groups (Shawnees, Conestogas, Tutelos, Conoys, Nanticokes, and others) became in effect a well-armed defensive shield for Pennsylvania as a whole. The Quaker province could safely dispense with a militia because it effectively outsourced defense to Indian allies whom no one expected to live according to pacificist principles.

This system worked amazingly well, and it made Pennsylvania the greatest success story in English North America. The absence of warfare (and Pennsylvania remained free from war for more than seven decades after its founding), the lack of any military obligation for the colonists, religious toleration, and the comparatively cheap and fertile soil of the colony combined to draw thousands of immigrants, primarily from the lowlands of Scotland, northern Ireland, and the war-ravaged Rhenish Palatinate in what is now southwestern Germany. Following the end of the War of the Spanish Succession in 1713, the press of immigrants grew ever greater, and showed no sign of diminishing as the century progressed. The colonists' large family sizes and generally healthful conditions of settlement kept mortality low, while the influx of settlers drove an astonishing increase in white population—approximately 150 percent per decade. Prosperity kept pace with population to such a degree that eighteenth-century Pennsylvania came to be known as "the best poor man's country on earth."

There was, inevitably, a price to be paid for so much growth. The colony's white farmers, with their large families and burgeoning livestock herds, needed space to expand, and hence ever more Indian land. From the very beginning, peace in Penn's province had depended upon the ability of Indians and white settlers to develop as parallel communities, each free to pursue its own interests without interference from the other. James Logan, the Penn family's "man of business" in Pennsylvania and the most powerful man in the colony, understood this fundamental truth, and saw that Pennsylvania's very success could become its nemesis. The expansion of Pennsylvania, he knew, might bring war down on a province that was wholly unprepared to defend itself.

As early as the 1720s Logan understood the Indians of Pennsylvania as the most immediate threat, for they both resented the growing pressure of whites on their lands and possessed far greater military capacity than the colonists. If they struck (as Logan knew they had nearly done in 1728 when white settlers in the Schuylkill Valley murdered three peaceful Indians), the result would be a bloodbath. Yet an even greater threat, he believed, came from the ability of the French to exploit their capacity for alliance-making to create an Indian uprising on a truly grand scale. The French had a vital strategic interest in keeping the British colonists confined to the area between the Atlantic and the Appalachians, for if Pennsylvania's mushrooming population continued to press westward, it would only be a matter of time until it breached the mountain barrier. Rather than let Britain's colonists flood into the Ohio River Valley, the French would surely mobilize their Indian allies to attack on a broad front, along the colonial frontier from New York to the Carolinas. Pennsylvania, lacking a militia to defend itself, would be the most inviting and vulnerable target of all. The consequences would be catastrophic.

William Penn was long dead by the time Logan reached these sobering conclusions, but to abandon Penn's pacifist policy and create a militia was impossible. Logan was not so committed a Quaker that he would have scrupled at establishing a self-defense force, but he knew the Quaker grandees who dominated the provincial assembly too well to imagine that they would abandon the Peace Testimony. The defense of the province, then, had to come from outside, and Logan knew that the Iroquois were the likeliest to provide it. As early as the 1640s Iroquois warriors had acted as musclemen for the Dutch in punishing the refractory Indians of the lower Hudson Valley; at the behest of the governor of New York in the 1670s, they had played a decisive role in putting down Indian uprisings in Massachusetts and Virginia. An alliance between Pennsylvania and the Iroquois, Logan believed, would give the notoriously weak province a means to discipline its own native people, while the exceptionally effective diplomats of the League could help fend off the threat from French-allied Indians farther west.

To this end, between 1721 and 1732 Logan worked to extend the Covenant Chain alliance to Pennsylvania, in order to have the province recognize the Iroquois as diplomatic spokesmen for the Delawares, Shawnees, and other Indians living in Pennsylvania. Making the Five Nations (or, following the admission of the Tuscaroras to the League in 1726, the Six Nations) custodians of the interests of Pennsylvania's Indians would confer not only the security benefits that Logan was desperate to achieve, but also add one more singularly great advantage: it would greatly ease the process of transferring lands from Indian ownership to the Penn family, whose interests Logan faithfully represented.

It took the heirs of William Penn thirteen years after his death to straighten out the tangled legal circumstances in which he had left the ownership of the province. Thus when the Court of Chancery finally rendered its decision and prompted the out-of-court settlement that at last determined the ownership of Pennsylvania in 1731, Richard, John, and Thomas Penn were more than eager to make the family's province a paying proposition. This meant acquiring substantial amounts of Indian land for sale to settlers. To adhere to their father's policy of buying that land from the Delawares, Shawnees, Conestogas, and other Indians who actually lived on it would have been time-consuming and prohibitively expensive. Logan's success in installing the Six Nations in a position of suzerainty over the Indians of Pennsylvania, however, allowed Penn's heirs the convenience of acquiring the land they wanted simply by dealing with the Iroquois.

Because the Six Nations were willing to sell land out from under the Delawares and other peoples, now conveniently defined as the wards of the League, the Penns were able to buy it in quantity and begin reselling it to white settlers. Niceties of law and equity did not unduly concern them, and they grew steadily bolder and more aggressive until, in 1737, they succeeded in perpetrating the so-called Walking Purchase. This spectacular land fraud, the most flagrant of the whole eighteenth century, dispossessed the Delawares of nearly three-quarters of a million acres of land near the confluence of the Lehigh and Delaware rivers. Iroquois enforcers, complicit in the fraud, prevented the victims from making any effective protest; the League confirmed the purchase by treaty in 1742, and forced a stubborn band of Delawares who had refused to leave to move to the Susquehanna Valley. Nothing indicates that the Penn brothers ever reckoned the costs to the Indians of the Walking Purchase and various other land deals, but they could hardly have escaped the realization that their own profits were enormous. Whereas William Penn had averaged £400 or less in annual income from land sales and had died deeply in debt, his heirs raked in an average of £7,150 in income from their dealings in Pennsylvania real estate every year from 1731 through 1760.

***Tishcohan*, by Gustavus Hesselius, 1735.** *The Delaware leader Tishcohan was one of several signatories to a deed confirming the infamous "Walking Purchase" of 1737. The Pennsylvania proprietors Thomas and John Penn, who commissioned this portrait, used Iroquois aid to press Tishcohan's people to abandon their lands in eastern Pennsylvania. Most moved to the Susquehanna Valley, nursing resentment over their dispossession.* (Courtesy of The Historical Society of Pennsylvania Collection, Atwater Kent Museum of Philadelphia)

By the time James Logan died in 1751, his attempts to secure Pennsylvania through diplomacy with the Iroquois League had yielded three important, if unanticipated, results. The once penurious Penns had become one of the richest families in England; the Iroquois League had achieved a level of power and diplomatic influence it had not seen in nearly a century;

and the Indians of eastern Pennsylvania had largely been driven from their homes. None of these outcomes, unfortunately, had done a great deal to achieve the goal of a defensible frontier that Logan had intended. Although he could not have known it when he died, the net result had been to move the province closer to war than it had ever been. When the war came, it would strike Pennsylvania with a fury that would make its seven decades of peaceful Indian relations seem as distant and irrecoverable as a half-remembered dream.

CHAPTER TWO

The Half King's Dilemma

In adopting an essentially high-handed approach to the Pennsylvania Indians, the Iroquois made a classic miscalculation. Although virtually all empires grow by the forcible extension of dominion over others, the most successful empires have maintained long-term control by encouraging subordinated groups to participate voluntarily in the larger imperial community. Typically this kind of cooperative relationship rests on a pair of complementary realizations. In the first place, client communities must be willing to believe that the advantages of membership in the empire—a greater degree of security, for instance, or the economic benefits of trading within an imperial market—outweigh the costs of subordination and the dangers of resistance. In the second, the empire's leaders must be able to recognize that it is neither possible nor desirable to use force constantly to maintain control. Ultimately the co-optation of local leaders and the consent of their communities are crucial to enduring imperial mastery. This was particularly true for the Six Nations. Iroquois warriors could strike with horrifying violence and intimidate other groups more or less at will, but lacked the capacity to undertake anything like a military occupation, or even to understand that concept as a meaningful one. The error that the leaders of the Six Nations made in dealing with the Delawares, Shawnees, and other Indians of Pennsylvania lay in assuming that they would accept subordination without resistance or complaint.

That they would not do. Instead, they moved west.

Native Peoples and European Empires, c.1750–1763

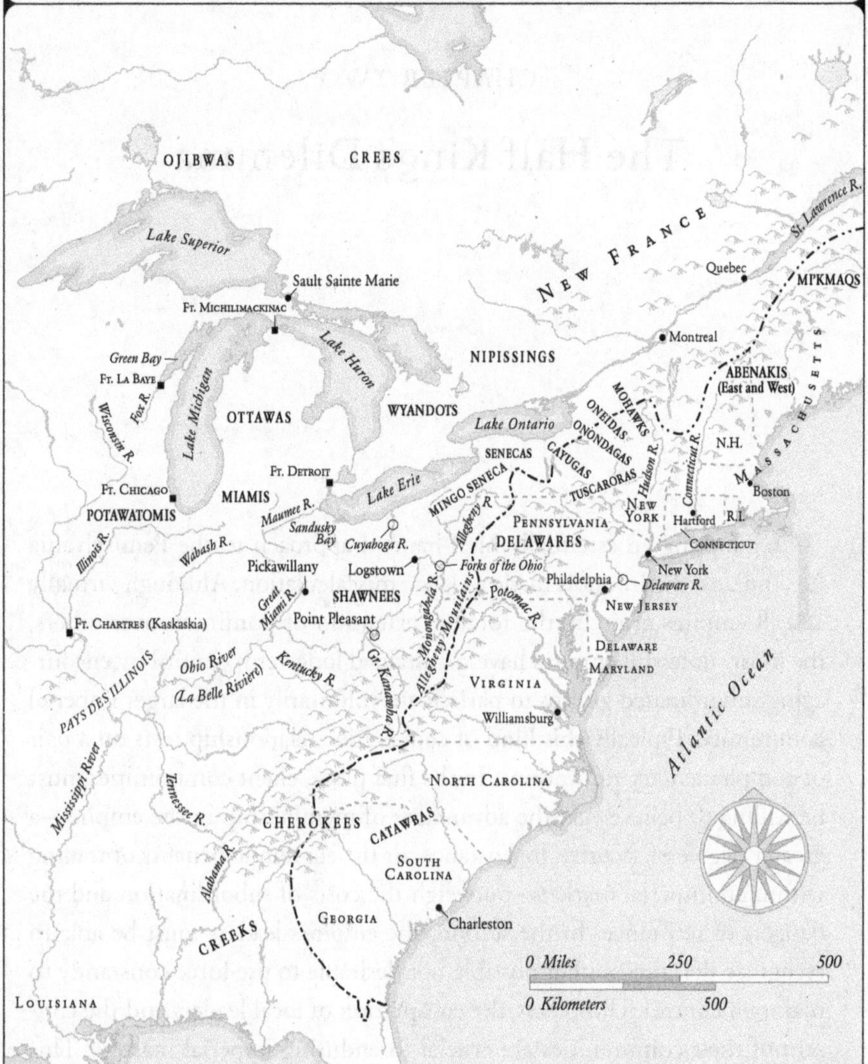

OJIBWAS
CREES
Lake Superior
New France
St. Lawrence R.
Quebec
MI'KMAQS
Sault Sainte Marie
Ft. Michilimackinac
Lake Huron
Montreal
Green Bay
Ft. La Baye
Lake Michigan
Fox R.
Wisconsin R.
NIPISSINGS
ABENAKIS
(East and West)
Massachusetts
OTTAWAS
WYANDOTS
Lake Ontario
MOHAWKS
ONEIDAS
ONONDAGAS
CAYUGAS
SENECAS
TUSCARORAS
Hudson R.
Connecticut R.
N.H.
Boston
Ft. Detroit
Lake Erie
MINGO SENECA
Allegheny R.
New York
Hartford
R.I.
Connecticut
Ft. Chicago
MIAMIS
POTAWATOMIS
Maumee R.
Sandusky Bay
Cuyahoga R.
Pennsylvania
DELAWARES
Illinois R.
Wabash R.
Pickawillany
Logstown
Forks of the Ohio
New York
Great Miami R.
SHAWNEES
Monongahela R.
Allegheny Mountains
Potomac R.
Philadelphia
Delaware R.
New Jersey
Ft. Chartres (Kaskaskia)
Point Pleasant
Delaware
Maryland
Pays des Illinois
Ohio River
(La Belle Rivière)
Kentucky R.
Gr. Kanawha R.
Virginia
Williamsburg
Atlantic Ocean
Mississippi River
Tennessee R.
North Carolina
CHEROKEES
CATAWBAS
Alabama R.
South Carolina
Georgia
Charleston
CREEKS
0 Miles 250 500
0 Kilometers 500
Louisiana
Gulf of Mexico

Proclamation Line, 1763
WYANDOTS Native tribes
Forts
Settlements

© 2005 Jeffrey L. Ward

It would have suited the purposes of the League ideally if the Delawares had merely relocated from the upper Delaware Valley (on the eastern edge of Pennsylvania) to the Susquehanna Valley in the center of the province, where most of the Shawnee villages were already situated. The headwaters of the Susquehanna lay in the heart of Iroquoia, and the route that Six Nations warriors took on raiding expeditions against the Cherokees and Catawbas followed the valley. To have client groups living there would give raiders passing through on the warriors' path places to rest and reprovision themselves, coming and going; and since any retaliatory raids would follow the same path north, the Delawares, Shawnees, and others living in the valley would form a defensive shield for Iroquoia.

Many Delawares did in fact move to the Susquehanna, and some decided to remain there permanently in villages around Shamokin, the principal settlement at the confluence of the river's west and north branches. Yet for most of the Delawares, and for the Shawnees of the valley as well, the Susquehanna was only a way station on a path whose ultimate destination lay far to the west, beyond the Alleghenies, at the Forks of the Ohio—the site on which Pittsburgh stands today. There, they believed, they would be beyond the reach of the land-hungry Pennsylvanians; beyond, indeed, the effective control of the Iroquois chiefs who had betrayed them in order to gain profit and power. In the Ohio country they might become independent once more, and reap the same kinds of benefits the Six Nations did from dealing as a neutral power with both the French and British empires.

Independence was a compelling vision, and for a time it seemed to be a realizable one. When the Delawares and Shawnees moved to the Ohio country, they were relocating to an area that had been depopulated of human beings for nearly a century, and which as a result had become the home to the greatest populations of game animals—especially deer, beaver, and bear—in North America. Because the traders who had long lived among them decided to follow them west, the migrants could translate this abundance of game into a higher standard of living by hunting commercially for pelts and skins. Continued access to weapons, ammunition, and trade goods of all sorts encouraged them to imagine that they could once more live on their own terms.

By the mid-1740s, at least twenty-five hundred Indians lived in valleys of the Allegheny, Monongahela, and Ohio, and their associated tributaries. The majority were Delawares and Shawnees, but large numbers of western Senecas, called Mingos, lived there as well. As members of the Seneca nation, the Mingos were of course Iroquois. Yet like the Delawares and Shawnees they too hoped to escape domination by the League. Descended mainly from nations the Iroquois had absorbed in the Beaver Wars—Eries, Neutrals, Monongahelas, and others—the Mingos moved west in order to reestablish themselves on ancestral lands. All three groups shared a strong impulse toward traditionalism. Whereas the Delawares and Shawnees who remained behind on the Susquehanna responded to the pressures of an encroaching white society by converting to Christianity, those who moved to the Ohio country embraced nativist beliefs as a key to recapturing cultural and religious autonomy.

At first the chiefs of the Six Nations viewed the departure of so many of the Pennsylvania Indians with equanimity, for they underestimated how deeply the migrants desired independence. The Iroquois benefited from having client peoples living on the Ohio because it strengthened their claim to ownership of the region—a claim ultimately based on having conquered it in the Beaver Wars. Suzerainty over the Ohio country was, in every sense, crucial to the Iroquois policy of neutrality. The French had long made it clear that they would recognize the Iroquois claim to the Ohio country provided the Six Nations kept the English out. For the French to build the forts necessary to occupy the valley would cost far more than they could hope to recover by trade. At the same time, the Ohio furnished the principal river connection between the western slope of the Appalachians and the Mississippi Valley, flowing directly into the heart of French settlement in the mid-Mississippi Valley, the *pays des Illinois.* If the numerous, prolific, aggressive English settlers colonized the Ohio Valley, they would, of course, be in a position to cut the great inland arc of French influence and alliances in two. The most immediate threat, however, was that English traders would invade the Ohio country. Britain's cheap, high-quality trade goods would become a magnet drawing away the native peoples who now traded with the French at Detroit and other posts. This in turn would weaken, and perhaps destroy, the system of alliances on which French power rested in the interior of the continent.

Traders from Pennsylvania, as we have seen, accompanied the Delawares

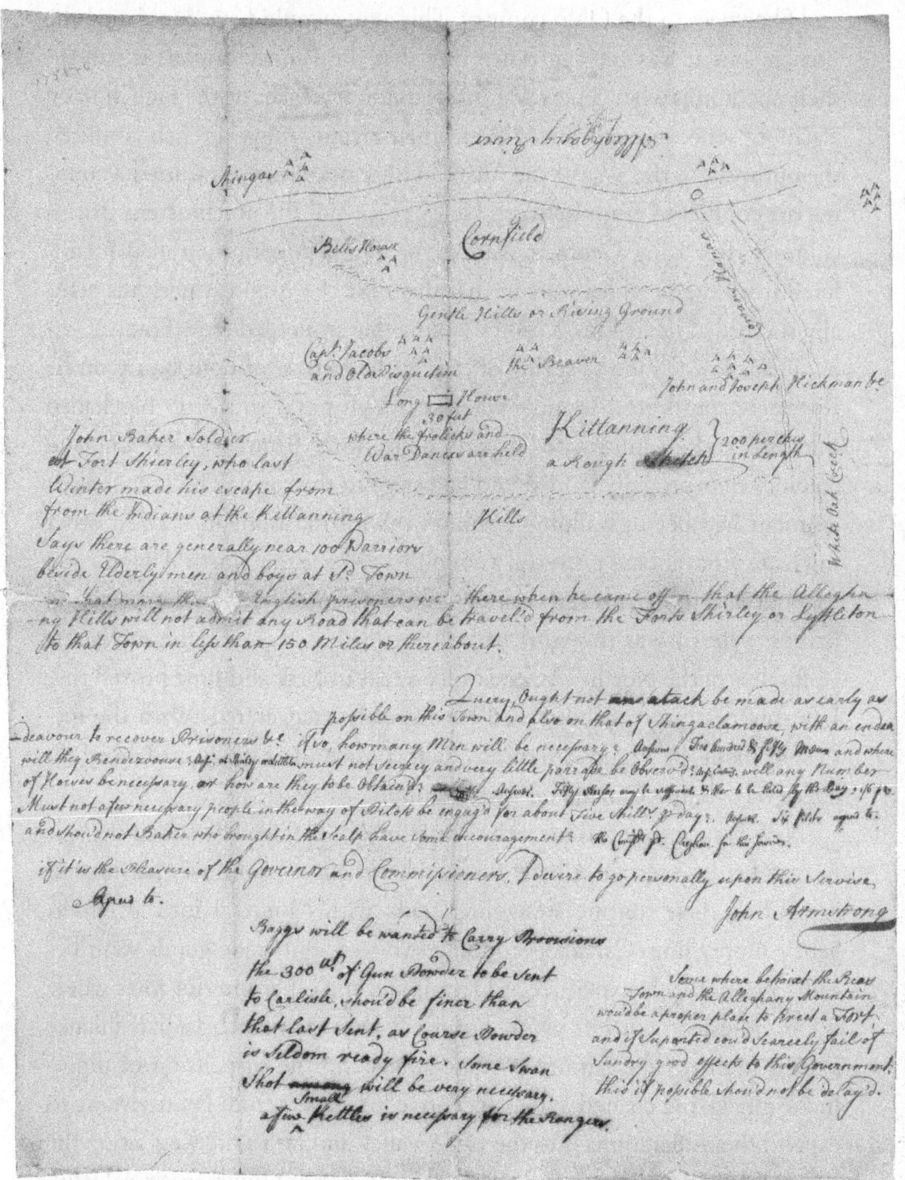

Map of Kittanning, 1756. *Delaware emigrants seeking freedom from colonial and Iroquois domination established the town of Kittanning in the 1720s along the banks of the Allegheny River north of present-day Pittsburgh. By 1756, when this map of the settlement was drawn, more than five hundred residents lived in several clusters of dwellings stretching for more than a thousand yards along the rich river bottomland.* (Courtesy of the American Philosophical Society)

and Shawnees to the Ohio country. This alone would have concerned the French, but it was the aggressive way that the Pennsylvanians expanded their operations when a new war broke out that awakened the French to an alarming set of circumstances. As in the previous Anglo-French conflicts, the outbreak of the War of the Austrian Succession in 1744 caused a counterpart conflict to erupt between New France and the northeastern British colonies. But King George's War, as the Anglo-Americans called it, differed from the previous wars in that this time the Anglo-Americans actually succeeded in striking a military blow that imperiled New France.

That blow fell in the spring of 1745 at the fortress of Louisbourg on Île Royale (Cape Breton Island), when a British naval squadron blockaded the port, and an improvised expeditionary force from the New England colonies unexpectedly landed and laid siege to the town. The French government had begun building Louisbourg's fortifications in 1720 in order to create a naval base powerful enough to protect the North Atlantic cod fisheries and to defend the Gulf of Saint Lawrence. By 1745 the town and harbor were (it was thought) so well fortified as to merit the nickname "Gibraltar of the North." A siege of six weeks in May and June proved that Louisbourg's impregnability had been greatly exaggerated. With the fortress in hand the Anglo-Americans took command of the Saint Lawrence, effectively sealing Canada off from resupply.

New France survived until the Treaty of Aix-la-Chapelle ended the war in 1748 because certain Albany fur merchants chose profit over patriotism, expanding their routine smuggling trade with Montreal into an emergency supply line. Canada's economy survived, but trade goods soon became prohibitively expensive at Detroit and the other interior forts where trade and diplomatic gift-giving ordinarily kept the Franco-Indian alliance system healthy. The famine in trade goods and the suspension of diplomatic gift-giving created a huge incentive for traders from Pennsylvania to expand their operations into the Ohio Valley and far to the west along the shore of Lake Erie. Among these the most important figure was a colorful, supremely confident Irish opportunist named George Croghan. Even before the war he had opened a trading post on the Cuyahoga River at Lake Erie (on the site of modern Cleveland). Now he took advantage of the trade-good famine in the interior by establishing a post at Logstown, about fifteen miles downstream from the Forks of the Ohio, and at Sandusky Bay on Lake Erie, just fifty miles from Fort Detroit.

By war's end Croghan was the greatest Pennsylvania trader in the West, and poised to expand his operations far down the Ohio Valley to a new post at Pickawillany on the Great Miami River. Pickawillany grew into a great emporium, an immense magnet for Indian groups that had formerly traded at Detroit. Meanwhile the Ohio Indians had begun to show more overt signs of independence than ever before, by seeking to establish direct diplomatic ties with Pennsylvania's government. At a treaty conference at Logstown in 1748, Pennsylvania's commissioner (abetted by the omnipresent Croghan) seemed willing to bypass the authority of the League and negotiate directly with the Ohio chiefs.

Aware that the French would intervene if the English presence on the Ohio continued to grow, the Iroquois now took action, appointing a regent to superintend the Mingos and other Ohio Indians. This chief, Tanaghrisson, was a Catawba by birth and a Seneca by adoption, and his status among the Ohio peoples was a matter of considerable ambiguity. The League Council at Onondaga authorized Tanaghrisson to speak on behalf of the Ohio Indians; that is, it made him solely responsible for conducting diplomacy on their behalf, thus rebuking them for their recent presumptions of independence at the Logstown conference. At the same time, however, any agreements Tanaghrisson might make were only conditional ones, which had to be ratified by Onondaga; hence his derisive nickname, "the Half King."

Unfortunately for the Half King (and for the hopes of the Iroquois Council that he might be able to defend its interests), his ability to influence the Ohio Indians depended on building a following among the chiefs who led them, especially the emergent Delaware leaders Tamaqua, Shingas, and Pisquetomen. That in turn meant that he needed a European ally to provide him with trade goods, as diplomatic gifts, to distribute among them, which they could in turn redistribute among their own followers. Croghan and his fellow Pennsylvania traders were already on the scene, and a new set of traders from Virginia had recently made its appearance as well, bearing ample gifts in the hope of forging connections of their own. Tanaghrisson had no choice but to turn to them for the necessary trade goods. In so doing, however, he also convinced the French, watching warily from Detroit, that the Iroquois had indeed lost the ability to keep the Ohio Valley free of English traders and English influence.

For the French this unbalanced state of affairs was intolerable. But what to do?

CHAPTER THREE

Confrontation on the Ohio

France did not have great plans for what its maps labeled *la Belle Rivière,* apart from keeping it out of British hands. French traders, soldiers, and priests rarely used the river to pass from the Canadian heartland to the *pays des Illinois.* To do so required a long, difficult initial portage from the south shore of Lake Erie to a shallow, unreliable tributary of the Allegheny. Only after many miles did the going become tolerable for the great cargo canoes that *voyageurs* used in trade. Travelers to the west preferred to take sailing vessels as far as Lake Michigan, then canoe to the Mississippi by one of two routes: either from Green Bay and the Fox River/Wisconsin River route to the upper valley, or from Fort Chicago by portage to the Illinois River, and thence directly to the midvalley settlements near Fort Chartres (Kaskaskia). The intrusion of Pennsylvania traders into the Ohio country, more than any other factor, made the French government place *la Belle Rivière* under the jurisdiction of the governor-general of New France in 1749. It was a first step toward direct involvement in the region, but only a tentative one. More information was necessary, so in June the governor, the comte de La Galissonière, dispatched Captain Pierre-Joseph de Céloron de Blainville of the *troupes de la marine* (Canada's regular infantry) to lead a force of 265 Canadians and Indians on a tour of the Ohio country.

That November, with thousands of miles of canoe travel behind him, Céloron made a discouraging report to La Galissonière's successor, the

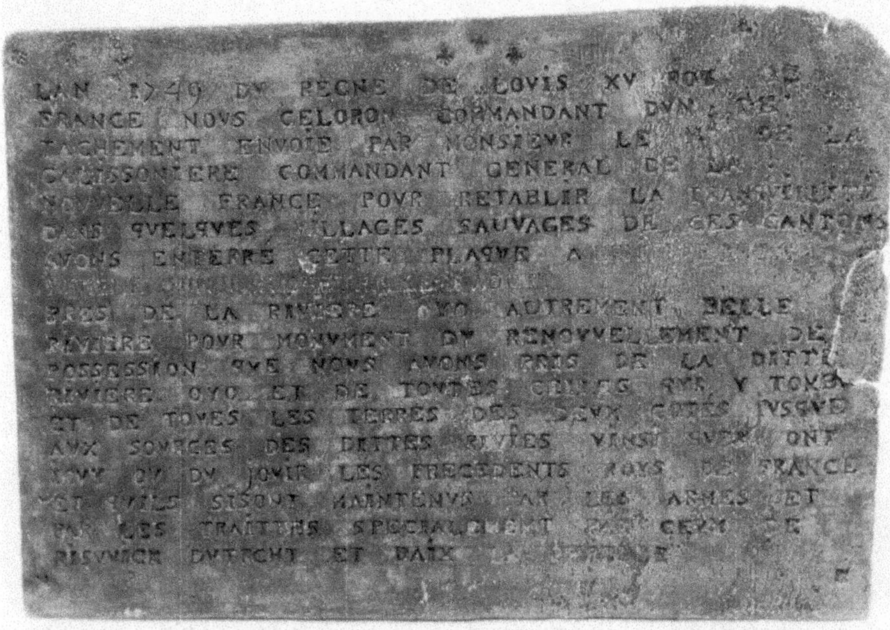

Céloron tablet. *Only two of the lead tablets planted along the Ohio River by Céloron de Blainville's 1749 expedition were ever found. Only this one has survived intact. It was discovered near the confluence of the Kanawha and Ohio rivers in the nineteenth century.* (Virginia Historical Society, Richmond, Virginia)

marquis de La Jonquière. The Ohio Indians had been surly, even hostile, in behavior. Céloron had met bands of Pennsylvania traders and warned them out; he had posted signs and buried lead tablets in the ground at various locations to renew His Most Christian Majesty's claims to the region. None of it, he knew, would prevent the traders from returning. Particularly sobering had been the numbers of Miamis and other French-allied Indians he found at Pickawillany on the Great Miami River, where George Croghan and his associates had established a trading post on a spot that dominated the major canoe route from Detroit to the Mississippi. The Indians' eagerness to trade with the English and their open contempt of Céloron's authority meant only one thing: the alliances south of the Great Lakes were at the point of dissolution.

La Jonquière contemplated taking action, but in the end only procrastinated. Two years passed before he authorized Céloron to take a larger force back to Pickawillany to compel the Miamis to return to their previous settlement on the Maumee. When few Indians at Fort Detroit volunteered to join him, Céloron had to call off the expedition. Meanwhile France's strategic position in the Ohio country grew even more tenuous when a new and aggressive set of intruders appeared in the valley in 1750. The previous year the Ohio Company of Virginia, a syndicate of twenty rich tobacco planters, had built a stockaded storehouse on the north branch of the Potomac at Wills Creek (the site of modern Cumberland, Maryland) in preparation for opening a route to the Ohio via the Youghiogheny and Monongahela rivers. Over the next two years the company's principal agent, an experienced Indian trader and surveyor named Christopher Gist, explored lands on both sides of the river from the Forks as far as the Falls of the Ohio (modern Louisville, Kentucky), making trade and diplomatic contacts as he went. His presence did not go unnoticed, either by the French or by George Croghan and his associates.

La Jonquière died in March 1752 without having taken any effective action. Both his immediate successor, acting governor Charles Le Moyne de Longueuil, and the new governor, Ange Duquesne de Menneville, marquis Duquesne, who arrived to take control in July, were less hesitant. Though they had differing opinions about how best to meet the English challenge, they saw the Pennsylvanian and Virginian intrusions into the Ohio Valley as two dimensions of a single, coordinated invasion. They were quite mistaken; the Pennsylvanians and Virginians were in fact bitter competitors. In overestimating the coherence of the English actions, the French effectively frightened themselves into taking steps that radically increased the likelihood of an armed confrontation over the Forks of the Ohio.

Unlike George Croghan and his associates—who had merely wanted to trade with the Indians and had as yet developed no coherent plans for encouraging white settlers to take up land on the Ohio—the Virginians saw the development of trade as a prelude to acquiring real estate for later sale. Virginia's gentry had grown rich by planting tobacco, but tobacco's tendency to exhaust the soil and the proliferation of enslaved African Americans by natural increase had made land speculation essential to the continued economic growth and social stability of the Old Dominion.

Short of slave rebellion itself, there was no greater nightmare for planters than a future in which relentlessly increasing numbers of slaves would crowd land holdings of steadily decreasing fertility. Planters therefore constantly hunted for new lands to bring under cultivation, and also to resell or rent out to tenants in order to supplement their income from tobacco.

Typically, the larger the planter, the more deeply he was engaged in buying cheap frontier land whose value would rise as the population of the province increased. Gentlemen with good political connections could easily acquire forty or fifty thousand acres of woodland at bargain rates in return for the promise to "seat" settlers on the land within a specified period. Then the speculators located their own younger sons on frontier property, gave them their inheritances in the form of slaves to clear and plant it, and designated them as agents for the sale or rental of the remainder of their holdings in the region.

In this way the gentry society of the Tidewater steadily reproduced itself on frontier after frontier, and avoided the Malthusian calamity that would surely have resulted in the absence of new lands to settle. Virginia's planters could literally see no end to the expansion of this system. Thanks to Virginia's charter of 1609, drawn up by royal officials who thought that North America might be at most three or four hundred miles across, the colony's southern boundary ran straight west to the Pacific on a latitude of 36 degrees 30 minutes, while its northern boundary proceeded northwestward from the mouth of the Potomac to somewhere in the neighborhood of the Bering Strait. Acting both as individuals and in groups (the members of which formed joint-stock corporations with a view to acquiring tracts of a quarter-million acres or more), rich Virginians looked constantly toward the future, identifying it above all with the West.

The Ohio Company, made up of investors from the northern part of the province, was thus only one of several land-speculating syndicates active in the 1740s. This group differed from the others, however, in one crucial way: its stockholders were effectively blocked from speculating in lands close to home by the Fairfax Grant—a Massachusetts-sized tract between the Potomac and Rappahannock rivers, from the Chesapeake to the Appalachian crest, that belonged to the only British nobleman who made his permanent home in America, Lord Thomas Fairfax, baron Cameron. The Ohio partners accordingly looked beyond the limits of the Fairfax proprietary to the broad, well-watered lands of the trans-Appalachian west, which seemed destined to become a magnet for farmers as soon as the mountain barrier could be breached by roads and waterways.

The Ohio Company coveted the Forks of the Ohio, to which the Youghiogheny and Monongahela rivers offered access by way of the upper Potomac. The opportunity to acquire lands there appeared, fortuitously, when one of the leading shareholders in the company was appointed as a commissioner to represent Virginia at a great conference with the Six Nations, at Lancaster, Pennsylvania, in 1744. The Iroquois League, now at the height of its influence and well aware of the benefits that it derived from close cooperation with the Penn family, offered to cede all of its remaining claims within the limits of Pennsylvania, Maryland, and Virginia in return for a substantial diplomatic gift, recognition of the Six Nations as sovereign over several southern Indian peoples, and free passage of Iroquois warriors through Virginia on their way to raid the Cherokees and Catawbas of South Carolina. The League's negotiators did not imagine that Virginia's claims extended farther than the western edge of the Shenandoah Valley. The Virginia delegation did not feel obliged to instruct them on the details of the charter of 1609.

The year after the Treaty of Lancaster, Virginia's legislature, the House of Burgesses, granted the Ohio Company rights to three hundred square miles of land at the Forks of the Ohio. The sole condition was that they seat two hundred families there; once they had done so, the grant would be further enlarged. King George's War kept the company from proceeding, but with the return of peace with the Treaty of Aix-la-Chapelle, the shareholders lost no time in resuming their program. Wills Creek Fort, completed in 1749, became the base of operations from which Christopher Gist explored the valley and established trade and diplomatic ties with the Ohio Indians in 1750 and 1751. The following year he opened a trading post, Gist's Plantation, in the valley of the Youghiogheny. Fully fifty miles west of Wills Creek and well within the watershed of the Ohio, the company expected Gist's settlement to become a way station on a thoroughfare from Virginia to the Forks of the Ohio.

Apart from careful planning and substantial capital investments, the Ohio Company took one more significant step to ensure its success: its members presented a share, as a gift, to Virginia's new lieutenant governor,

A

TREATY,

Held at the Town of

Lancaster, in PENNSYLVANIA,

By the HONOURABLE the

Lieutenant-Governor of the PROVINCE,

And the HONOURABLE the

Commissioners for the PROVINCES

OF

VIRGINIA *and* MARYLAND,

WITH THE

INDIANS

OF THE

SIX NATIONS,

In *JUNE*, 1744.

PHILADELPHIA:

Printed and Sold by B. FRANKLIN, at the New-Printing-Office, near the Market. M,DCC,XLIV.

Treaty of Lancaster, 1744 (title page). *Benjamin Franklin printed these minutes of a treaty negotiated at Lancaster, Pennsylvania, in June 1744, by which Iroquois leaders, hoping to strengthen their ties to Pennsylvania and Virginia, approved a vague cession of their claims to lands along the Allegheny Mountains. Virginia construed this as authorizing the Ohio Company to establish trade and promote settlement near the Forks of the Ohio, alarming French and Canadian officials, who responded by building forts from Lake Erie to the Forks.* (Beinecke Rare Book and Manuscript Library, Yale University)

Robert Dinwiddie, upon his arrival in the province in 1751.* This furnished what amounted to an ironclad guarantee that the most important man in Virginia's government, and the person with the most reliable connections to the crown, would pay scrupulous attention to the company's welfare. Dinwiddie soon proved that he was indeed a friend; it was with his approval that Gist proposed a treaty council at Logstown in the spring of 1752, to gain Tanaghrisson's approval for an Ohio Company "strong house," or fortified trading post, at the Forks of the Ohio.

Tanaghrisson accepted a thousand pounds' worth of diplomatic gifts at the Logstown conference and agreed to the construction of the post knowing full well that the Virginians' other proposal, to create a white settlement near the trading center, was unlikely to be approved by the Iroquois Council at Onondaga. He desperately needed the resources the Ohio Company offered because he strongly suspected that Céloron de Blainville would not be the last French officer to appear on the Allegheny at the head of an expedition. He knew, too, that when the French returned, it would likely be with sufficient force to impose their control over the region. Unless he had an ally strong enough to stand them off, the influence of the Iroquois League on the Ohio would be a dead letter. Offensive as the proposed Virginia settlement at the Forks was to the Delawares, Shawnees, Mingos, and other groups in the valley, Tanaghrisson accepted the company's present as an earnest of the support he hoped would continue to flow his way thereafter.

---

*As lieutenant governor, Dinwiddie represented Virginia's governor, the earl of Albemarle, a courtier who collected the governor's annual salary of £1,665 and never once set foot in the colony from the time of his appointment in 1737 to his death in 1754. Such absentee arrangements were common in colonial British America, and gave the lieutenant governors, who exercised considerable power but received salaries far smaller than those of the governors, huge incentives to maximize their incomes by indulging in various forms of graft and speculation. The shareholders of the Ohio Company were hardly unaware of these conditions when they offered Dinwiddie one of the corporation's twenty shares. The company's original capitalization, at £4,000 sterling, meant that Dinwiddie's share had an immediate cash value of £200, equivalent in purchasing power to perhaps $40,000 today. Even as a bribe this would have been a tidy sum, but the real significance of the share was that it gave Dinwiddie a 5 percent stake in the future profits of the Ohio Company, and hence an incentive to look out for its best interests as if they were his own. Which, of course, they were.

George Mercer's map of Ohio Company lands. *The Ohio Company agent George Mercer drafted this map of the area surrounding the Forks of the Ohio after the 1752 Treaty of Logstown. The location originally selected for the company "strong house" (fort) and settlement is at the base of "Fort Hill," an eminence known in today's Pittsburgh as McKee's Rocks.* (The National Archives of the UK [PRO])

Meanwhile, in Canada, the future that Tanaghrisson dreaded was rapidly taking shape. The acting governor, Longueuil, approved of an expedition by more than two hundred Ojibwa and Ottawa warriors under Charles-Michel Mouet de Langlade, the son of a French trader and an Ottawa Indian mother, to discipline the breakaway Miamis at Pickawillany and destroy the trading post that had drawn so many other Indians away from the French alliance. In June, a few days after the Logstown conference ended, Langlade's force attacked Pickawillany, destroying the settlement, looting its trading post, and taking five of its six resident traders captive. The sixth trader, who had been wounded in the attack, they killed. The

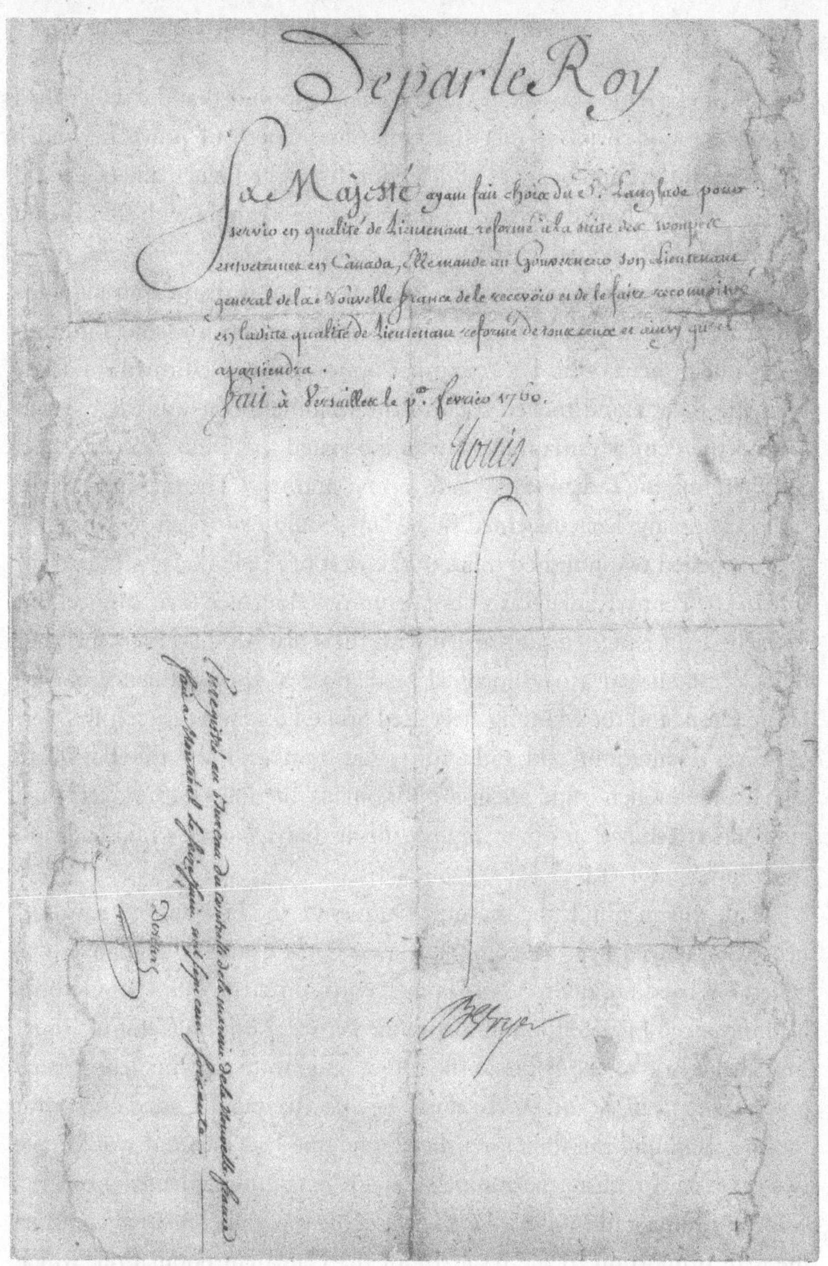

De par le Roy

Sa Majesté ayant fait choix du Sr. Langlade pour servir en qualité de Lieutenant reformé à la suite des troupes entretenues en Canada, Elle mande au Gouverneur son Lieutenant general de la Nouvelle France de le recevoir et de le faire reconnoître en laditte qualité de Lieutenant reformé de tous ceux et ainsy qu'il appartiendra.

Fait à Versailles le 1er fevrier 1760.

Louis

Berryer

Charles de Langlade's commission. *Charles-Michel Mouet de Langlade (1729–1801), the son of a French trader and his Ottawa Indian wife, was appointed cadet in the colonial* troupes de la marine *in 1750. He led his Ottawa kinsmen against the Miami Indians at Pickawillany in 1752. Langlade received this lieutenant's commission, signed by Louis XV, shortly before the fall of New France in 1760.* (Courtesy of the Neville Public Museum of Brown County)

Miami chief Memeskia—such a consistent Anglophile that the traders had called him Old Briton—met the same fate. Then, to prove beyond a doubt what the consequences of defection from the French alliance could be, the warriors boiled the trader's heart and ate it, along with Old Briton *tout ensemble,* in a ritual feast.

The message was not lost on the Indians of Pickawillany, who soon discovered that Pennsylvania had no intention of sending arms and ammunition to help them resist. Lacking other options, they reaffirmed solidarity with the French and moved back to the Maumee. Nor was the message lost on the Pennsylvania traders, who evacuated the Ohio country, effectively ending the Indian trade there in 1752 and 1753. The members of the Ohio Company, less concerned than they should have been by what had just happened two hundred miles to the west of the Forks, saw the departure of the Pennsylvanians as an opportunity to enhance their connections with the Half King. Forging ahead with their plans for a settlement, they quickly established a new fortified storehouse at the confluence of Red Stone Creek and the Monongahela. Red Stone Fort lay a dozen miles west of Gist's Plantation, and only thirty-seven miles from the Forks. In Canada the French could see in the Virginians' boldness nothing less than a defiant continuation of an English threat that Langlade's raid had not, somehow, eradicated.

With this in mind, the marquis Duquesne, the bull-headed naval officer who arrived in Quebec on July 1, 1752, as Canada's new governor-general, moved rapidly to assert French control on the Ohio. In October he announced his intention to fortify the key locations on Céloron's route from Lake Erie to the Forks of the Ohio, and create a permanent French presence on *la Belle Rivière.* To do so he effectively put Canada on a war footing. Building the four forts that Duquesne had in mind would take two years and require the mobilization of two thousand men from the colony's militia and *troupes de la marine.* This was a phenomenal commitment in proportion to the total size of the Canadian population, which had only about eleven thousand able-bodied men between the ages of sixteen and sixty. More than four hundred workers lost their lives by accident and disease in the construction of Fort Presque Isle (on the site of modern Erie, Pennsylvania), Fort de la Rivière au Boeuf (or Fort Le Boeuf, in modern Waterford, Pennsylvania), Fort Machault (near today's Franklin, Pennsylvania), and Fort Duquesne at the Forks of the Ohio. The cost of four million livres—equivalent to about £180,000 sterling, with roughly the purchasing power of 30 million of today's dollars—imposed a tremendous financial burden on the colony.

Only a man with Duquesne's force of will, and sheer disdain for the Canadians who begged him not to proceed, would have undertaken such

***Charles-Jacques Le Moyne, Second Baron de Longueuil,* artist unknown, c. 1730–1740.** *The Canadian nobleman Charles Le Moyne was an experienced colonial regular officer and acting governor of New France when the marquis Duquesne arrived from France in July 1752. Like many Canadians, he opposed Duquesne's program of military action on the Ohio River, advocating commercial competition with British traders and reliance on the Iroquois Confederacy to keep the region free of settlements.* (Oil on canvas; Collection of the Musée d'art de Joliette, Quebec, long-term loan of Historical Society of Longueuil; Photo: Richard-Max Tremblay)

a heroic expenditure of the colony's resources in pursuit of a goal that could have been much more cheaply achieved by diplomacy. The most dangerous of the British, the Pennsylvania traders, had already fled the Ohio. The Virginians could have been countered by making substantial diplomatic gifts to the Ohio Indians and opening a subsidized trade among them. If Duquesne had done so, the Delawares, Shawnees, and Mingos would have had the resources they needed to defy the attenuated power of the Iroquois League and to resist the Virginians' efforts to found a settlement at the Forks. It would have put them in a position to begin playing off one empire against the other, thus enabling them to secure the independence of action they most desired. But that alternative would have required Duquesne to trust the negotiating expertise of Canadian colonists (whom he disdained as provincials) and to rely on Indians (whom he understood as savages) to carry out policy. Neither were actions that he, as a metropolitan aristocrat and servant of the crown, could have found acceptable.

Instead Duquesne pursued a plan that could only provoke a confrontation between the French and British empires. In opting for direct military occupation of the Ohio, Duquesne had not yet chosen a path that would lead inevitably to war. It was, however, a path that made violence infinitely more likely when the confrontation occurred, and war infinitely harder to avoid in its aftermath.

CHAPTER FOUR

"Thou Art Not Yet Dead, My Father"

To Robert Dinwiddie in the Governor's Palace at Williamsburg, the news that the French were building the first three forts—Presque Isle, Le Boeuf, and Machault—in the summer of 1753 looked unmistakably like an attempt to prevent Virginia from expanding settlement within its legitimate boundaries. Dinwiddie accordingly informed the duke of Newcastle and other leaders of His Majesty's government of what he characterized as a brazen French attempt to seize lands that belonged by right of ancient claim to the king of Great Britain. The ministers found the news deeply troubling. The last war with France had ended only five years before, and France had emerged from it in a far stronger position than Britain. Apart from the taking of Louisbourg, the British had won no victories. Desperate for peace in 1748, Britain had essentially forced its ally Austria to sign a treaty that surrendered the rich province of Silesia to France's ally, Prussia. Bad feelings between the Austrians and the British had persisted. Were the French even now moving toward another war, to take advantage of the weakened Anglo-Austrian alliance? Fearful of this possibility, the ministers concluded that only a forceful response would deter the French from whatever devious and subtle plan they were pursuing in North America.

The cabinet therefore sent a circular letter to Dinwiddie and his fellow governors authorizing them to remove the French from any "encroachments" they had made on the frontiers of their colonies. Since Dinwiddie's

Robert Dinwiddie, **artist unknown, c. 1760–1765.** *Virginia's lieutenant governor, Robert Dinwiddie, labored through the summer and fall of 1753 to build support for a campaign to forestall French occupation of the Ohio River. As a result, British imperial authorities approved his plan to confront encroaching French forces at the Forks of the Ohio in the summer of 1754.* (National Portrait Gallery, London)

case had pertained most directly to Virginia's frontiers, he received a separate, more detailed set of instructions outlining the actions he was to take. First, he was to demand that the French withdraw from the posts they had built. Second, he was authorized to erect "forts within the king's own territory" and "to repel force with force" should the French seek to eject Virginia's troops from them. Finally, if the French refused to leave forts they had built within "the undoubted limits of His Majesty's dominions," Dinwiddie was authorized "to enforce by arms (if necessary)" their evacuation. Cannon and ammunition were sent to help him arm and defend whatever forts he needed to build on Virginia's frontier.

The officers of the crown, in effect, gave Dinwiddie all the authority and armaments he needed to build a fort at the Forks of the Ohio. Had he been on good terms with the House of Burgesses at the time his instructions arrived, and had the members of the House not had excellent reason to suspect that he planned to promote the fortunes of the Ohio Company at public expense, Dinwiddie might have mustered the support he would have needed to build a fort without delay. Ever the stickler for collecting every penny due to him, however, the governor had lately antagonized the legislators in a dispute over the terms of his compensation, creating a legislative impasse. Until the dispute could be sorted out by authorities in England, all that Dinwiddie could do about the French was to send an emissary out to demand that they leave the posts they had recently completed. The man the governor chose to carry the message was George Washington.

Why the governor picked a twenty-one-year-old major of the Virginia militia for this mission—a man who spoke no French, had little formal education, and utterly lacked diplomatic experience—may not seem intuitively obvious. Young Washington, however, had several qualifications. He had the backing of Lord Thomas Fairfax, who approved of the work Washington had done for him as a surveyor; he had an intense ambition to prove himself worthy of public trust and thus to rise in the ranks of the planter gentry; and he had both the willingness and the hardihood to undertake a five-hundred-mile journey under miserable conditions, in the late fall and winter of the year. Moreover, Washington had a powerful personal desire to see the Ohio country. His late half brother, Lawrence, had been one of the original shareholders in the Ohio Company. While Washington himself did not hold stock in it, his experiences as a surveyor on Fairfax lands in the Shenandoah Valley had convinced him that his future fortunes would be tied to the development of the West.

Major Washington left Williamsburg on November 1, 1753, with little idea of what lay ahead. Luckily he had Christopher Gist, who knew the Ohio Indians and the region they lived in as well as anyone in Virginia, to accompany him as a guide, translator, and negotiator. Luckily, indeed, for Gist also had the strength and presence of mind to save Washington's life on two occasions on the journey, thus allowing the major to return to Williamsburg in mid-January 1754 and report what he had seen to Dinwiddie. The French, Washington explained, were well established on

Honble Sir King George Cty. June 10th 1752

Being impatient to know Col°. Fitzhughs result; I went to Maryland as I returned Home. He is willing to accept of the Adjutancy of the Northern Neck, if he can obtain it on the terms he proposes, which he hardly expects, will be granted Him: The inclosed is his Letter, wherein I believe he informs of his intention. He told Me, he would, when conveniency admitted, build a House in Virginia, at which, he should sometimes reside. If I could have the Honour of obtaining that, in case Col°. Fitzhugh does not; or either of the other two; should take the greatest pleasure in punctually obeying from time, to time, your Honours commands; and by a strict observance of my Duty, render my self worthy of ye trust reposed in Me: I am sensible my best endeavours will not be wanting, and doubt not, but by a constant application to fit my self for the Office, could I presume your Honour had not in view a more deserving Person

Washington's letter to Dinwiddie, June 10, 1752. *This letter from George Washington requesting a militia appointment from Lieutenant Governor Dinwiddie marks the beginning of the young Virginian's military career. Enjoying the support of Lord*

I hope Capt. Mackay will have more sense than to insist on a very unreasonable distinction tho' he & his have commissions from his Majesty. Let him consider that we are greatly inferior in respect to profitable advantages yet we have the same spirit to serve our Gracious King as they have & are as ready and willing to sacrifice our lives for our Country's good as them — and here once more for the last time I must say that will be a canker that will grate some Officers of this Regiment beyond all measure to serve upon such different terms when their lives, their fortunes & their Characters are equally & I dare say as effectually exposed as those who are happy enough to have King's Commissions —

N.B. This occurred when Braddock arrived in Virginia

Thomas Fairfax and other members of the governor's council, Washington was appointed adjutant of Virginia's southern militia district in December. (Courtesy George Washington's Fredericksburg Foundation)

flatter myself I should meet with the approbation of
the Gentlemen of the Council

I am Yr Honours most
Obt & very Hble Servt
G Washington

the Allegheny. He had visited forts Machault and Le Boeuf; both were sturdy and well supplied. At Fort Le Boeuf he had found the regional commander, Captain Jacques Legardeur de Saint-Pierre of the *troupes de la marine,* and delivered Dinwiddie's message to him. That veteran soldier, who had seen service at posts from Nova Scotia to Lake Winnipeg to Tennessee, had politely declined to leave; the decision, he explained, was not his to make. Moreover, Washington had seen canoes and bateaux on the banks of the river and in the woods near Fort Le Boeuf, hundreds of them: a clear indication that the next stage of the French occupation would be to build a fourth fort, at the Forks of the Ohio, in the coming year.

The single most alarming thing about Washington's report, ironically, was a fact that seems not to have greatly concerned either him or the governor: although Tanaghrisson had accompanied Washington's party to Fort Le Boeuf, he was able to persuade only one Mingo war chief, Guyasutha, and two other Mingo warriors to make the journey with them. Had Washington known more of Indian diplomacy, he would have found cause for worry in such a small escort and especially in the complete absence of Delawares and Shawnees from the Half King's entourage. Legardeur de Saint-Pierre, vastly more experienced in such matters, understood precisely what it meant: whatever Tanaghrisson might say, the Ohio Indians were unwilling to commit themselves to an alliance with the British. The Half King clearly had only slender support among the people he was supposed to lead. If the French could beat the English to the Forks in the spring, they would meet no effective resistance from the natives.

Dinwiddie quickly dispatched a copy of Washington's journal to the duke of Newcastle and other British authorities, who agreed that the governor should build a fort at the Forks as quickly as possible and recruit a Virginia provincial regiment to defend it. He had a harder time persuading the members of the House of Burgesses, but in the end they appropriated £10,000 to pay for the fort and two hundred soldiers. Neither the amount of money nor the number of men was adequate, but they gave Dinwiddie what he needed to proceed. Later he would ask for supplementary funds and men, and the burgesses, grudgingly, would comply.

Washington, who now knew the upper Ohio region better than any other qualified officer, asked to be appointed as the regiment's lieutenant colonel. Dinwiddie gladly agreed, and issued the necessary orders to allow

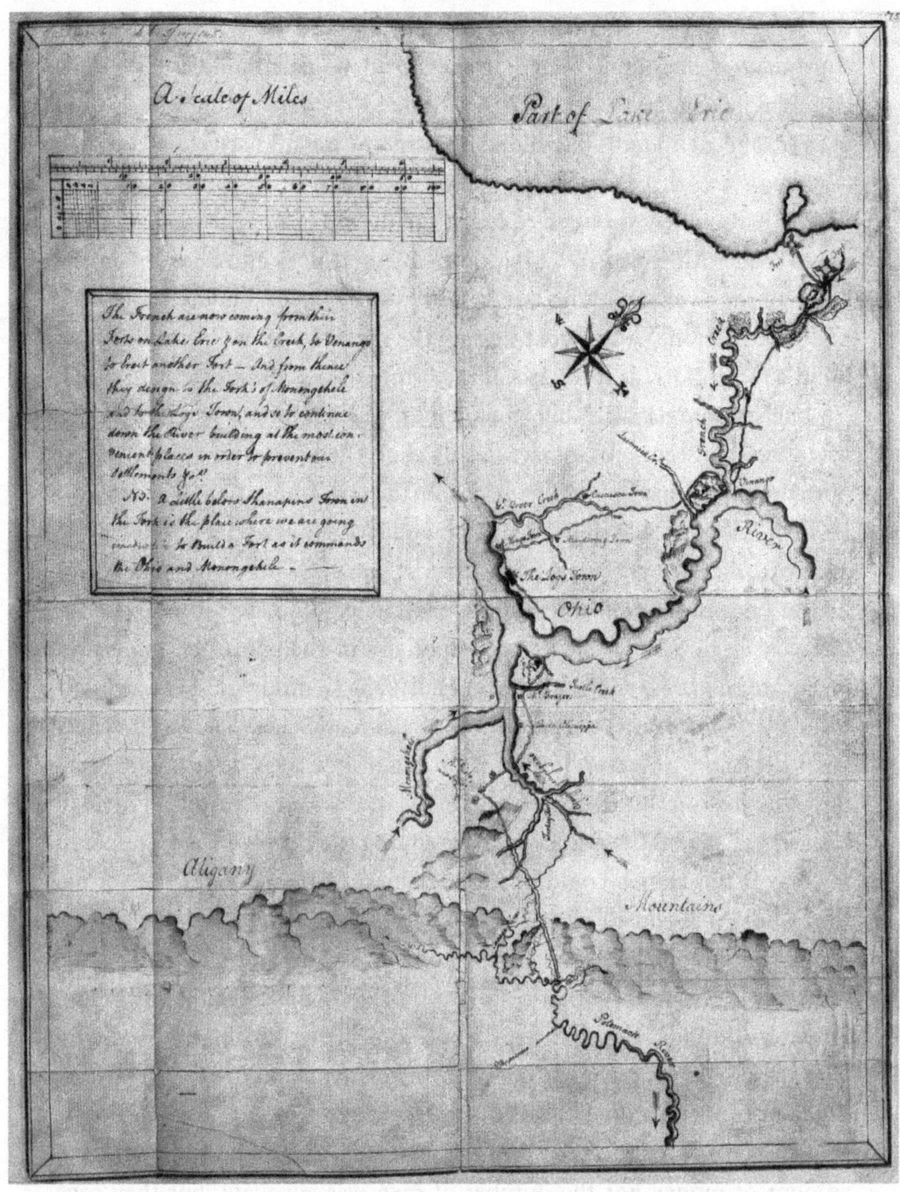

Washington's map of the Ohio River region, 1754. *Major Washington turned a trained surveyor's eye to the landscape during his arduous journey westward from the Ohio Company storehouse at Wills Creek on the Potomac River to the French posts in the upper Ohio Valley. His journal and testimony, together with this manuscript map of the region, convinced Dinwiddie and his council of the need to counter the French encroachments.* (The National Archives of the UK [PRO])

him to enlist men for the unit. The governor also issued commissions appointing several Pennsylvania traders who had taken refuge at Red Stone Fort as officers in the Virginia militia; they were to raise a company of carpenters and begin building a fort at the Forks as soon as possible.

The new lieutenant colonel had a terrible time convincing men to volunteer. In large part this was because the skinflint burgesses had approved a daily wage for the common soldiers that was less than half of what a common laborer could earn, a paltry sum that was to be supplemented by a modest grant of land to be awarded at the end of service. By mid-April, when Washington marched the unit west toward Wills Creek, he had only 159 soldiers under his command. They were far from a promising lot. Many were paupers and vagabonds who had been coerced into service. The regiment as a whole was poorly clad, poorly shod, poorly supplied, and as yet wholly untrained.

Washington cut a more dashing figure than his men, but did not know a great deal more about what he was doing than they did. All that he understood of military service he had learned from reading books and quizzing his older half brother, Lawrence, who had once held a captain's commission in the British army. This did not particularly concern him, because he was accustomed to learning by experience, and therefore eagerly anticipated the arrival of the regiment's commanding officer, Colonel Joshua Frye, whom he expected to supply the expertise he lacked. Frye was to bring more troops and supplies to a rendezvous with Washington at the Wills Creek fort; in addition, Washington knew, the Virginia Regiment would be joined by a company of British regulars from South Carolina. Once the reinforcements arrived and the men had been drilled enough to know their duty, they would march for the Ohio and defend the new post at the Forks. Fort Prince George, named for the heir apparent to the throne, would (Washington believed) stand up to attack if the French were to be so foolish as to try to eject the Virginians from the Forks. That, at least, was the plan.

Washington had been at Wills Creek only a couple of days when on April 22 the commander of the carpenters' company arrived to inform him that hundreds of French troops had appeared on the Allegheny in a flotilla of canoes and bateaux on April 17, carrying with them no fewer than eighteen cannon. With his forty men desperately short of food, arms, and ammunition, he had taken one look at what seemed to be a thousand Canadians and surrendered the recently completed stockade. Washington absorbed the news, took stock of his own underequipped and untrained men, wrote the necessary reports to Dinwiddie, and ordered the regiment to make ready to march. Despite the unpromising state of his command and his own lack of experience, he intended to comply with Dinwiddie's orders to "make prisoners of or kill and destroy" any "Offenders" against the king's authority who had sought to "obstruct the works" at Fort Prince George. He would move his force to Red Stone Fort and wait for Frye and his reinforcements there; then they could take back the Forks.

The regiment marched from Wills Creek on April 30. By May 24, it had built a crude wagon road over fifty of the eighty miles that separated Wills Creek from Red Stone Fort, and encamped in a valley between two formidable mountains, Chestnut Ridge and Laurel Hill. The spot, called Great Meadows, was a quarter-mile wide, rather boggy, grassland perhaps a mile in length with a creek meandering down its center. Washington saw what it had to offer—fodder for his draft animals and a constant supply of water—and decided that it would be a useful way station. He ordered a pause for his men to clear brush, cut fodder, and construct a storehouse.

On the morning of May 27, Christopher Gist rode into camp to tell Washington that a party of French soldiers had passed his trading post at noon on the previous day. He estimated that they were now within five miles of the Great Meadows. Washington, fearing an attack, sent half his men west toward the Monongahela to look for them. At sunset, a Mingo warrior arrived in camp with a message from Tanaghrisson saying that the French had bivouacked about seven miles to the north. Only then did Washington understand that he had sent his men in the wrong direction. Hurriedly he gathered up half of his remaining troops and led them off, behind the Indian guide, for Tanaghrisson's camp. All that night the Virginians blundered through the woods in a heavy rain, arriving at the Indian camp around sunrise. Tanaghrisson and the handful of warriors he had with him offered to lead Washington and his wet, weary men to the French camp, which was not far off.

When they arrived at the top of a rock wall overlooking a small glen, Washington saw that the French were just crawling out of their bark shelters and beginning to prepare their breakfast. He quietly arrayed his men above the hollow. Tanaghrisson and his warriors slipped off below to block the escape route.

The shooting that broke out soon thereafter may have started (as Washington maintained) when the French, suddenly seeing men on the rocks above them, seized their muskets and fired; or it may have begun (as the French attested) when the English unleashed a volley at them without warning. At any rate the confused firefight soon ended when the French officer in charge, wounded, called out for a cease-fire. One Virginian was dead, and three wounded; the French had suffered fourteen casualties among the thirty-five men in the camp.

The French commander, a thirty-five-year-old ensign in the *troupes de la marine* named Joseph Coulon de Villiers de Jumonville, was among the wounded. Now, through an interpreter, he tried to explain his mission to Washington. He had been sent by the commandant of the new fort at the Forks, Fort Duquesne, on a diplomatic mission: he was to deliver a letter to Washington ordering him to evacuate the lands of the king of France or suffer the consequences. The translation of the letter was proceeding when Tanaghrisson stepped up to Jumonville, raised his hatchet, and smashed open the ensign's skull. His warriors then began to kill the rest of the wounded, scalping and stripping them of arms and clothing. By the time Washington gathered enough of his wits to intervene, only one of the wounded men was left alive.

Why had it happened? Washington himself could scarcely have fathomed the reason at that moment, but the words that Tanaghrisson spoke to Jumonville immediately before he killed him made it clear: *"Tu n'es pas encore mort, mon père"*—"Thou art not yet dead, my father." When he called Jumonville "father," Tanaghrisson evoked the role that representatives of the French king had traditionally claimed in alliances with native people; then he denied the power of that name by killing the man who bore it. Tanaghrisson had committed a murder, but he had also made a diplomatic statement. He was declaring war—on his own behalf and that of the Virginians.

Tanaghrisson committed this horrible, desperate, calculated act for a reason that would have been apparent to Washington if only the Virginian had known how to interpret what he had earlier seen at the Indian camp. The Half King had perhaps eighty people with him. At most a dozen were

"Habillemens des Coureurs de bois Canadiens," no. 2. *This rare eighteenth-century sketch illustrates the common working dress of Canadians engaged in war and the fur trade, which borrowed heavily from American Indian fashion. Ensign Jumonville's party was composed almost entirely of such men, whose lack of military uniforms probably exacerbated the confusion of the skirmish with Washington's Virginians on May 28, 1754.* (Yale Collection of Western Americana, Beinecke Rare Book and Manuscript Library)

warriors; the rest were women, children, and old men. All, or virtually all, of them were Mingos. It was, in other words, a refugee group, driven from the Forks by the loss of Tanaghrisson's status as a leader. The Delawares, Shawnees, and hundreds of remaining Mingos were—had to be—dealing directly with the French. Tanaghrisson's only hope of restoring his own position, and the influence of the Iroquois League, was to return to the valley with a powerful ally. Jumonville's blood had sealed what the Half King intended to be an unbreakable covenant with Washington and the Virginians, and through them with the king of England.

Washington, confused, tried to cover up what had been at the least a colossal humiliation by writing misleading reports of the action and sending them back to Dinwiddie along with the twenty-one Canadian militiamen who had survived. The Canadians, he cautioned, were spies. Nothing they might say about being on a diplomatic mission should be believed.

The massacre took place on May 28; the reckoning came five weeks later. In the interim, Washington learned by a letter from the governor that Colonel Frye had fallen from his horse and died; Dinwiddie had promoted Washington to the rank of colonel and commandant of the regiment. Two hundred more troops had arrived at Great Meadows from Virginia, hauling light artillery. Shortly thereafter the British regular infantry company from South Carolina had reached the camp, bringing forty beef cattle with them. Word had come that a great supply train was on its way; and Tanaghrisson, who moved his encampment to Great Meadows, professed confidence that the Ohio Indians would join the British if only Washington showed resolve. In view of these developments, Washington decided to attack Fort Duquesne.

It was a move that only a neophyte would have made, and it ended in a fiasco. An attempt to move men and supplies forward reached Gist's Plantation only on June 18, when the Delaware chief Shingas, together with Shawnee and Mingo leaders from the valley, appeared to confer with Washington and Tanaghrisson. Three days of negotiations revealed that the Ohio Indians had no intention of joining in an attack on the French. This ended Tanaghrisson's hopes of reestablishing himself, and Iroquois authority, on the Ohio. Knowing that the French would retaliate, he returned to Great Meadows, gathered his followers, and moved them a hundred miles east to take refuge at George Croghan's trading post on Aughwick Creek. The Half King understood perfectly well that the fort that Washington had built—a small circular stockade around the storehouse that Washington had named Fort Necessity, which Tanaghrisson called "that little thing upon the Meadow"—was useless. If Washington had chosen to doom himself and his command, Tanaghrisson saw no reason that he, his family, and his followers should share their fate.

Incredibly, despite the departure of Tanaghrisson and the knowledge that the Ohio Indians would not help him, Washington tried to move ahead toward Red Stone Fort; Indian aid or no, he intended to attack Fort Duquesne. His resolve lasted until June 28, when Scarouady, an Oneida leader who had remained on the Ohio and who had perforce become

Tanaghrisson's successor as representative of the Iroquois League, arrived at Red Stone. A large French and Indian reinforcement had reached Fort Duquesne, he informed Washington, and a detachment was preparing to march against him. Washington's fellow officers urged him to return to Fort Necessity. He agreed.

The retreat, a two-day forced march, left Washington's men exhausted. They did what they could to strengthen their position, digging trenches outside the palisade of Fort Necessity to afford some shelter when the attack came. The stockade was too small to protect more than sixty or seventy men, and more than that many were too sick and weak to fight. That night it began to rain. The morning light of July 3 showed the trenches filling with water. Roll call disclosed that only three hundred of the four hundred men at the fort were fit for duty.

At eleven o'clock the French appeared—six hundred regulars and Canadian militiamen, together with a hundred Indian warriors, primarily Ottawas, Nipissings, and other allies from the Great Lakes—and launched their attack. Within minutes they had taken positions under cover on the wooded hillside that overlooked the fort, firing down on the men who huddled in the sodden trenches. The canopy of leaves above them enabled the attackers to keep their powder dry, and their muskets operable, for a long day of slaughter. The defenders, by contrast, quickly lost the capacity to fire back, and became little more than targets. By nightfall thirty of them were dead and another seventy had been badly wounded. The demoralized survivors, knowing how little chance they stood if the French and Indians renewed their attack the following morning, broke into the rum supply. Any sense of order and subordination that had survived the hellish day now fell to pieces; Washington contemplated the utter humiliation of a defeat that might well end in the annihilation of his command. Then something that seemed miraculous happened: the French ordered a cease-fire and proposed a parley on terms of capitulation.

The French commander, who happened to be Captain Louis Coulon de Villiers, Ensign Jumonville's older brother, had more reason to be merciful than Washington knew. His men had come lightly armed and with only the ammunition they could carry; the long day's firing had used up most of what they had. As a professional officer, he was concerned about the extent of his legal authority over the defeated force; unlike the amateur

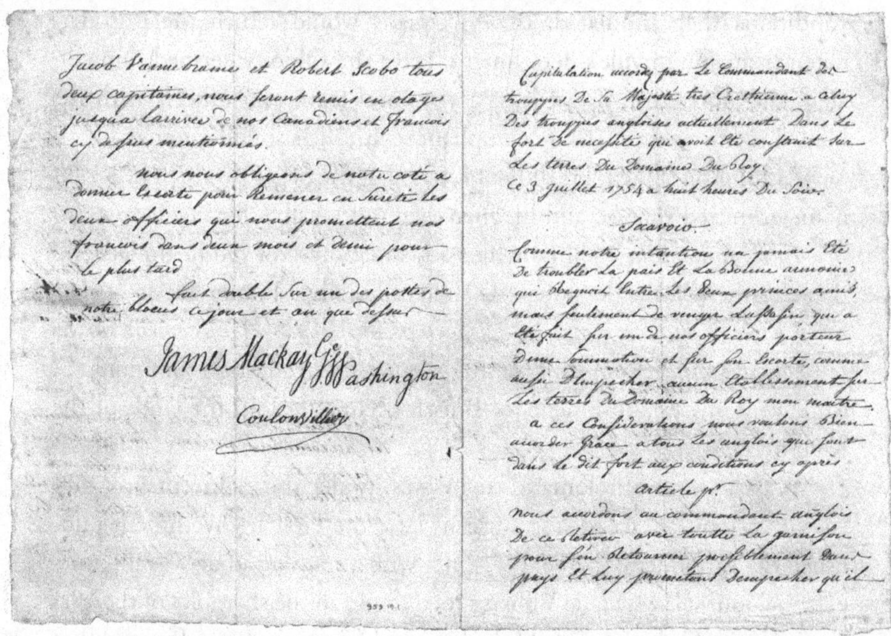

Jacob Vambrame et Robert Scobo tous deux capitaines, nous seront remis en otage jusqu'a l'arrivée de nos Canadiens et François cy dessus mentionnés.

nous nous obligeons de notre coté a donner Lescorte pour Ramener en Sureté les deux officiers qui nous promettent nos françois dans deux mois et demi pour le plus tard

fait double sur un des postes de notre blocus a jour et an que dessus

James Mackay Go Washington

Coulonvillier

Capitulation accordé par le Commandant des troupes de Sa Majesté tres Crethienne a celuy des troupes angloises actuellement dans le fort de necessité qui avoit été construit sur les terres du Domaine du Roy.

Ce 3 juillet 1754 a huit heures du Soir.

Scavoir.

Comme notre intention na jamais été de troubler la paix et la bonne armonie qui Regnoit Entre les deux princes amis, mais seulement de venger Lassassin qui a été fait sur un de nos officiers porteur dune sommation et sur son Escorte, comme aussy Dempecher aucun Etablissement sur les terres du Domaine du Roy mon maitre.

a ces Considerations nous voulons bien accorder grace a tous les anglois qui sont dans le dit fort aux conditions cy apres

article pr.

nous accordons au commandant anglois de se Retirer avec toutte sa garnison pour s'en Retourner paisiblement dans son pays et luy promettons dempecher qu'il

Document of capitulation at Fort Necessity (first and last pages). *Lieutenant Colonel George Washington, Captain James Mackay, and the French commander Captain Louis Coulon de Villiers (Ensign Jumonville's brother) signed this capitulation at eight in the evening on July 3, 1754. Washington was humiliated to learn later that the document twice referred to his "assassination" of Jumonville; he blamed Captain Jacob Van Braam, his subordinate, for making an incompetent translation.* (With permission of the Royal Ontario Museum © ROM)

Washington, who in his ignorance had sent twenty-one Canadian militiamen to Williamsburg, de Villiers knew that in the absence of a state of war he had no authority to make anyone a prisoner of war. Even if he had wanted to consider the Virginians as criminals, there was no place to hold them at Fort Duquesne, and no way to transport them to Canada for trial. Moreover, he had come on a punitive expedition, and clearly had accomplished his mission of chastisement. He therefore offered the Virginians the conventional military compliment of a surrender "with the honors of war," which allowed the defeated soldiers to keep their arms, colors, personal property, and one symbolic piece of light artillery. All that Washington had to do was to sign articles of capitulation and adhere to the conditions they stipulated: the Virginians would return the prisoners taken from Jumonville's detachment, leave the Ohio watershed immediately and not return for at least a year, and leave two officers with the French as hostages, to ensure compliance with the surrender terms.

Washington signed. He did not know that the pages to which he set his name admitted that he and his men were responsible for *"l'assassinat du S[ieu]r de Jumonville"*—Jumonville's assassination. Nor did he understand that elsewhere in the document de Villiers described Jumonville as *"nos officier porteur d'une sommation . . . d'empecher aucun Etablissement sur les terres du domaine du Roy mon maitre"*—"our officer carrying a summons . . . to prevent any establishment [of British occupation] on the lands of the King my master."

To assassinate a diplomatic envoy was, under the eighteenth-century law of nations, an act of war. Months later the French government published the surrender document together with a translation of Washington's personal journal, which de Villiers's men found in the shambles of the Virginian camp. Only then would the king and his ministers understand that George Washington had done much more than simply fail to eject the French from the Forks of the Ohio. He had handed Louis XV all the justification he would ever need to declare war on Great Britain.

PART TWO

LA GUERRE SAUVAGE

CHAPTER FIVE

Intervention

Despite having a perfectly serviceable casus belli in the murder of Ensign Jumonville, the French crown did not declare war on Britain in 1754. The marquis Duquesne was spoiling for a fight, but when he asked his superior, the minister of marine, if he should anticipate hostilities, the minister sent back a negative reply. This baffled and outraged the impetuous governor-general, but France had good reasons to cling to peace. It was replacing its navy with ships of the most sophisticated design, an expensive endeavor that was only halfway to its goal of creating a fleet the size of the British navy. Public finance as a whole was stable, thanks to a long program of paying off Louis XIV's debts. But retiring those staggering obligations had pushed taxes up to a level that left little room for new ones. If the nation went to war, Louis XV would have to fund it by borrowing, and that would put an end to the prudent fiscal program France had pursued since 1726. Finally, diplomacy was at a delicate stage, with Austria secretly suggesting it might abandon its half-century-old alliance with Britain if France would support it in regaining Silesia. As pleased as Duquesne was with himself for wrong-footing the British in the interior of North America, and concerned as he was about what would happen if they recovered their balance, he was well ahead of the king and his ministers in the lunge toward war. Despite Washington's provocation, His Most Christian Majesty preferred to negotiate with Britain on the question of imperial boundaries. Rather than issuing an ultimatum to

Britain, the French foreign ministry calmly proposed that the Ohio country from the Forks of the Ohio to the Wabash be declared a neutral zone, and permanently demilitarized.

French medal, 1754. *This silver medal struck in France in 1754 commemorates the shipbuilding and modernization program France undertook following the War of the Austrian Succession. Inscribed "DANT OTIA VIRES" ("Repose gives strength"), this piece reflects the official French policy of restoring military and financial strength before resuming conflict with Britain.* (J. C. Roettier, © National Maritime Museum, London)

In London, meanwhile, George II's leading minister, the duke of Newcastle, reacted to the news of Fort Necessity with an alarm that verged on panic. At his urging the crown offered Virginia £120,000 to shore up its defenses and contemplated a plan to dispatch regular army officers to train provincial troops so that they could in turn remove the "encroachment" of Fort Duquesne. He also made diplomatic overtures to various European states for support—notably to Austria, which he did not know was negotiating secretly with Versailles—in the hope of putting France on the defensive. Newcastle's goal was to force a resolution in America favorable to British interests without going to war. A hawkish faction within Newcastle's cabinet, however, favored sterner measures than the duke, and set about undermining his authority to achieve its goals. Ultimately it intended to displace Newcastle from his position of leadership altogether.

Appealing to William Augustus, duke of Cumberland—George II's favorite son, captain-general of the British army, and a major influence in the politics of Parliament and the court—the insurgent ministers pushed for sending troops to America. Cumberland proposed the Forty-fourth and Forty-eighth Regiments of Foot, to be commanded by one of his favorite officers, Major General Edward Braddock of the Coldstream Guards. Two more regular regiments, the Fiftieth and Fifty-first Foot, were to be raised in America and placed under the command of Governor William Shirley of Massachusetts and Sir William Pepperrell, who had planned and led the expedition against Louisbourg in 1745. Those four regular regiments, together with several thousand provincial soldiers recruited for a year's service, were to undertake a complex set of missions. Braddock himself would use the Forty-fourth and Forty-eighth to dislodge the French from the Forks and then expel them from Forts Machault, Le Boeuf, and Presque Isle. The Fiftieth and Fifty-first were to destroy Fort Niagara at the head of Lake Ontario. A provincial expedition with Iroquois support would demolish Fort Saint Frédéric on Lake Champlain, while another provincial force operating under regular command would level two forts the French had lately built at the Nova Scotia frontier, on the isthmus of Chignecto. Braddock, as commander in chief of British forces in North America, was to coordinate all these missions. Moreover, in addition to his purely military powers, his commission gave him authority over the governors of the colonies, as well as the authority to instruct the assemblies of the provinces to raise soldiers and contribute to a "common fund" that would pay for the campaigns.

Braddock's broad powers effectively made him Britain's viceroy in North America: a radical departure from previous British policies toward the colonies, which had largely left matters of military defense to the colonists themselves. Part of the reason for this was the duke of Cumberland's faith that military force could solve almost any difficult problem; he had earned his nickname, "the Butcher," in the exceptionally thorough and violent way his redcoats had suppressed a great rebellion of the Highland Scots in 1745–46. A more important stimulus to centralization, however,

His Royal Highness WILLIAM Duke of CUMBERLAND.
Done from an Original Painting in the Possession of the Honourable Lieut: General ONSLOW.
To whom This PLATE is most Humbly Dedicated, By His Honours most Obedient Servant, T. Burford

Portrait of William Augustus, Duke of Cumberland. *William Augustus, duke of Cumberland (1721–1765), the third son of George II and commander of Britain's land forces, shaped the planning of Braddock's 1755 North American expedition. Lionized by Britons throughout the Atlantic world for his success in crushing the 1745–1746 Highland Rebellion against his father's rule, Cumberland was a popular subject for artists and printmakers.* (William L. Clements Library, University of Michigan)

was the North American colonists' inability to cooperate among themselves. New York's extraordinary behavior in King George's War, when it had essentially pursued its own foreign policy of neutrality while New England provincials had beset Louisbourg with the frenzied enthusiasm of a terrier attacking a rat, was only the most striking example of intercolonial self-interest, competition, and fragmentation. There were many more.

In an attempt to remedy this chronic problem, the crown had ordered the colonial governments to send delegates to a general congress at Albany

Covenant Chain wampum belt, 2004. *This modern reproduction depicts the great wampum belt that British colonial delegates presented to the Iroquois Confederacy at Albany in 1754. It represents graphically the nine colonial governors present (in person or by proxy) and the six Iroquois nations joined in amity (represented by a heart) under the protection of King George II (represented by GR, for Georgius Rex).* (Courtesy of Duane Schrecengost)

in the summer of 1754, in order to renew the Covenant Chain with the Iroquois Confederacy and coordinate measures for defense. The Albany Congress, however, fostered little in the way of intercolonial cooperation. Pennsylvania's delegate Benjamin Franklin had indeed proposed a Plan of Union to create an umbrella government for the mainland colonies, with a crown-appointed "President General" and an elected legislature with the power to levy taxes for defense. But the colonial assemblies had proven strikingly indifferent to the plan when it was submitted to them for debate and ratification after the congress ended. Only Massachusetts showed even a slight inclination to pursue the idea of intercolonial union; the rest of the provinces rejected it out of hand. It was clear to Britain's colonial administrators, therefore, that any coordination among the colonies would have to come from above. Braddock's extensive authority thus reflected a British determination to impose a degree of unity on the colonists that they had never before known.

The British government made no attempt to conceal Braddock's appointment or the ordering of the Forty-fourth and Forty-eighth Regiments from Ireland to North America. This thoroughly alarmed the French, who responded by sending seventy-eight regular infantry companies—the equivalent of six regiments—to Canada. These *troupes de terre* numbered

Benjamin Franklin, "Join, or Die" woodcut. *Franklin's famous political cartoon urged support for the Albany Plan of Union that few contemporary colonists, wary of their fellow Americans, shared. Britain's response to the unwillingness of colonies to cooperate was to send Major General Edward Braddock as commander in chief with the authority over colonial governors and instructions to impose unity in the face of French encroachments.* (Courtesy American Antiquarian Society)

approximately three thousand men, four times the number of troops Braddock took with him from Ireland, and included some of the best-trained soldiers in the French army. Their commander was Jean-Armand, baron de Dieskau, a *maréchal de camp* (brigadier general) with considerable experience in the previous war, especially in the use of irregular auxiliary forces. The departure of these troops early in the spring of 1755 was timed to bring them to Canada at the earliest possible moment after the Saint Lawrence cleared of ice. The British navy, alerted to their departure from Brest, tried to intercept them, but captured only the *Alcide* and the *Lys,* carrying ten companies (about four hundred men). Thus by the time Braddock and his troops arrived, the French had augmented the total military manpower of New France by 25 percent. At the beginning of the campaigning season reinforcements were in place and ready to defend strategic strongpoints from Louisbourg to Lake Champlain.

In many ways Braddock resembled the marquis Duquesne. Stubbornness, impetuosity, and disdain for the capacities and views of both colonists and native peoples were among the most obvious of their shared traits, but they resembled each other most significantly in their faith in the superiority of European military professionalism over the types of war-making that had evolved in North America. When Braddock convened a meeting of governors from Virginia, Maryland, Pennsylvania, New York, and Massachusetts at Alexandria, Virginia, in April 1755, he accordingly showed less interest in learning about the temper of their colonies' assemblies or the readiness of the colonists for war than in instructing the governors in their responsibilities, as if they were so many subordinate commanders. He informed them of what each province would provide in support of the campaigns, and ordered them to have their assemblies create the common fund forthwith. He was not happy to hear that the assemblies were deeply protective of their self-supposed right to originate tax bills, and thus unlikely to create that fund without protest. He was, however, pleased to find that a good deal of progress had already been made in mobilizing the New England colonies.

The energetic governor of Massachusetts, William Shirley, had been officially warned in December about the coming campaigns and therefore knew more than most of his colleagues about what was afoot. He and Governor Charles Lawrence of Nova Scotia, on their own initiative, had planned a campaign to suppress unrest among that province's French-speaking population and to destroy the forts, Beauséjour and Gaspereau, that the French had constructed on the Chignecto Isthmus. Shirley had, indeed, already persuaded the assemblies of Massachusetts, Connecticut, and New Hampshire to raise provincial troops and money for the expedition.

Shirley was a lawyer by training and a superb political operative, arguably the most effective of all the colonial governors. He knew how to make things work, even in a colony as refractory as Massachusetts, by manipulating patronage, and was well aware that a war would produce money, military positions, and supply contracts to reward his supporters. Shirley's greatest triumph in that respect had come in King George's War, when he had masterminded the 1745 New England attack on Louisbourg and used the patronage that venture created to build an impressive political machine. At Alexandria he learned to his surprise that he had been commissioned as a regular-army major general and Braddock's second-in-command. He was to have the direction of the northern campaigns, and would personally command the expedition against Fort Niagara. To have this position and the financial and political capital that came with it pleased Shirley greatly, even though he knew nothing of military administration or the procedures of command; he also remained the governor of Massachusetts, with all the responsibilities that entailed. He willingly undertook the responsibilities that he had been given, and set about his new job with characteristic vigor. His instincts, however, remained those of a politician. That, and his utter lack of experience in command, gave him greater cause for caution than he realized.

The second surprise at the Alexandria conference was Braddock's announcement that New York's commissary of Indian affairs, William Johnson, had been named Indian Superintendent for the northern colonies—a new royal office designed to take over responsibility for relations with native peoples that the colonial governments had previously exercised in disorderly and competitive ways. Thanks to a remarkable ability to adapt himself to the culture of the Mohawk Indians, in whose homeland he had lived since 1738, Johnson had become an exceptionally capable intercultural diplomat and a rich man; because of his family's political connections in Britain, he was also a man who could wield great influence on the other side of the Atlantic. His close connections with the Six Nations, of course, tended to magnify the already powerful tendency of British imperial policy to align with Iroquois interests. Johnson's affiliation with an Albany-based political faction in New York made him a rival of William Shirley, whose connections ran strongly toward a competing faction rooted in New York City and its surrounding areas. That would have been problematic at any rate, but it became even more so when Braddock revealed that in addition to his new office as Indian Superintendent, Johnson would also be given command of the provincial expedition that was to march north from Albany to Lake Champlain and destroy Fort Saint Frédéric, at Crown Point. All this reflected remarkably bad planning. Johnson was as much a military amateur as Shirley, and their rivalry was certain to make their expeditions, both of which were to be launched from Albany, into bitterly competitive ventures.

CHAPTER SIX

Braddock's March

When the Alexandria conference broke up, Edward Braddock prepared to march on Fort Duquesne. The plan was to use the road that Washington's Virginia Regiment had opened from Wills Creek to Red Stone Fort the previous summer, improving it to allow heavy artillery and a large supply train to pass. To perform this feat of engineering and execute the siege that would follow, he would rely on the old soldiers and new recruits of the Forty-fourth and Forty-eighth Regiments (about fourteen hundred in all), as well as companies of provincial soldiers from Virginia, Maryland, and North Carolina (a total of another thousand). In addition to these twenty-four hundred soldiers, four or five hundred civilian teamsters, horse wranglers, herdsmen, sutlers, and female camp followers also accompanied the expedition, providing support services from transportation to cooking, laundry, and nursing that the soldiers could not efficiently perform themselves.

Because the regulations that governed precedence in the army dictated that no provincial field officer (that is, major, lieutenant colonel, or colonel) should be superior in rank to any regular field officer, the provincials were organized as independent companies and included no officer above the rank of captain. Washington was eager to serve, but had too keen a sense of honor to accept demotion from provincial colonel to provincial captain. Braddock therefore invited Washington to join his official household as a "volunteer" and aide-de-camp—that is, as a civilian

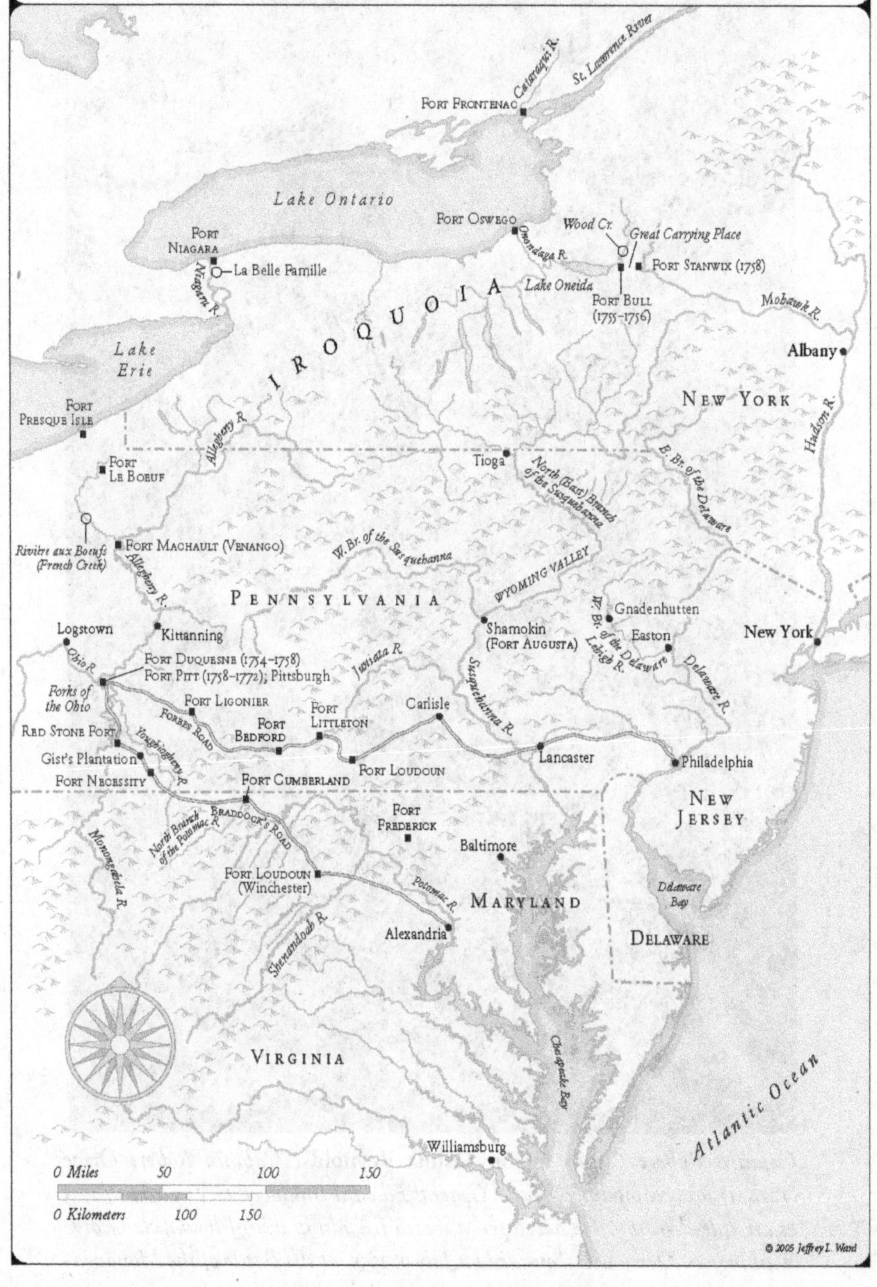

WESTERN THEATER OF OPERATIONS, 1754–1760:
The Pennsylvania-Virginia Frontier to the Great Lakes
St. Lawrence River
Cataraqui R.
FORT FRONTENAC
Lake Ontario
FORT OSWEGO
Wood Cr.
Great Carrying Place
Onondaga R.
FORT NIAGARA
La Belle Famille
FORT STANWIX (1758)
Lake Oneida
Niagara R.
IROQUOIA
FORT BULL (1755–1756)
Mohawk R.
Lake Erie
Albany
FORT PRESQUE ISLE
NEW YORK
Hudson R.
Allegheny R.
Tioga
B. Br. of the Delaware
FORT LE BOEUF
North (East) Branch of the Susquehanna
Rivière aux Boeufs (French Creek)
FORT MACHAULT (VENANGO)
W. Br. of the Susquehanna
Allegheny R.
WYOMING VALLEY
PENNSYLVANIA
Gnadenhutten
Logstown
Kittanning
Shamokin (FORT AUGUSTA)
W. Br. of the Delaware
Easton
New York
Ohio R.
FORT DUQUESNE (1754–1758)
FORT PITT (1758–1772); Pittsburgh
Juniata R.
Lehigh R.
Delaware R.
Forks of the Ohio
FORT LIGONIER
Susquehanna R.
FORBES ROAD
FORT LITTLETON
Carlisle
RED STONE FORT
FORT BEDFORD
Youghiogheny R.
Gist's Plantation
Lancaster
Philadelphia
FORT NECESSITY
FORT LOUDOUN
FORT CUMBERLAND
NEW JERSEY
BRADDOCK'S ROAD
North Branch of the Potomac R.
FORT FREDERICK
Monongahela R.
Baltimore
FORT LOUDOUN (Winchester)
Potomac R.
MARYLAND
Delaware Bay
Shenandoah R.
Alexandria
DELAWARE
VIRGINIA
Chesapeake Bay
Atlantic Ocean
Williamsburg
0 Miles 50 100 150
0 Kilometers 100 150
© 2005 Jeffrey L. Ward

Captain Robert Orme, by Sir Joshua Reynolds. *Captain Robert Orme (1732–1790) accompanied Major General Edward Braddock to Virginia in 1755 as an aide-de-camp. He developed a warm friendship with fellow aide George Washington. Orme was wounded on July 9, 1755, at the Battle of the Monongahela, and returned to Britain, where he posed for this portrait commemorating his American service.* (© National Gallery, London)

performing the same duties as Braddock's other two aides, both regular-army captains. He would receive the same rations and respect as they, but no pay. Such arrangements were common in the British army, and service for a campaign as a gentleman volunteer often furnished the means for ambitious young men to gain appointments as officers. Braddock had a number of blank commissions to use in filling vacancies as they occurred, and Washington understood that one would eventually go to him.

Braddock assembled his expedition's forces, wagons, and draft animals in May at Wills Creek, where he ordered a fort—which he named Cumberland, for his patron—to be built across the Potomac from the Ohio Company's storehouse. What he needed above all was intelligence concerning the enemy's strength and circumstances, and that could come only from Indian sources. To that end he had obtained the services of George Croghan, whose linguistic and cultural skills William Johnson had already recognized by appointing him as his deputy superintendent. Croghan in turn had used his contacts with Tanaghrisson's band (Tanaghrisson himself had died at Croghan's trading post the previous October) to invite Indians from the Forks to meet with Braddock at Fort Cumberland. In late May a delegation appeared, including the Oneida chief Scarouady, Tanaghrisson's successor as Half King, and the Delaware chiefs Shingas and Delaware George. One member of the group, a Mohawk called Moses the Song, brought with him a plan of Fort Duquesne drawn by Captain Robert Stobo, one of the two officers whom Washington had left as hostages with the French in 1754. The delegates presented it in a gesture of goodwill that the general, in his ignorance, entirely disregarded.

The Ohio Indians were in fact quite interested in helping Braddock remove the French and the hundreds of French-allied Indian warriors—Potawatomis, Ottawas, Abenakis, and others—who had accompanied them to the Forks. They now dominated the region in ways infinitely more intrusive than the Iroquois ever had, depriving the Delawares, Shawnees, and Mingos of the self-rule they longed to exercise. All that Shingas and his fellow chiefs asked was that Braddock promise no permanent English settlement would be established in the Ohio country once the French had been driven out. Braddock, however, understood neither how much he needed the Indians nor how much they wanted his aid in establishing their independence. Thus when the chiefs asked him what he planned for

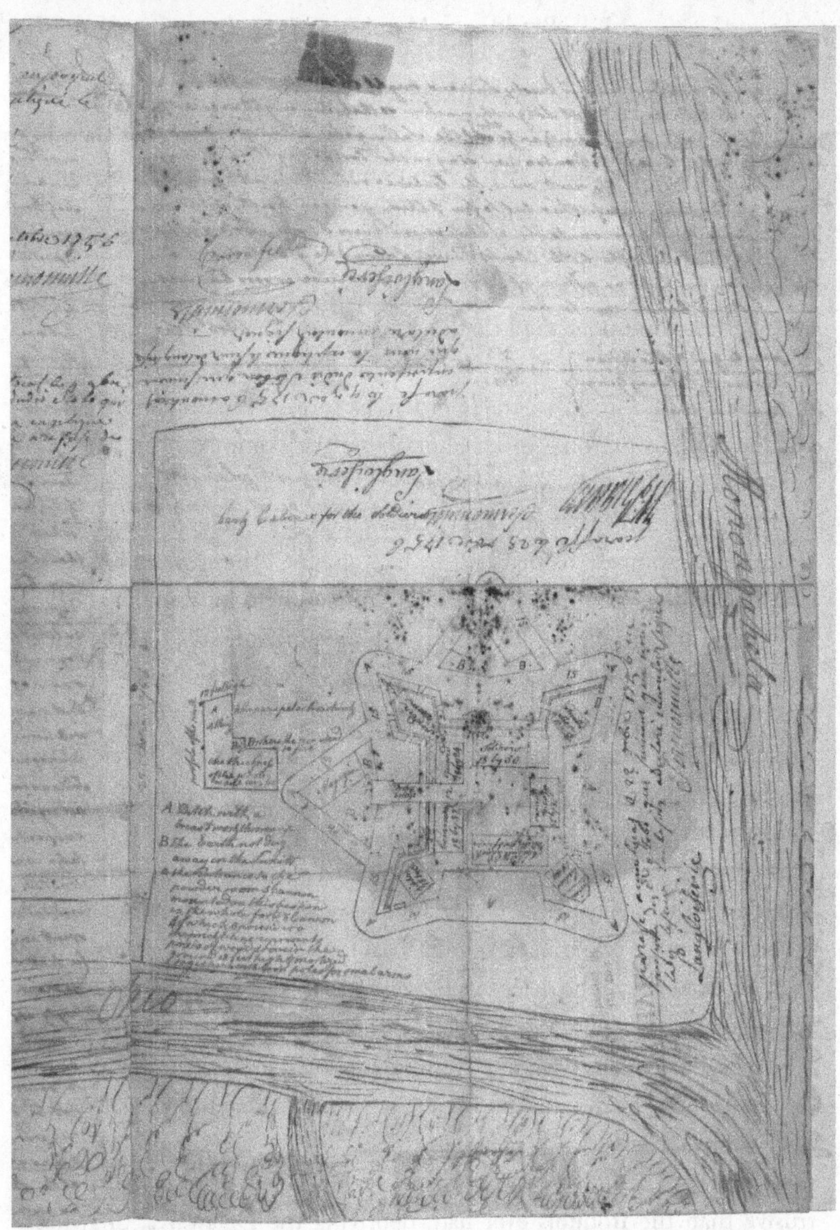

Stobo's map of Fort Duquesne. *Following the Fort Necessity capitulation, two Virginia captains, Robert Stobo and Jacob Van Braam, returned to Fort Duquesne as hostages to ensure the repatriation of the surviving members of Jumonville's party. Moses the Song, a Mohawk who was closely associated with Scarouady and Tanaghrisson (the Half King), smuggled Stobo's plan of Fort Duquesne to Major General Braddock.* (Archives nationales de Quebec—Centre de Montreal, Fonds Juridiction Royale de Montreal, TL4, S1, D6128)

the future of the Forks, he bluntly replied "that the English should inhabit and inherit the land." Would he at least allow the Indians to live among the English, they asked, and leave them sufficient hunting grounds to support their families? Braddock's gruff reply, "No savage should inherit the land," convinced them that they had come to the wrong man for help. Replying that "if they might not have liberty to live on the land they would not fight for it," all the Ohio chiefs but Scarouady returned to their homes and came to terms with the French.

Braddock, unconcerned at their departure, anticipated no problem in removing the French and their allies, for he was convinced he needed no Indian help to do it. "Savages," he remarked to Benjamin Franklin, who had come to Fort Cumberland to help procure wagons and horses for the army, "may indeed be a formidable enemy to your raw American militia; but upon the king's regular and disciplined troops, Sir, it is impossible they should make any impression." It was a mistaken view, expressed by a man who had little personal experience with battle—least of all of the kind of battle that, in a little more than six weeks, would cost him his life.

Braddock's column, perhaps two miles in length and gravid with cannon and supplies, left Fort Cumberland on May 29. Croghan had persuaded only Scarouady and seven Mingo warriors to accompany it, an entirely inadequate number of scouts. The march went slowly enough that Braddock, growing impatient at the end of the first week, decided to split the army into two divisions, and proceed with a "flying column" of twelve hundred picked men, together with about 250 camp followers and wagoners. The remainder of the army, under the command of Colonel Thomas Dunbar, would follow with most of the baggage and the heaviest artillery, improving the road as it went. The distance between the two bodies steadily lengthened; ultimately the flying column would be sixty miles ahead of the main body.

The march of the flying column went remarkably well, with Braddock deploying flanking parties for security and progressing at a rate of five or more miles per day. They knew they were being observed from the forest by French-allied Indians but, apart from a very small number of men taken and killed, suffered little as a result. In the small number of skirmishes with enemy scouts, the Indians fled at the first volleys, increasing Braddock's confidence in the superiority of his men. By the time the column crossed the Monongahela a few miles southeast of Fort Duquesne early in the afternoon of July 9, he had no reason to expect anything but success. His troops had been most vulnerable to attack while fording the river. The absence of opposition at this critical moment seemed to indicate that the French had simply decided to abandon the Forks as indefensible. At any moment, Braddock thought, he might hear the roar of a great gunpowder explosion as the defenders demolished the fort and fled.

Rather than fleeing, however, the commandant of Fort Duquesne had dispatched nearly 900 men—637 Indians, 146 Canadian militiamen, and 108 *troupes de la marine,* or half his total force at the Forks—to intercept the invaders. Not knowing precisely where Braddock's force would be, the defenders collided with it on the trail not far from the crossing, about six miles from the Forks. In the initial confusion of what eighteenth-century soldiers called a "meeting engagement," the French captain who had been leading the force was killed by a random, long-range musket shot. Croghan, Scarouady, and the Mingo scouts retreated along with the advance party of British soldiers under Lieutenant Colonel Thomas Gage. The sudden death of the French leader confused and disorganized the militia and *troupes de la marine,* but the Indians continued the attack without need of direction. Largely made up of northern warriors (among whom were Charles Langlade and his Ottawa kinsmen from Detroit) but also including substantial numbers of Shawnee, Delaware, and Mingo fighters, they dispersed into the woods on both sides of the road and began picking off the scarlet-coated enemy.

The British made it substantially easier for the Indian marksmen to do their work. Hearing firing erupt ahead, the main body of the column rushed forward, colliding with the retreating advance guard. Tangled in confusion on a road little more than twelve feet wide, the British made a splendid, defenseless target. Unable to see the Indians who sniped at them from cover, the British troops fought as best they could, directing volleys blindly into the woods—and also, all too often, into one another.

Braddock, splendidly brave, sat astride his horse in the midst of the chaos, trying to direct his men's fire and attempting to re-form them into coherent units. Two of his aides, wounded, could not carry on their duties; the third, Washington, remained untouched as he rode beside Braddock despite having three horses shot from beneath him and his coat and hat repeatedly pierced by bullets. For all their confusion and fear, however, the British troops did not flee until a musket ball smashed into Braddock's back, knocking him from his horse after three full hours of fighting. By then more than two-thirds of the 1,450 men and women in the British column had been killed or wounded. Sixty of Braddock's eighty-six officers were among the casualties.

Though no one in Braddock's shattered force knew it, the moment the survivors were the safest they had been all day was the moment they broke and ran, following the wounding of Braddock. The Indians, having won a great engagement, now concentrated on seizing plunder and captives. Finding the army's stock of rum—two hundred gallons of it—in the abandoned supply wagons soon distracted them further, and an increasingly disorderly celebration ended what had been a remarkably lopsided battle. The Indians and French had suffered casualties of just twenty-three dead and sixteen wounded. For the panicked, exhausted British the next two days of flight became a new kind of hell. Men too seriously wounded to walk were left to die as their comrades stumbled down the road without food or water, convinced that the enemy would fall upon them at any moment. Braddock, carried from the battlefield on an ammunition cart, jostled along in agony for days, dying only when he reached the army's rear element, near the site of the Jumonville massacre. His sole unwounded aide, Washington, arranged to have him buried in the road, so the army could march over the grave and obliterate any trace of it. The intention was to keep the body from being exhumed and mutilated by the Indians, who, the British believed, might attack once more. It is not impossible that many of the battle's survivors welcomed the opportunity to grind their heels into the grave of the man who had led them to slaughter.

Once the survivors had reunited with Colonel Dunbar's troops, the British force numbered two thousand, with more than thirteen hundred men fit for duty—a strength great enough to renew the campaign against Fort Duquesne. The demoralized and frightened Dunbar, however, found it impossible to order the men back down the road. Had he been able to, they would have arrived to find the fort virtually defenseless. The Ottawas and other northern Indians, having acquired the plunder and captives they had come to take, went home after the battle, leaving the commandant with too few men to withstand a siege. Not knowing this, and fearing that

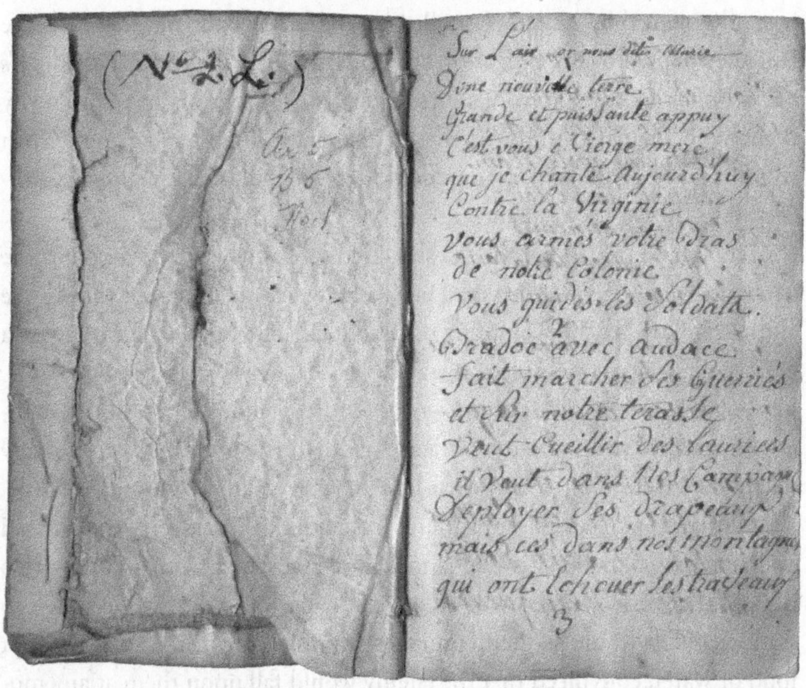
(No. 2. L.)

Sur L'air or nous dites Marie
D'une nouvelle terre
Grande et puissante appuy
C'est vous ô Vierge mere
que je chante aujourd'huy
Contre la Virginie
vous armés votre bras
de notre Colonie
Vous guidés les soldats.
2
Bradoc avec audace
fait marcher ses guerriers
et sur notre terasse
Veut Cueillir des lauriers
il Veut dans nos Campagnes
Deployer ses drapeaux
mais cas dans nos montagnes
qui ont Echouer les travaux
3

"D'une nouvelle terre" (lyrics). *The Catholic chaplain Denys Baron penned these lyrics at Fort Duquesne following Braddock's defeat. Thanking the Virgin Mary for the surprising victory, Baron concluded with a premonition of the bitter struggle to come:*

a French and Indian force might materialize from the forest at any time, Dunbar ordered the remnants of the largest military force British America had ever seen to destroy supplies, mortars, and ammunition and march for Philadelphia with all possible speed. There he completed the redcoats' humiliation and disgrace by demanding, in July, that the city provide them with winter quarters.

The survivors of the Virginia provincial companies—those who did not desert—remained at Fort Cumberland. There Governor Dinwiddie ordered them reconstituted as the Virginia Regiment and offered Washington the command. The reappointed colonel thereupon undertook the task that occupied him for the next three years: defending more than three hundred miles of backwoods settlements along the whole length of the Shenandoah Valley. To the north, Pennsylvania's frontier had no defenders at all. Using Braddock's road as their warrior's path, Ohio Indian raiding

3

meprisant les alarmes
Diore et de Baston
nous porterons les armes
Sous Votre auguste Nom
Donnes nous la Victoire
Sur tous nos ennemis
vous Seulle aurés la Gloire
de les avoir Soumis

4

plains d'un nouveau Courage
Sont nos braves françois
vont avec les Sauvages
au Devant des Anglois
S'appuyant Sur marie
plus que Sur leur Vailleur
Bientot Chacun S'ecrit
Loüis est le Vainqueur

5

quinze Cents Sur La place
Viennent d'être immoler
Quinze Centa Sur La Place
Vaincu et desolés
Succede a la ardiesse
L'epouvante et l'effroy
marie est la maitresse
tous flechir a Sa Voix

6

Soutenés grande mere notre
pauvre pays
il est Votre demaine faites
fleurir nos lis.
L'anglois Sur nos frontiers
porte leur étandars
exaucés nos prieres
fortifier nos Rampard.

"Great Mother, support our poor country that belongs to you / Make our lily flowers bloom / The English are raising their flags at our own border / Answer our prayers, fortify our ramparts." (Archive du Monastère des Augustines de l'Hôtel-Dieu de Quebec)

parties now brought devastation down upon the frontiers of two of the richest, most populous colonies in British America. Western settlers by the thousand fled their farms for the presumed safety of settlements farther east. Thus began the greatest refugee crisis in the history of the colonies, and the most widespread war British North America had ever known.

CHAPTER SEVEN

A Lake Defended, a Province Purged

The remaining campaigns of 1755 began more promisingly for the Anglo-Americans, but even so the results were hardly reassuring. All three of the remaining expeditions fell under the charge of William Shirley, the political virtuoso and military novice who unexpectedly found himself commander in chief of British forces in North America. All three showed the mark of Shirley's creative thinking and the signature of his military inexperience.

The three campaigns—directed against Fort Niagara on Lake Ontario, Fort Saint Frédéric on Lake Champlain, and the French forts on the Chignecto Isthmus in Nova Scotia—proceeded almost simultaneously. Shirley assumed personal control of the campaign against Niagara, which was arguably the most strategically important of the three. Niagara, dominating the portage between Lake Ontario and Lake Erie, controlled the supply route to the Ohio forts, Detroit, and points west. If that post could be taken, all French influence in the interior of North America would wither. To reach Niagara, however, was no easy task: it was at least four hundred miles away from Albany by way of the Mohawk River, Wood Creek, Lake Oneida, and the Onondaga River, as well as Lake Ontario itself. Thus the expedition had to proceed in two stages, pausing at the old trading fort of Oswego on Lake Ontario, where a base of supply could be established and vessels built to carry the siege guns, supplies, and troops up the lake.

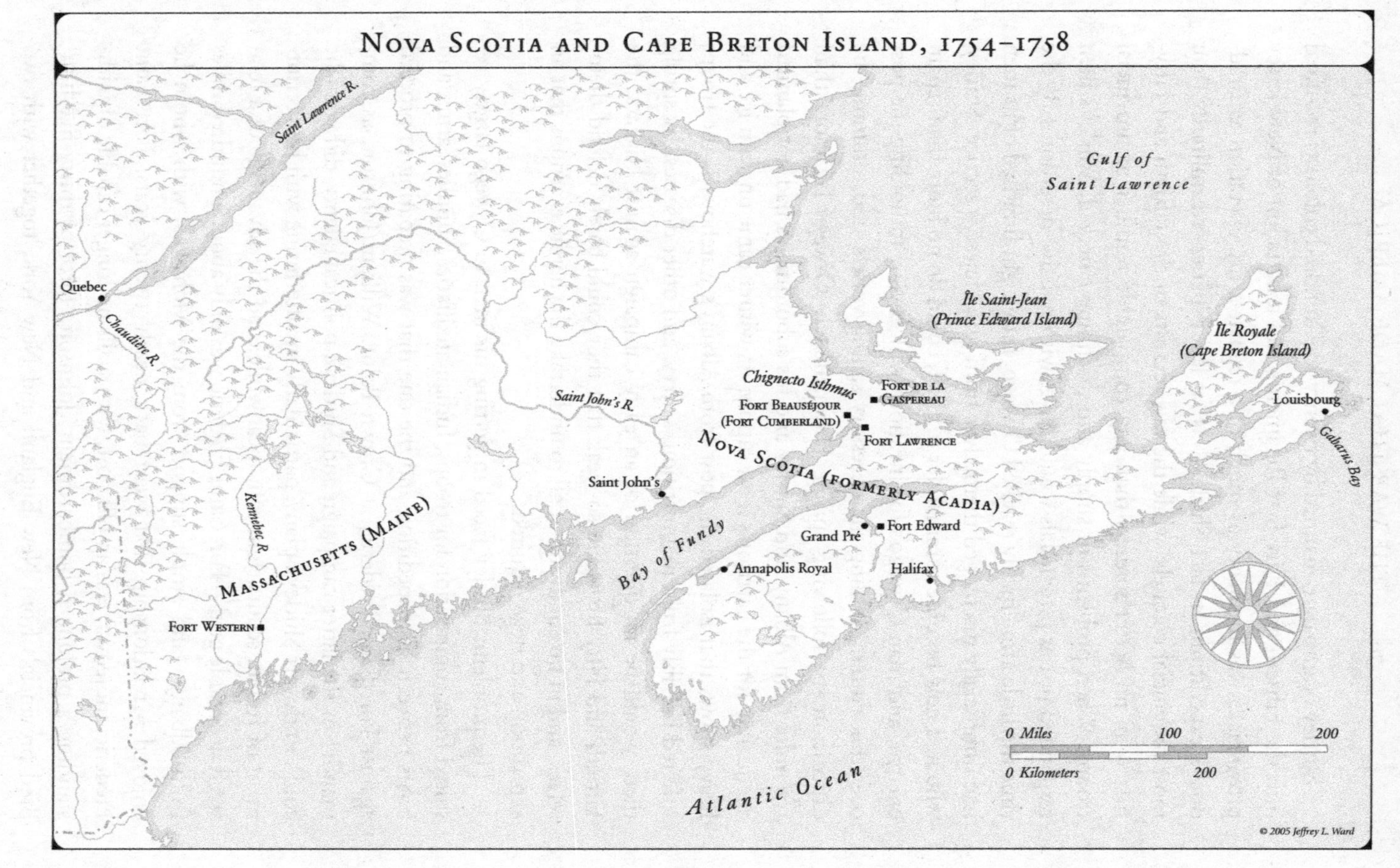
Nova Scotia and Cape Breton Island, 1754–1758
Saint Lawrence R.
Gulf of
Saint Lawrence
Quebec
Chaudière R.
Île Saint-Jean
(Prince Edward Island)
Île Royale
(Cape Breton Island)
Chignecto Isthmus
Fort de la
Gaspereau
Louisbourg
Saint John's R.
Fort Beauséjour
(Fort Cumberland)
Fort Lawrence
Gabarus Bay
Nova Scotia (formerly Acadia)
Saint John's
Kennebec R.
Massachusetts (Maine)
Fort Edward
Grand Pré
Bay of Fundy
Annapolis Royal
Halifax
Fort Western
0 Miles
100
200
0 Kilometers
200
Atlantic Ocean
© 2005 Jeffrey L. Ward

Shirley's campaign, manned by twenty-five hundred colonists recruited into the Fiftieth and Fifty-first Regiments and a battalion of New Jersey provincials, was in theory as much of a regular-army operation as Braddock's expedition. In fact Shirley was far less experienced militarily than most provincial colonels, while the raw recruits of the Fiftieth and Fifty-first were no better soldiers than any comparable number of provincial troops. When problems of supply and discipline emerged, Shirley's men responded just as provincials would have, with massive desertions. By the time the little army finally reached Oswego, fully eight hundred of its men had unofficially discharged themselves from His Majesty's service. Shirley, who had now become commander in chief, could do no more than repair, enlarge, and man Oswego's fortifications with a view to holding the post over the winter, building the necessary sailing vessels, and resuming the expedition the following spring. Unfortunately Oswego lay more than 150 miles from Albany, and Shirley and his subordinates had not planned adequately for the garrison's food supply. As winter came on with ice and heavy snows that isolated the post from Albany's warehouses, the troops suffered horribly from malnutrition, scurvy, and other diseases. By spring there would be no question of an early campaign against Niagara; the Fiftieth and Fifty-first were so weak that they could barely defend themselves, and in no condition at all to undertake the heroic exertions that an expedition and siege required.

The problems Shirley faced in getting his men to Oswego largely resulted from competition for troops, Indian auxiliaries, supplies, arms, and boats between his expedition and the one that was preparing to proceed against Fort Saint Frédéric, at Crown Point. William Johnson, as commander of the latter campaign and Shirley's political enemy, did what he could to thwart Shirley's plans, particularly by interfering with his recruitment of Indian scouts. Johnson, meanwhile, had the advantage of a relatively accessible goal—Fort Saint Frédéric was only about a hundred miles from Albany—and ample support from the Mohawks, with whom he enjoyed a relationship that went back nearly twenty years. Fort Saint Frédéric, moreover, was an old post, with walls no longer capable of withstanding a prolonged bombardment. Johnson's force of thirty-five hundred provincials from New England and New York, together with two

***Portrait of William Shirley*, by Thomas Hudson, 1750.** *Massachusetts governor William Shirley (1694–1771) sat for the English artist Thomas Hudson in 1750, shortly before the resumption of Anglo-French conflict in North America. Shirley succeeded Braddock as British commander in chief in North America in 1755, only to find that his lack of military experience and training would expose him to severe censure once his successor, Lord Loudoun, arrived the following year.* (National Portrait Gallery, Smithsonian Institution/Art Resource, NY)

hundred Mohawk warriors, should have stood a superb chance at success. What happened, however, was anything but a quick march to victory.

Like Shirley's expedition, Johnson's had to proceed in two stages, cutting a road from its base of supply at Fort Edward on the upper Hudson to the head of Lac Saint-Sacrement, sixteen miles to the north, the body of water by which the expedition would gain access to Lake Champlain. At the lake (which Johnson renamed Lake George in honor of his king) the force was to pause and construct the boats it needed to advance to Crown Point, which lay only fifty miles to the north. The men had only barely made camp at Lake George, however, when it became clear that they were not alone in the woods. On September 3, scouts from the contingent of Mohawk warriors headed by Chief Hendrick (Theyanoguin) reported seeing the tracks of more than a hundred native warriors just a few miles away; on the seventh they reported seeing the tracks of several hundred Europeans. Hurriedly Johnson's men felled trees around the Lake George camp, dragging them into barricades and clearing fields of fire. The next morning Johnson dispatched one-third of the men in his command—a thousand provincials, with two hundred Mohawks—to reinforce Fort Edward, which had been left only lightly defended, with its fortifications still in a rudimentary state. If the French seized that vulnerable post, Johnson would be unable to remain at the lake and the campaign against Crown Point would have to be abandoned.

A force of fifteen hundred French regulars, Canadians, and Indians was waiting for the provincials and Mohawks, about four miles away, at a point where the road to Fort Edward ran along the floor of a steep-walled ravine. The baron de Dieskau had arrived safely in Canada with more than sixty companies of *troupes de terre* in June, and had deployed them largely at Fort Saint Frédéric. From there he had taken a smaller force, made up of two hundred *troupes de terre,* six hundred Canadian militiamen, and seven hundred Abenakis and Catholic Mohawks from the *réserve* of Caughnawaga, and ascended Lac Saint-Sacrement to disrupt Johnson's expedition. Although Dieskau was every inch a professional officer, he was by no means a conventional one. His service as an aide-de-camp to France's greatest field marshal, the comte de Saxe, during the War of the Austrian Succession had alerted him to the value of partisan irregulars, the *grassins*

***Chief Hendrick*, engraving.** *Theyanoguin (1692–1755), also known as Hendrick, persuaded about three hundred Iroquois warriors (mostly fellow Mohawks) to accompany the provincial major general William Johnson's 1755 expedition against Fort Saint Frédéric. This engraved portrait may commemorate Hendrick's 1740 trip to London. He died in the sharp fighting with Canadian Indians and militia in the Bloody Morning Scout on September 8, 1755.* (Colonial Williamsburg Foundation)

and *pandours* who operated as raiders in the penumbra of regular forces. Dieskau had no difficulty in seeing an analogy between his own Indians and Canadian militiamen and those dangerous European partisans, and had no objection to using them in the same way.

He had been encouraged in this kind of thinking on the ship that carried him to Canada by one of his fellow passengers, Pierre de Rigaud de Vaudreuil de Cavagnal, marquis de Vaudreuil, who had lately been appointed as governor-general of New France. A Canadian by birth, Vaudreuil had served in the *troupes de la marine* as a young man and knew war in the eastern woodlands intimately; his service as governor of Louisiana from 1743 to 1752 had given him a matchless sensitivity to the conduct of intercultural diplomacy. He had urged Dieskau to understand the Indians as allies, not auxiliaries, and to give them a wide scope in fighting the common enemy. That was precisely what Dieskau did on September 8; so much so, indeed, that he used his regulars as auxiliaries to the Indians.

The provincial and Mohawk force that marched into the ambush that Dieskau and his Indians had prepared was similar in size to Braddock's, yet for a variety of reasons it did not suffer Braddock's fate. When the Catholic Mohawks in Dieskau's force saw that the warriors in the advance guard were Mohawks from New York and hence their kinsmen, they called out a warning. Chief Hendrick, who was mounted on horseback at the head of the column, rode forward to investigate, only to be felled by a shot, probably from one of the French troops. The Mohawks, however, had already had enough warning to retreat, while the lead unit of Massachusetts provincials tried to assault the ambushers and then withdrew fighting, in a more or less orderly way, alongside the warriors. This melee, known as the Bloody Morning Scout, was the opening phase of what came to be called the Battle of Lake George. Casualties on the English side were substantial—about thirty Mohawks and fifty provincials—but far from catastrophic. The bulk of the provincials farther back in the column simply ran for the camp—an inglorious but effective response that undoubtedly saved the men's lives.

When the survivors streamed into the fortified camp, they found their comrades, alerted by the sound of firing, busy reinforcing the barricade with overturned wagons and boats, and positioning four cannon to cover the road. The sight of this improvised defensive line stopped the Indians in Dieskau's pursuing force in their tracks. Seeing that they had no interest in throwing their lives away in a frontal assault, Dieskau encouraged them to take cover and fire at the provincials manning the barricade while he organized his regulars—all of them grenadiers, the biggest, strongest men of the *régiments* Languedoc and La Reine—into a compact column and ordered them to charge the guns. He hoped that if they forced their way into the camp, the Indians and Canadians would follow. The grenadiers had to cover about 150 yards from the forest's edge to the barricade, and when they fixed bayonets and charged with a shout they showed all the courage and élan for which the French army was famous. They were halfway to the

Drawing of Thomas Williams's powder horn, by Rufus Grider. *The Massachusetts native Thomas Williams (1718–1775) served in the provincial corps commanded by his brother, Colonel Ephraim Williams, who fell mortally wounded in the Bloody Morning Scout. Thomas's engraved powder horn, made in 1755 and sketched by the nineteenth-century antiquarian Rufus Grider in 1888, commemorates the Battle of Lake George.* (Accession number 1907.36.97, negative number 34425. Collection of The New-York Historical Society)

barricade when the guns opened up with grapeshot that cut "lanes, streets, and alleys" through their formation, killing a third of them in a matter of seconds and convincing the Mohawks and Abenakis that Dieskau (who was himself wounded) must be a madman. Thereafter the Canadians and Indians continued for most of the afternoon to fire from long range at Johnson's men, who suffered comparatively few casualties as a result. When it was all over, the French and Indian force retreated to Fort Saint Frédéric, leaving the wounded Dieskau to be taken prisoner.

Both sides lost about the same number in the battle, somewhat more than three hundred men dead, wounded, and missing. Because the French withdrew from the field, the Anglo-Americans were able to claim that they had won a victory. But it was a hollow one on two counts.

First, Johnson's men were too shocked and demoralized by the battle to pursue the enemy, who regrouped at Crown Point and then set out to build a new fort at the foot of Lake George, on the promontory of Ticonderoga. Fort Carillon, as they called it, would become both the main obstacle on the Lake Champlain invasion route and a base for raids against the New England frontier. To counter it, Johnson's men built a post of their own on the site of the battle: Fort William Henry, named for two of George II's sons. Over the next four years, the forty miles of lake and shoreline that separated the forts would mask the grim reality of war in deceptively lovely vistas of island, water, and balsam forest.

Second, the Mohawks had seen with unmistakable clarity that the price of their alliance with the British would be bloody confrontations with their Canadian Catholic cousins. At the end of the battle they withdrew to their homes to mourn the dead, taking with them several French prisoners, whom Johnson quietly gave them, knowing full well what their fate would be. He hoped that once the Mohawks had mourned their dead, they would return. They did not. In their absence the British struggled mightily to develop scouts to replace them, enlisting frontiersmen and Christian Indians from Stockbridge and other Massachusetts "praying towns" as "rangers" in a desperate, and largely frustrated, attempt to replace an Iroquois ally they could ill afford to lose. The paucity of scouts on the British side, and the shortage of intelligence about enemy movements and strength that resulted from it, would heavily contribute to the indecisive nature of operations on the New York frontier for the next four years.

The final Anglo-American campaign, in Nova Scotia, proceeded with a speed and decisiveness missing from the Crown Point and Niagara ventures. Unlike the others, this offensive had been planned well in advance; indeed as early as mid-1754 Shirley and Nova Scotia's acting governor, Charles Lawrence, had proposed removing the pair of forts—Beauséjour and Gaspereau—that the French had built on the isthmus of Chignecto in 1750. These "encroachments," as the British called them, served a double purpose. Practically speaking, they enabled the French to maintain overland communication between Louisbourg and Quebec. Symbolically, and of greater concern to the British, was that they reminded the twenty thousand or so Catholic and Francophone Acadians that even though they lived under the jurisdiction of a British government, they had not been forgotten; in the event of a new war, they would have a refuge defended by French troops to which to flee.

The two forts probably concerned British officials more than they interested the Acadians, who were for the most part peasant farmers with little interest in involving themselves in imperial disputes. Ever since France had ceded Acadia to the British by the Treaty of Utrecht in 1713, the French population of the peninsula had enjoyed both the freedom to practice Catholicism and the privilege of remaining neutral in conflicts between France and Britain. Because the colony's Anglophone population consisted primarily of soldiers and sailors (an army garrison at Annapolis Royal and a naval base at Halifax), in 1755 the Acadians still outnumbered the British by nearly ten to one. This worried the British greatly, because those numerous Acadians enjoyed a close relationship with the three thousand Mi'kmaq Indians of the peninsula—a group that was also Catholic, and overtly hostile to the British. A British attempt to change the character of the province by settling German-speaking Protestants near Halifax had enjoyed only small success. By 1755 the Germans were too few in number to make a dent in the Acadian dominance, and showed little eagerness to take up arms in behalf of the British crown.

Over the previous four decades the fear of an Acadian fifth column had repeatedly driven British governors to demand that the Acadians take loyalty oaths; the Acadians had repeatedly refused, fearing that to swear allegiance to a Protestant monarch meant abjuring their spiritual allegiance to the pope. Always before, the British had backed down because they had had no way to force the Acadians into taking the oath. The arrival of thousands of Anglo-American troops for the Chignecto campaign, however, gave the British a kind of coercive capacity they had previously lacked. That the Acadians had always been a peaceful people mattered less than the strategic threat that seemed implicit in their intimacy with the Mi'kmaqs and the fact that Acadian farms had been the main source of provisions for Louisbourg since the founding of the fortress in 1718. Seizing the Chignecto forts, Shirley and Lawrence believed, eliminated the possibility that they would serve as sources of arms and sedition, should relations between Britain and France collapse into war.

What else Shirley and Lawrence intended to follow from the destruction of the forts became clear only after the brief June campaign in which two thousand New England provincials under Major General John Winslow, together with 270 British regulars under Colonel Robert Monckton, besieged and took Fort Beauséjour, and then occupied Fort Gaspereau, which surrendered without a fight. With the forts neutralized, Governor Lawrence demanded that the Acadians take an unconditional oath of loyalty. When they refused, Winslow's provincials and Monckton's regulars swept down on their communities, rounding up as many of them as they could catch, herding them on board ships, and deporting them to mainland colonies from Massachusetts to Georgia. In order to discourage them from returning, the Anglo-Americans systematically devastated their farmsteads, burning buildings, killing or dispersing livestock, and breaking the dikes by which the Acadians had reclaimed coastal lands for agriculture. By the end of 1755, approximately seven thousand Acadians had been deported as de facto prisoners of war. Shirley and Lawrence expected that most would be sold as indentured servants in the colonies to which they were sent, to serve for whatever contractual period local authorities cared to stipulate. They believed that the Acadians would soon learn to speak English, forget their Catholic religious identity, and assimilate into colonial populations as loyal British subjects.

Two-thirds of the Acadians in the peninsula escaped the first deportations. Some made their way to Île Royale; others established refugee settlements in the Saint John River Valley in what is now New Brunswick; still others took refuge with the Mi'kmaqs, beginning a long guerrilla struggle against British power in the peninsula. The British used companies of

Charles Deschamps de Boishébert et de Raffetot, Marquis de Boishébert, **artist unknown, c. 1753.** *The Canadian nobleman Boishébert (1727–1797) entered the colony troops as a cadet in 1739 and gained military experience raiding the frontiers of New York and Nova Scotia in the 1740s. After leading the advance detachment of Governor Duquesne's Ohio expedition in 1753, Boishébert spent much of the war organizing partisan resistance to British forces in Acadia and on Cape Breton Island.* (Accession number M967.48, McCord Museum of Canadian History, Montreal)

rangers, mainly raised in New England, to wage ruthless campaigns aimed at clearing Nova Scotia's lands of all Mi'kmaqs and any refugee Acadians they harbored. The goal was what the late twentieth century would label ethnic cleansing: to transform a purged province by resettling it with Protestant immigrants from New England, Scotland, and Germany.

This remained impossible so long as the French maintained a military presence in the area, and while Louisbourg remained unconquered the refugees who had avoided deportation could hope to return. When British forces seized the fortress in 1758, however, a second great roundup followed on Île Royale, netting most of those who had escaped in 1755. Two years later, the British and the Mi'kmaqs negotiated a peace that guaranteed the surviving Indians their hunting and fishing rights and opened trade on favorable terms. Notwithstanding these efforts, however, surprising numbers of Acadians managed to continue living in Nova Scotia, evading capture by Anglo-American and British patrols until the mid-1760s. With the return of peace, these fugitives became a valuable source of labor for the new wave of Anglophone immigrants, and were allowed to remain. Most Acadians, however, never returned after what they called

A View of the Plundering and Burning of the City of Grimross, **by Thomas Davies, 1758.** *The British commander Robert Monckton led an expedition in 1758 to destroy French settlements along the Saint John River in present-day New Brunswick. More than two thousand Acadians, many of them refugees from the British expulsions, had gathered in the area. Many fled overland to Quebec, where food shortages and smallpox created further suffering and death.* (National Gallery of Canada, Ottawa. Purchased 1954)

le grand dérangement. Instead they dispersed to settle in the Saint John Valley, Quebec, the littoral of the Gulf of Saint Lawrence, the west coast of Newfoundland, the islands of Saint Pierre and Miquelon, and the bayou country of Louisiana.

The Acadian episode illuminates, within a small frame, several important issues. The essential requirements for membership in the eighteenth-century British imperial community were few: willingness to affirm allegiance to the king of England, adherence to some form of Protestantism, anti-Catholicism, and Francophobia. Those who met these criteria could find a place in the empire even if (like the Germans) they spoke no English, claimed no ethnic connection to British populations, and had no previous experience with English political or legal institutions. This ease of entry permitted the empire to operate primarily on a voluntarist basis, and created a surprisingly robust social and political order within a remarkably diverse community. It was not, however, an imperial order that welcomed those who refused to embrace its fundamentally anti-Catholic and anti-French spirit. Nor did it offer much of a place to those native groups who refused to surrender lands coveted by white farmers and remove themselves beyond the pale of Anglo-American settlement.

The willingness, even eagerness, of New England provincials to participate in the ethnic cleansing of Nova Scotia beginning in late 1755 indicated how fully they participated in the anti-French, anti-Catholic, anti-Indian spirit of British imperialism. Like the New Englanders, Anglo-American colonists generally wanted to think of themselves as partners with metropolitan Britons in a great war for empire, a crusade that would eliminate forever the threat of popery and savagery, secure a lasting peace, and open the lands of North America to occupation by people like themselves. In the bleak dawn of a war that would change their world forever, it had not yet occurred to most Anglo-American colonists that British authorities might have reason to think about the future of the empire, and the colonists' place in it, in entirely different ways.

CHAPTER EIGHT

La Guerre Sauvage

For Governor-General Vaudreuil there was no mystery about how to fight effectively against the British colonies, no matter how vastly their populations outnumbered that of New France. Vaudreuil had literally grown up with war. His father, another governor-general, had enrolled him as an ensign in the *troupes de la marine* when he was still a boy, and he had risen to the rank of major before he became governor of Louisiana. Everything in his experience convinced him that the most effective way to defend New France was to encourage its Indian allies to raid the frontiers of the British colonies at will.

Attacks by Indians on backcountry settlements terrified the settlers, and reliably created panic. Facing massive refugee crises, British colonial governments had no choice but to fortify their frontiers, spending massive amounts of money, tying down militiamen and provincial soldiers as garrison troops, and diminishing their capacity to take the initiative. Expensive as they were to build and man, however, the Anglo-American forts were always too far-flung to create a genuine shield for the colonies that built them, and so generally accomplished little more than reassuring those settlers who chose not to flee that they would have a place to take shelter in case of attack.

In practice the forts were as much targets as shields. Because they attracted so many people and held large stocks of supplies and arms, the loss of a major fort could have a disproportionally devastating effect. When

Pierre de Rigaud de Vaudreuil de Cavagnal, Marquis de Vaudreuil (1698–1778), **unknown French artist, c. 1753–1755.** *The Canadian-born marquis de Vaudreuil was already an experienced military officer, colonial administrator, and intercultural diplomat when he was appointed governor-general of New France in 1755. His strategy of frontier raiding against the British colonies produced a string of early victories.* (Library and Archives Canada/C-147538)

Delaware warriors attacked Fort Granville on the Juniata River in south-central Pennsylvania on July 30, 1756, for example, they killed or captured its entire garrison, together with all the settlers who had sought refuge there. Granville had been a major supply depot; without it, posts that lay farther west had to be abandoned, and the colony's defensive line fell back to Carlisle, just a hundred miles from Philadelphia. French forts, by contrast, supported offensive actions at the same time that they defended strategic passes. Fort Duquesne and Fort Saint Frédéric, notably, served as advanced bases for Indian warriors, offering them the weapons and ammunition they needed to carry on raids and acting as collecting points where prisoners and loot could be brought to be exchanged for trade goods. French posts thus functioned less as defensive bulwarks than as magnets for the warriors—some from hundreds of miles away—on whom the security of New France depended.

Pursuing what amounted to a strategy of guerrilla war had two drawbacks: it placed the initiative in Indian hands, and it encouraged native warriors to fight according to their own cultural norms. Both would have made it difficult for the marquis Duquesne, with his metropolitan and militarily conservative perspective, to embrace fully *la guerre sauvage.* Neither feature, however, bothered Vaudreuil. From the time of Braddock's

Stove plate, 1756. *Central European immigrants to Pennsylvania continued the tradition of heating their homes with iron stoves that often displayed biblical references and other decoration. The inscription on this cast iron side plate—"DIS IST DAS IAHR DARIN WITET" ("This is the year in which rages")—continues on an end plate: "DER INCHIN SCHAR" ("the Indian War Party").* (From the collection of the Moravian Historical Society, Nazareth, Pennsylvania)

defeat through 1757, he happily took advantage of the willingness of Indians to fight for their French father on whatever terms they pleased. At Fort Duquesne, Fort Niagara, Fort Saint Frédéric, and Fort Detroit he offered arms, supplies, and modest numbers of *troupes de la marine* and Canadian militiamen to provide whatever guidance and aid native raiders were willing to accept. Essentially, however, the western Indians were free to conduct a war of their own devising, and they did so with enormous success. With the governments of Virginia and Pennsylvania entirely preoccupied with defending their own frontiers and unable to contribute much in the way of men or money to efforts to attack Canada, Vaudreuil could concentrate on defending the likeliest invasion route, the Lake Champlain–Richelieu River corridor, while deploying enough men to besiege posts of high strategic value on the New York frontier.

The first fort to offer itself as a potential target was Oswego, the old New York trading post on Lake Ontario that William Shirley's forces had occupied, at great cost, through the bitter winter of 1756. Vaudreuil had intended to wipe it out in 1755, before the Anglo-Americans could complete their fortifications there, but he found New France under attack from so many different directions that he was forced to hold off until the following year. By that point the need to strike Oswego had become critical. The fort allowed the British to threaten critical sites in two directions: Fort Frontenac on the north shore of Lake Ontario, which guarded the head of the Saint Lawrence (and hence controlled access to Montreal by the river); and Fort Niagara at the western end of the lake, which protected the portage to Lake Erie and hence controlled communication to all interior posts. Oswego could not be ignored.

Fortunately for the French, Oswego was also vulnerable. The withdrawal of the Mohawks from active alliance with the British after the Battle of Lake George and the resumption of a more or less uniform Iroquois policy of neutrality between the combatant empires had made it so, because the long supply route on which Oswego depended could be attacked at will, provided that the Iroquois gave permission for the attackers to pass through their lands. Vaudreuil took advantage of this in late March 1756 by sending a raiding party on snowshoes to destroy Fort Bull, the main way station between Albany and Oswego. This stockaded storehouse complex guarded the portage between the upper Mohawk and Wood Creek,

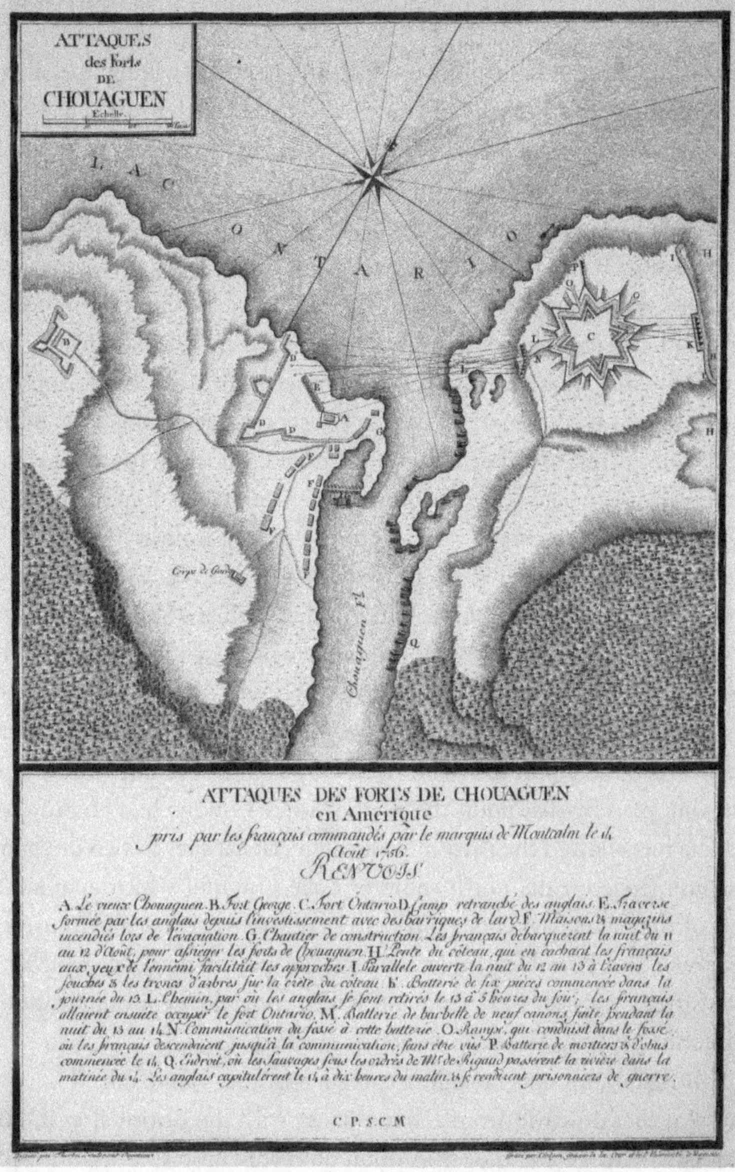
ATTAQUES des Forts DE CHOUAGUEN
Echelle
LAC ONTARIO
Chouaguen Fl.
Corps de Garde
ATTAQUES DES FORTS DE CHOUAGUEN
en Amérique
pris par les français commandés par le marquis de Montcalm le 14 Aout 1756.
RENVOIS
A. Le vieux Chouaguen. B. Fort George. C. Fort Ontario. D. Camp retranché des anglais. E. Traverse formée par les anglais depuis l'investissement avec des barriques de lard. F. Maisons & magazins incendiés lors de l'évacuation. G. Chantier de construction. Les français débarquèrent la nuit du 11 au 12 d'Aout, pour assiéger les forts de Chouaguen. H. Pente du côteau, qui en cachant les français aux yeux de l'ennemi facilitait les approches. I. Parallele ouverte la nuit du 12 au 13 à travers les souches & les troncs d'arbres sur la crête du côteau. K. Batterie de six pièces commencée dans la journée du 13. L. Chemin, par où les anglais se sont retirés le 13 à 5 heures du soir; les français allaient ensuite occuper le fort Ontario. M. Batterie de barbette de neuf canons faite pendant la nuit du 13 au 14. N. Communication du fossé à cette batterie. O. Rampe, qui conduisit dans le fossé où les français descendaient jusqu'à la communication, sans être vus. P. Batterie de mortiers & d'obus commencée le 14. Q. Endroit, où les Sauvages sous les ordres de Mr de Rigaud passèrent la rivière dans la matinée du 14. Les anglais capitulèrent le 14 à dix heures du matin, & se rendirent prisonniers de guerre.
C.P.S.C.M

"Attaques des Forts de Chouaguen." This finely detailed topographical map of Oswego (called Chouaguen by the French) shows the arrangement of defenses and siege lines at the time of Montcalm's attack, August 10, 1756. The original fort, a fur-trading post, lies west of the river's mouth within a triangular entrenchment. Fort Ontario, an eight-pointed star, stands on a low hill to the east; the small, isolated Fort George ("Fort Rascal") looks down from the top of a bluff to the west. Warehouses and traders' houses line the riverbank just south of Fort Oswego's entrenchments, near the small harbor. (Library and Archives Canada/C-041106)

which in turn gave access to Lake Oneida, the Onondaga River, and Lake Ontario. The raiding party was modest in size—slightly more than 350 Canadians, Indians, and *troupes de terre*—but exploited the advantage of surprise so completely as to annihilate the hundred-man garrison. Fort Bull's destruction left Oswego in a perilous state, for all that spring French and Indian war parties beset supply convoys on the river with ease. It was May before the first boatloads of supplies arrived from Albany, and June before the depleted, disease-ridden garrison had recuperated sufficiently to begin strengthening the fort's defensive works. Only then did the garrison resume building the whaleboats, sloops, and other vessels that were to carry troops in the expedition against Fort Frontenac that General Shirley had ordered for the summer of 1756.

The expedition never happened. French and Indian pressure on Oswego's supply lines did not diminish as summer advanced, and the garrison's strength increased only moderately. By the beginning of August the three forts in the Oswego complex (Old Oswego, Fort Ontario, and New Oswego, an outlier stockade so small and contemptible that the troops called it "Fort Rascal") sheltered only about 1,800 souls, a number that included not only the 1,135 regular troops of the Fiftieth and Fifty-first Regiments, but hundreds of boat-builders and other civilian artificers, traders, and sailors, and a considerable number of women and children camp followers. The reinforcements from Albany that Oswego's commander, Lieutenant Colonel James Mercer, needed in order to move against Fort Frontenac never materialized. Instead, on August 10, three thousand French and Indian enemies did. Four days later Mercer was dead and Oswego was theirs.

The siege of Oswego was, as Vaudreuil had planned it, a joint operation involving *troupes de terre, troupes de la marine,* Canadian militiamen, and Indian warriors. The commander on the scene, and the man who accepted the British surrender, was not Vaudreuil but Dieskau's successor, Louis-Joseph de Montcalm, marquis de Montcalm-Gozon de Saint-Véran. Like the governor-general, the forty-four-year-old Montcalm had been an army officer since boyhood; commissioned an ensign at age nine, he had entered on active duty at twenty as a captain and gone on to serve in eleven campaigns, in the course of which he had suffered five wounds. A small, charming man with an acid wit, Montcalm differed in every way—

except perhaps in egotism—from the bearish, affable Vaudreuil. The potential for friction between the two was in no way diminished by the fact that Montcalm had come to New France as a major general, with orders that designated him as commander of troops in the field and therefore subordinate to Vaudreuil. Montcalm had arrived at Quebec in May accompanied by his staff and two fresh regiments of *troupes de terre,* but assumed command of the Oswego expedition only at the end of July; thus he had little part in the planning or organization of the campaign, which had been Vaudreuil's alone.

It was therefore with some justice that Vaudreuil called the taking of Oswego "my victory" and took pride in having secured control of the Great Lakes and the west. Montcalm, however, disapproved. He had intended to conduct a formal siege with a prolonged artillery bombardment, in the hope of luring a relief column west from Albany. Once those reinforcements were well along the way, troops whom he had previously positioned at Fort Carillon had orders to strike Fort William Henry and if possible Fort Edward. That design had been frustrated by the quickness with which Oswego's surrender followed the death of its commandant, Lieutenant Colonel Mercer; when a cannonball beheaded him not long after the bombardment began, his unnerved second-in-command asked for a truce and then capitulated. Montcalm, outraged that a professional officer would surrender before losing at least three or four hundred men, denied the surrendered garrison the honors of war.

An impulsive reaction, Montcalm's decision spoke volumes about the depth of his concern for conducting the war according to the norms of European military culture.* What appalled him most in this connection, however, was the behavior of the 260 or so Indian warriors who had taken part in the expedition. During the siege they had swarmed within musket shot of Fort Ontario, utterly disregarding the disciplined, professional rituals of approach and attack. After the surrender they had broken into Oswego's hospital, where they killed at least thirty of the wounded and

---

*This was by no means a wise choice, because it meant that the surrendered garrison had to be made prisoners of war and transported back to Canada, where they would place further stress on an agricultural system that could barely feed the colony's own population and the thousands of French soldiers who had lately come to defend it.

sick; and they had taken captives with the usual purposes of adoption and torture in mind. Vaudreuil, who was not on the scene, would have understood this behavior, and tolerated it as the price of *la guerre sauvage.* Montcalm, horrified, did his best to put a stop to it. In the end he redeemed the captives at great expense in trade goods and brandy, thereby convincing the Indians that captive-taking had the potential to enhance both their martial reputations and their material well-being.

Although Vaudreuil retroactively supported Montcalm's decision to ransom prisoners, the taking of Oswego marked the opening of a rift between the two men. It would widen as Montcalm's disgust with *la guerre sauvage* grew, and with it his scorn for the provincial aristocrat who clung to it with undiminished conviction. To Montcalm nothing could have been clearer than the folly of taking "a few scalps, or . . . burning a few houses," the "petty means" that served only to "waste material and time," when he had thousands of trained professionals, men who knew what war was supposed to be, at his disposal. With these *troupes de terre* he could defend Canada in the classic way, strengthening the forts that defended its heartland and capital, compelling the Anglo-Americans to fling themselves at his defenses and wear themselves out in a long, civilized war of attrition. The West, strategically meaningless in such a war, could safely be left to the savages. But Vaudreuil understood a strategy of conventional defense as doomed by Britain's overwhelming numbers and naval strength, and so refused to consider it. His continued promotion of Indian alliances and adherence to guerrilla strategies would produce military successes—to Montcalm's chagrin—for another year.

The British, meanwhile, had yet to find the formula for capitalizing on their manifest advantages. During the previous winter the accidental commander in chief, William Shirley, had proposed campaigns for 1756 that would concentrate on defending the frontiers of Pennsylvania and Virginia while pressing two offensive expeditions through New York. Regulars from the Fiftieth and Fifty-first Regiments were to make the attempt—foiled with the loss of Oswego—to take Fort Frontenac, and thus to cut Fort Duquesne and the other interior posts off from Canada. At the same time an expedition made up entirely of provincial troops from New England would attack Ticonderoga (Fort Carillon) and Crown Point (Fort Saint Frédéric). Shirley's was a plan that no professional general could have approved, for it assigned responsibility for a major campaign to several thousand half-disciplined provincials, under the command of officers who were scarcely more proficient than their men.

That William Shirley was no professional general was not lost on the duke of Cumberland and Secretary at War Henry Fox, who began moving during the early months of 1756 to replace him with one of Cumberland's protégés, John Campbell, the fourth earl of Loudoun. Like the mills of the gods, however, the wheels of Whitehall ground exceeding slow. Even though Shirley knew in April that he would be superseded, he remained in command until June 25, when Loudoun's second-in-command, Major General James Abercromby, arrived to relieve him of his duties. Meanwhile the campaigns had proceeded along the deeply irregular paths that Shirley had marked out for them.

While Shirley's military amateurism was unmistakably evident in his unorthodox campaign plans, he had excellent political reasons to make the choices he did. The assemblies of the New England provinces were eager to seize the French forts at Ticonderoga and Crown Point, and even to invade Canada, to bring an end to Indian raids against the northern frontier. They feared two British policies, however, as much as they feared the French and Indians, and refused to appropriate money and raise troops until they had been reassured that neither would be implemented. First was a ruling by the British solicitor general from 1754, which stipulated that whenever provincial soldiers served jointly with regulars in North America they would be under the direct command of regular officers and therefore subject to the same rigorous discipline as the regulars. Second was a royal proclamation of 1754 that made all provincial officers junior in rank to all regular officers, effectively subjecting even provincial colonels and generals to the commands of fuzz-faced redcoat ensigns. The solicitor general's ruling would inhibit voluntary enlistment, for the ferocious discipline of the redcoats, whose courts-martial regularly sentenced men to floggings of a thousand lashes, was only too well known in the colonies; the royal proclamation would ensure that no gentleman with any self-respect would offer his services as a provincial officer. Shirley's simple, direct solution had been to separate the provincials and regulars into two entirely distinct expeditions, linked only insofar as he had ultimate supervision of both. Thus he guaranteed that neither unduly strict discipline nor loss of honor would diminish Yankee engagement in the war effort. The New England assemblies, understanding Shirley's solution as a concession to their interests, responded with great enthusiasm, authorizing the enlistment of seventy-five hundred men for the Crown Point expedition. By the end of June the provincials' regiments were nearly full.

All this was lost on General Abercromby, who saw only an astonishingly disordered state of affairs when he assumed command from William Shirley in late June—so disordered, indeed, that he hesitated to proceed with either expedition until his superior, Lord Loudoun, arrived. His lordship finally stepped on the quay at New York only on July 23, as Montcalm's troops were making the final preparations to embark against Fort Oswego. Meanwhile the colonels of the New England regiments at Lake George were debating what would happen, and what actions they would take, if the new commander in chief decided to subject them and their troops to direct redcoat authority. The colonels concluded that the result would be "a dissolution of the army": the common soldiers would desert en masse and most officers would resign their commissions.

Lord Loudoun, an officer so professional that he had planted hundreds of trees on his Ayrshire estate "in the form of a regiment drawn up in review, a tree to a man," was dumbfounded by the attitudes and behavior of the provincials. He rejected Shirley's bizarre campaign plans immediately and set about making the wholesale corrections he thought necessary. He encountered little but frustration. His powers were even more extensive than Braddock's had been; he was a viceroy in all but name, and his commission gave him direct authority over all colonial civil officers, including governors. Yet he found that he could do nothing to counteract the provincial soldiers' and officers' determination to stand by what they thought were their rights, and to insist on the binding nature of the contracts under which they served. Nor did Loudoun arrive in time to deploy the eight fresh regiments of regular troops he had brought with him to save Oswego from destruction. Nor indeed could he prevent his panicky subordinate on the New York frontier, Major General Daniel Webb, from responding to the fall of Oswego by pulling his advanced forces back from the Great Carrying Place to German Flats, fully forty miles down the Mohawk River.

By mid-August the New York frontier had unraveled in confusion, and

John Campbell, Fourth Earl of Loudoun, **by Allan Ramsay, c. 1754.** *The Scottish artist Allan Ramsay painted Lord Loudoun (1705–1782) several times between 1747 and about 1754, when Britain's former commander in chief in North America sat for this portrait. Loudoun's American command (1756–1758) was marked by acrimonious disputes with provincial forces, legislatures, and officials over royal prerogative and colonial rights.* (Fort Ligonier, Ligonier, Pennsylvania)

all Loudoun could do was blame Shirley for having made it happen. Incapable of regaining Oswego and unwilling to trust the provincials to move against the French at Ticonderoga and Crown Point, he embarked on a campaign to have his predecessor cashiered from the army and stripped of civil office. Loudoun's initial impulse was to send him back to England in chains; in the end he settled for sending a list of charges to London. Shirley returned to Boston, where he attended to his duties as governor while (good lawyer that he was) he gathered documents with which to defend himself before the secretary at war and the grave, serried ranks of treasury auditors who awaited his arrival. He sailed for London in October 1756. He would be cleared of wrongdoing only in 1758. The audits would drag on until 1763, at which point he would finally be released from scrutiny.

With Shirley out of the way and headed (Loudoun hoped) for disgrace, and with nothing more to be done militarily but to wait out the year and send his regulars into winter quarters, the commander in chief turned to the organizational tasks at which he excelled. There, he knew, he could make real progress, and the reforms he instituted in procurement, provisioning, and transport services would indeed stand the British war effort in good stead for years to come. His lordship would prove less successful in dealing with the colonists and their governments, however, in large part because his formal powers exceeded both his political resources and his fund of common sense. Nevertheless, by the end of the campaign year in 1756, he was beginning to understand what he was up against. The colonists and their legislatures, insistent on what they called their rights, would cooperate at best grudgingly with the demands for money and men that he made on the king's behalf. But Loudoun was not discouraged. Like young soldiers unaccustomed to discipline, colonial officials and legislators would simply have to be shown their duty. Then, and only then, could the war against New France be won.

CHAPTER NINE

The European War Begins

While frontier settlements burned and Oswego fell, as Shirley's planned campaigns stalled out in confusion and disarray, war between France and Britain finally began in Europe. The occasion was a French attack on Minorca, Britain's main naval base in the Mediterranean, in May—a target, and a moment, that Versailles chose with care. The ministers of Louis XV had been building up France's armed forces as rapidly as possible in anticipation of a war that they believed, in light of British aggressions in America since 1754, his Most Christian Majesty had every right and reason to declare. By the spring of 1756 France had approximately eighty ships of the line (vessels mounting between fifty and a hundred guns on two or more decks) either on active service or ready to join the fleet. More were on the stocks, and being completed at a rate that suggested France might achieve parity with the British navy's hundred line-of-battle ships in the foreseeable future. The French army, with 150,000 infantry, 30,000 cavalry, and nearly 4,000 artillerymen, was by far Europe's largest. Fully half of its regiments were stationed along the English Channel with an intent made unmistakable by the six hundred troop transports that lay at anchor in the Channel ports. Britain's fleet, while still larger than France's, was widely scattered. Its army numbered only about thirty thousand men—so few that it had to respond to the invasion threat by importing twenty thousand German mercenaries from Hanover and Hesse to man its Channel defenses. Taking all this into account, Versailles thought it unlikely that Britain could assemble enough ships and troops to relieve Minorca once French forces blockaded Port Mahon and laid siege to its citadel, Saint Philip's Castle.

In order to launch the expedition, all that the French decision-makers needed was to be certain that Austria would abandon its half-century-old alliance with Britain in favor of a new alignment with France. Disillusioned with the British as they had been since the Treaty of Aix-la-Chapelle, the Austrians hesitated to cut the cord until British diplomats began making overtures to King Frederick of Prussia—the mortal enemy who had annexed the Austrian province of Silesia during the previous war. The duke of Newcastle and his ministers, worrying that King George II's other realm, the north German state of Hanover, would be overrun in case of war, had thought it prudent to conclude a treaty of friendship with Frederick. On January 16, 1756, at the Convention of Westminster, Britain and Prussia pledged to unite their forces against any aggressor who might disturb the peace of "Germany," a term vague enough to include both Hanover and Prussia. This was entirely too much for the empress-queen of Austria, Maria Theresa, to stomach. On May 1 the Austrian and French crowns laid old enmities aside in the Convention of Versailles, a pledge by each to come to the other's aid in the event that either should come under attack on the continent of Europe. (The specification of a land attack was crucial to Austria, which intended to strengthen its position while still avoiding war; France's planned attacks on British maritime interests would not require Austria to take up arms against the United Kingdom.)

The Convention of Versailles completed the inversion of the alliance system that had structured European diplomacy for a half-century, and gave France the insurance it needed to launch an attack on Port Mahon in May. The British frantically dispatched a relief squadron under Admiral John Byng, declaring war on May 18. Byng encountered a French squadron under the marquis de La Galissonière off Minorca on May 20, fought an inconclusive action, and prudently withdrew to Gibraltar for repairs. Byng's withdrawal doomed the garrison of Saint Philip's Castle. Even so, its eighty-four-year-old commandant, General William Blakeney, held out until June 28 before surrendering. Blakeney's resolve made him a hero, a Knight of the Bath, and a baron; Byng's prudence made him a scapegoat. Recalled to England, he was tried by a court-martial for failure to do his

The Shooting of Admiral Byng, **unknown engraver, 1757.** *The British admiral John Byng was tried by a court-martial and condemned to death for having failed to prevent the French from seizing Britain's Mediterranean naval base on Minorca in the spring of 1756. His execution, on the quarterdeck of H.M.S.* Monarque *on March 14, 1757, prompted Voltaire to observe that the British found it desirable to shoot an admiral on occasion* "pour encourager les autres" *("to encourage the others").* (National Portrait Gallery, London)

utmost in the face of the enemy, found guilty, and executed by firing squad on the quarterdeck of his flagship on March 14, 1757. Widely understood as a travesty of justice even at the time, Byng's execution spoke clearly of Britain's desperation and fear. Parliamentary politics descended into a kind of numb impotence; for more than three months after the admiral's death it seemed as if no one in the government was actually in charge of policy, or the larger war effort.

France, meanwhile, was prepared to fight a war that, its leaders believed, would consist mainly of actions against Britain's main source of commercial strength, its empire. There was no real intention to use the troops stationed in Brittany and Normandy to invade England, only to tie down Royal Navy and army units in coastal defense, making it safer and easier to attack British overseas possessions in North America and the Caribbean, and perhaps to seize the British East India Company's trading factories at Calcutta and Madras. Chances seemed excellent that a weakened Britain would beg for peace in three or at most four years' time. At that point concessions could be extracted to limit British expansionism and render Canada and France's other New World colonies permanently secure. Had it not been for two unpredictable developments, things might well have worked out in exactly that way.

The first, France's failure to persuade Spain to enter the war as its ally, was a kind of nonevent, but a crucial one. The addition of the Spanish navy to that of France would have produced a decisive advantage in line-of-battle ships over Great Britain, magnifying the vulnerability of British colonial possessions. As significantly, the ability of Spanish officials in Florida to encourage a slave revolt in South Carolina (as they had done in 1739, when promises of freedom had triggered the largest slave uprising in the colony's history, the Stono Rebellion) could add much to the uncertainty and travail of the British colonies. Spain's King Ferdinand VI, however, had proven far more resistant to the overtures that France's ambassador made on behalf of Louis XV than a fellow member of the Bourbon family might have been expected to be.

French diplomats assumed that Spain would cooperate in their efforts to stymie British expansionism because they knew that the Spanish feared British interlopers in the commerce of the Caribbean Basin and South America. The Anglo-Spanish War of 1739–43 (the War of Jenkins' Ear) had been fought over just that concern. Yet to the consternation of Versailles, Ferdinand remained steadfastly neutral in the new Anglo-French confrontation until his death in 1759. In part this was a matter of temperament, for Ferdinand was notably timid, and much under the influence of the French-born Anglophile Irishman Don Ricardo Wall, who served as Spanish foreign minister from 1754 onward. While Wall's Anglophilia was real enough, it explained his commitment to neutrality less well than his meticulous calculations of Spain's national interest. Because Spain's control of the Philippines depended on its ability to ship silver by the ton from Mexico to Manila, Madrid feared incursions into the Pacific by other European powers. After Captain George Anson's capture of the Manila galleon in 1743, it was clear enough that the British had the capacity to conduct naval operations in the Pacific. What Versailles did not realize was that Spain feared that France also had designs on Mexico's silver, and perhaps on the Pacific itself. Since 1749 fragmentary reports from New

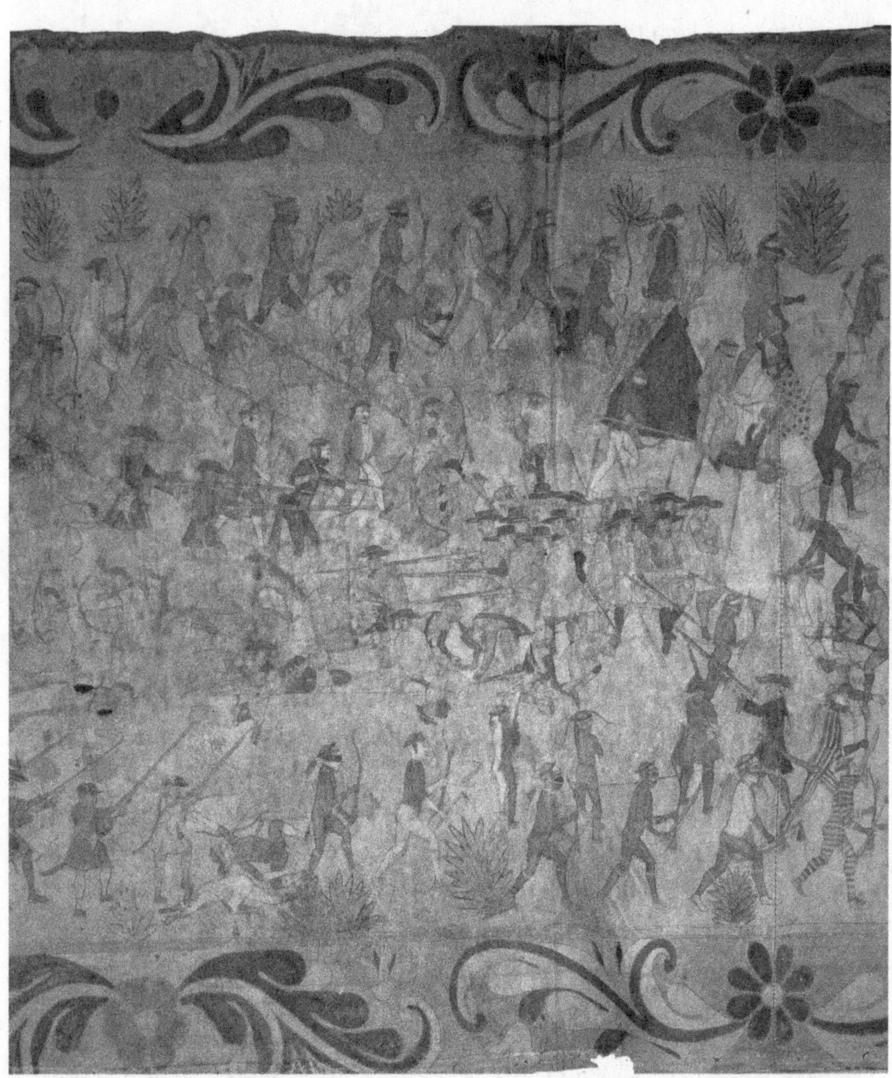

Segesser buffalo hide painting (detail), c. 1720–50. *Spain's concern about French imperial designs on the riches of New Mexico influenced its decision to remain neutral when Britain and France declared war in 1756. This was no groundless fear: France and Spain had clashed in the North American interior before. This painted buffalo hide depicts a 1720 skirmish between Spanish and French forces and their Indian allies—Apaches and Pawnees respectively—in what is now Nebraska. (The painting, almost certainly by a Native American eyewitness, was collected by Father Philipp von Segesser, a Jesuit missionary in New Mexico, in the mid-eighteenth century. His family preserved it in Switzerland until 1986, when it was returned to New Mexico.)* (Courtesy Palace of the Governors [MNM/DCA], neg. # 158345)

Mexico and Panama had given the Spanish foreign ministry grounds to worry that the French had discovered the Northwest Passage. If so, France would pose at least as grave a threat to Spain's dominance of the Pacific as the English. If two such dangerous powers wished to wear themselves out in a war, Wall and his king reasoned, Spain was best advised to stand aside and let them do it.

The lack of Spanish naval support made it difficult, though not inconceivable, for France to carry out a series of seaborne strikes against Britain's colonies. What ultimately did make that impossible, and what altered the nature of the war altogether, was the decision of Frederick of Prussia to launch a surprise attack in August 1756 on Saxony, a component of the Holy Roman Empire and hence under the protection of the empress-queen Maria Theresa. Britain and France had both altered their diplomatic alignments in the hope that these alliances would prevent a European war from complicating their colonial and maritime operations. Now, thanks to the towering ambition of a diminutive Prussian, the Conventions of Westminster and Versailles operated inexorably to bring Britain and France to the aid of their allies.

The explosion of a general war in Europe destroyed France's plans for a limited Anglo-French confrontation beyond the seas. All the preparation that Versailles had done could do nothing to control the direction of events. As 1756 ended and 1757 began, the gathering momentum of a general war in Europe preoccupied government leaders in France and Britain alike, while the war in North America proceeded according to a violent logic of its own.

CHAPTER TEN

The Making of a "Massacre"

Lord Loudoun's experiences with Britain's North American colonists in the fall of 1756 had hardly encouraged him to think of Americans as an asset in the war effort. In several important cities and towns, including Albany, the site of his campaign headquarters, civilian authorities had refused to provide quarters for his men. Faced with similar reluctance, the adaptable Shirley had purchased the goodwill of local governments and landlords by paying well for the shelter and provisions his men needed, and in so doing had drained his discretionary funds dry. Loudoun, cut from a different cloth, would have none of such irregular, extravagant practices. Finding that his requisition orders produced not accommodations but protests and lectures from mayors and town councils explaining how the English Bill of Rights forbade the billeting of troops on civil populations, Loudoun simply seized the quarters he needed, by force.

Once local officials saw that the choleric Scot was willing to chuck them out of their own houses at bayonet point, they appealed for help to their provincial legislatures, which eventually knuckled under and built barracks for the troops whom Loudoun wished to quarter. It was a deeply unpopular solution among colonial politicians, who saw the forcible taking of housing for troops as an act of tyranny, and who understood being compelled to appropriate public funds for barracks as tantamount to forced taxation. Loudoun, however, concluded that the colonists would respond to coercion, and he grew only more contemptuous of colonial assertions of rights. "I do expect to get through" the colonists' resistance, he assured the secretary at war, "for the People in this Country, tho' they are very obstinate, will generally submit when they see You [are] determined."

Loudoun was also determined to use provincial troops on terms that he, not the colonial assemblies, would set. Thus for the 1757 campaigns he demanded that colonial legislatures raise soldiers to fill standardized hundred-man companies, which could be placed under the command of regular regimental officers. This measure, he believed, would avoid the problems that went with raising provincial regiments of the sort he had encountered in the summer of 1756, manned by troops who insisted that their enlistment contracts be honored and commanded by field officers who refused to serve under regulars of lower rank than themselves. He intended to use most of the provincials as garrison troops at Fort Edward and Fort William Henry, where they would back up two redcoat regiments in preventing a French attack on Albany. Most of the remaining regulars in North America would participate in Loudoun's main expedition of 1757, an attack on Louisbourg.

Seizing control of the Saint Lawrence was critical to Britain's plans for success in the American war. So long as the French could supply reinforcements and arms and provisions by sea, there was no realistic hope of weaning the western Indians from their historic alliance, no way to stop the raids that continued to scorch the Anglo-American frontiers from New York to North Carolina. Louisbourg, while formidable, was by no means unassailable. Three thousand provincials and a small Royal Navy squadron had taken it in 1745; six thousand of His Majesty's best troops, trained in siege warfare and operating in conjunction with a far larger naval task force, could scarcely fail to duplicate their success in 1757.

As Loudoun knew only too well, the element of surprise was critical to the success of any such assault, while the elaborate preparations necessary for a combined army-navy operation were impossible to conceal. It was also clear to him that information about the expedition would fairly hemorrhage from North America's ports once preparations began; the French would know about it before Loudoun's transports could sail because merchants in all of the northern cities were keeping up a brisk, barely concealed trade with enemy correspondents in Canada and the French West

Indies alike. That treasonous trade, which Loudoun saw as typical of the self-interested behavior of Americans, disgusted him, and he longed to punish those who profited by it as much as he needed to prevent the flow of intelligence to the French. He soon hit on a way to accomplish both: in early March he used his vast powers as commander in chief to decree an embargo on all shipping from North American ports, excepting only those vessels that he or his representatives cleared for military missions. The closure of the ports would last until seven days after the invasion fleet had sailed from New York.

The fleet did not weigh anchor until June 20. For nearly four months virtually all economic activity in the colonial ports ceased. The price of bread skyrocketed in Boston, while the price of flour plummeted in the glutted market of Philadelphia. In the Chesapeake hogsheads of tobacco grew musty in warehouses and shipholds while London and Glasgow merchants looked sharp for other suppliers; New England's cod fishermen could not make their spring voyage to the Grand Banks. Everywhere sailors lounged about the docks with hands in pockets, unemployed and restless; everywhere merchants anxiously eyed their dwindling cash reserves, fretted over their inventories, and worried about their mounting debts. Only New York, insulated by heavy military demand for supplies and shipping, remained immune to the economic chaos Loudoun's order had unleashed. Dismissive of the complaints that made it to his ears, the commander in chief did not look up from his endlessly involving tasks of organization and planning to contemplate an American scene in which he was rapidly becoming more hated than Louis XV and more reviled than the marquis de Montcalm.

By the time Loudoun's fleet sailed, the principal French expedition of the summer was well under way at Montreal and Fort Saint Frédéric. News of the ransom Montcalm had paid for prisoners after the fall of Oswego traveled back into the upper Great Lakes along with the Ojibwa and Menominee warriors who had participated in the siege; from there it spread deep into the interior. With spring, warriors began to appear in unprecedented numbers at Montreal. In all nearly two thousand warriors, from thirty-three native nations, offered their services to their French father. Fewer than half of them were from Caughnawaga, Saint François, and the other Christian *réserves* that the Jesuits sponsored in New France.

***H.M.S.* Sutherland *Leaving New York for Halifax, 1757,* by Robert Wilkins.** *The fifty-gun* Sutherland *carried Lord Loudoun from New York to Halifax, the staging area for his intended attack on the fortress of Louisbourg, in June 1757. The ship had earlier served as a temporary prison for detained Acadian leaders, and would later serve in combined land and sea operations at Louisbourg (1758) and Quebec (1759).* (© Queen's Printer and Controller of HMSO, 2004. UK Government Art Collection)

The rest represented peoples from across the *pays d'en haut* and even beyond. One group came from what is now Iowa, speaking a language for which no interpreter could be found.

Vaudreuil welcomed them all, for he intended to use them in the time-tested way, as a loosely directed allied force that would harass and terrify the defenders of the expedition's objective, Fort William Henry, making the woods around the post a no-man's-land and preventing any hope of relief. Montcalm dreaded what they might do, and knew that their very diversity and lack of a common language would make them hard, if not impossible, to control. When Ottawa warriors returned to Fort Saint Frédéric from preliminary scouting expeditions with prisoners whom they ate in ritual feasts, he sensed that he might well have to confront behavior even worse than what he had witnessed after the fall of Oswego.

Despite the growing tensions between Montcalm and Vaudreuil, preparations for the largest military adventure yet undertaken from New France proceeded apace. In all about eight thousand men—*troupes de la marine, troupes de terre,* Canadian militiamen, and Indians—assembled at Fort Carillon in early July. Some sixty-five hundred of them would proceed by foot and boat down the length of Lake George in the last days of the month, bringing with them a train of thirty cannon. They did not expect an easy victory. The English garrison at Fort William Henry had originally consisted of about eleven hundred men fit for duty, together with perhaps sixty carpenters, eighty women and children, and several sutlers. When it became clear in late July that the fort was about to come under siege, the regional commander at Albany, General Daniel Webb, sent reinforcements to bring the defensive force up to nearly twenty-four hundred. Moreover, the fort was a stout one, built under the supervision of a regular-army engineer, and well provisioned. It was also formidably armed; its walls mounted eighteen heavy cannon and a variety of lighter ones. For all these reasons, as well as the still-sharp memory of Oswego, the marquis de Montcalm was determined to make his operations against Fort William Henry match, as much as possible, those of a European *siège en forme.* He knew that such a siege, properly conducted, would reduce even the strongest fortress in six or (at most) eight weeks' time, provided that no outside force arrived to relieve it.

Montcalm understood well the elaborate etiquette of the siege. Before the formal opening of operations he would advance a flag of truce and offer the English commandant the chance to surrender; his opponent, if he was an honorable man, would naturally refuse. The digging of approach trenches and transverse trenches would then begin outside cannon range, inching forward until batteries of heavy guns could be brought to bear on the walls of the fort. From that point on, if no relief column appeared from Fort Edward, the siege would proceed inexorably to its conclusion. Cannon would batter the wall and bastions nearest them with direct fire, while mortars would lob high-trajectory explosive shells, called bombs, into the interior of the fort. As the bombardment progressed, the defenders would see their own cannon blasted, one by one, from the embrasures on the walls; would see comrades dismembered by cannon shot, blown to pieces by bombs, mutilated by shell fragments; would grow increasingly demoralized from fear and lack of sleep. Meanwhile the cannonade would hammer the walls of the fort relentlessly, weakening them to the point of collapse. When sections of the wall gave way, Montcalm would raise a flag of truce and offer another proposal for surrender, this one—provided that the defenders had held out manfully under fire—promising an honorable capitulation and hence a means of escape for the battered garrison. Should the fort's commandant be so foolish as to refuse, he and his men would face the certainty of annihilation when the besieging army stormed through the breaches in the wall. It was virtually certain that he would accept terms that offered the honors of war: few commanders had ever declined them. Montcalm and his men would salute as the foe marched off with colors flying, personal property intact, and a symbolic cannon to testify to their valor; then Montcalm would order the fort razed and proceed with the campaign. Fort Carillon and Fort Saint Frédéric, and the invasion route they guarded, would be more secure than ever before.

And so it went—almost. Montcalm's second-in-command, a tough Gascon brigadier, François-Gaston de Lévis, arrived on August 3 with three thousand Canadian militiamen and Indian warriors, having marched overland from Fort Carillon. Quickly they succeeded in infiltrating the woods around the fort and cutting it off from communication with Fort Edward. Montcalm landed his artillery and established a siege camp that same day and politely invited Lieutenant Colonel George Monro to surrender. When Monro, a veteran officer from the Thirty-fifth Regiment of Foot, refused, the French set to work; meanwhile, the Indians harassed the garrison with sniper fire. From the time the bombardment began on August 6 it took only three days for Montcalm's gunners to disable or dismount most of the fort's great guns, and to position a nine-cannon "breaching battery" at point-blank range before a weakened western wall. Having satisfied the demands of honor, and knowing—thanks to a captured message that Webb had tried to send to Monro, which Montcalm obligingly delivered—that no relief force was on its way, Monro accepted Montcalm's offer of an honorable surrender.

By midday on August 9 all the particulars were agreed to, and all the preparations for turning over the fort to the French were in place. In return for the promise that neither he nor his men would fight again for eighteen months, Monro and the defenders of Fort William Henry would be allowed to march off for Fort Edward as "parolees," carrying their personal effects, arms, colors, and a symbolic brass fieldpiece. The sick and wounded of the fort were to be cared for by the French and returned under flag of truce when they recovered. Monro agreed to see to it that all French prisoners in English custody would be repatriated, and that the fort and all its supplies would be surrendered to Montcalm. Then, as befit the conclusion of business between professionals, Colonel Monro treated the marquis de Montcalm to a handsome dinner, complete with the best of the wine that remained in the cellar of the officers' mess. War might be nasty, brutal work, but it was no occasion for incivility between gentlemen.

It was a model capitulation, thoroughly in keeping with European regular-army practices, but in offering it Montcalm took no account of the wishes of his Indian allies. After the articles had been signed, he summoned the war chiefs to explain to them that they and their warriors would have none of the prisoners or plunder they believed they had fought to obtain. The chiefs listened impassively to what they regarded as an utterly dishonorable set of prohibitions, then returned to their followers with the news that the little man they had called Father was no father at all, for he intended to deprive them of what was rightfully theirs. If they were to have the prisoners, trophies, and plunder they had come for, they would have to take them by force, and Montcalm could be damned.

The next morning at five o'clock, as the long column of surrendered regular and provincial troops and their camp followers prepared to march for Fort Edward with a small French escort, the Indians took what they believed they had earned. The assault was brief, vicious, and chaotic, focused on the rear of the long column, where the Massachusetts provincials and camp followers marched. Within minutes the corpses of between 70 and 185 soldiers and camp followers lay scalped and stripped on the road and in the woods beyond. As many as five hundred more were taken captive. Then the warriors left. By nightfall on August 10, only three hundred or so Christian Abenakis and Nipissings remained with Montcalm's army. The rest of his erstwhile allies were paddling northward down Lake George, heading home with the rewards they had fought to gain.

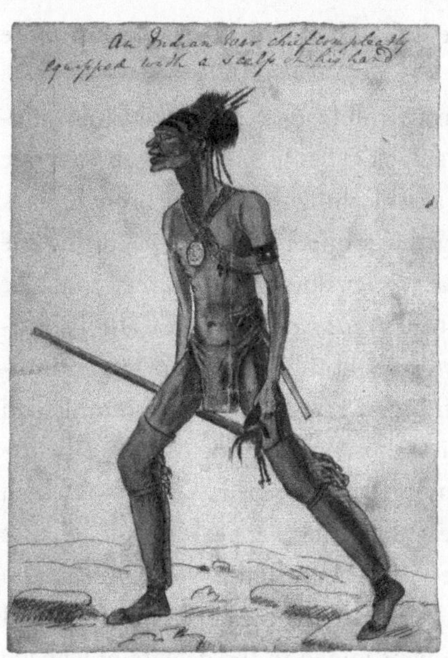

"An Indian War Chief Completely Equipped with a Scalp in His Hand," by George Townshend, c. 1758. *A military leader of modest gifts, Brigadier General George, Viscount Townshend (1724–1807), was a caricaturist of great, if merciless, talent. This image, taken from life, captures much about both the subject and the artist: it accurately depicts the light dress and arms favored by native warriors, reflects the European fascination with scalping, and bespeaks the casual racism of Townshend's view of Indians.* (National Portrait Gallery, London)

In the aftermath of what the Anglo-American colonists called "the massacre of Fort William Henry," Vaudreuil and Montcalm both did their best to ransom prisoners. They ultimately recovered all but about two hundred of them, at an average price of 130 livres in trade goods and thirty bottles of brandy per captive. Montcalm was desperate to redeem as many as he could to salvage his reputation as an honorable commander; Vaudreuil was equally concerned to pay handsomely in order to prevent damage to the alliance with the Indians of the Great Lakes Basin and the interior. Neither succeeded. The reports of the survivors convinced British authorities that the killing had been Montcalm's calculated blow against defenseless prisoners and resulted in the official voiding of the capitulation agreement. No British commander in North America would offer any defeated French force the option of surrender with the full honors of war for the rest of the conflict. In the view of the redcoat command, the "massacre" had left an ineradicable stain on the reputation of Montcalm and his fellow officers. Popular outcries, meanwhile, exploded in New England, stoking an already fierce anti-French, anti-Catholic rage. The colonists blamed the episode on Montcalm's premeditation, and found in it every reason to indulge the indiscriminate Indian-hating that became only more prevalent as the war dragged on.

The western Indians carried home a full load of anger and disillusionment, and something far worse: smallpox. The disease had been endemic at the fort, and the captives, scalps, and clothing the Indians brought back touched off an epidemic that ravaged the upper Great Lakes during the latter 1750s. This disaster meant that few warriors would journey from the region to join the French in the critical year 1758, and even Catholic warriors from the Saint Lawrence *réserves* would show markedly less enthusiasm. Higher proportions of mission Indians turned out in 1759 to defend against an Anglo-American invasion, but that was in the context of a life-or-death struggle that the missionary priests explained as a war to defend the Catholic faith. In that same year the fervent appeals of missionaries and *officiers* at remote posts on the Great Lakes and beyond produced a resurgence in the numbers of western and northern Indians. In the end approximately eighteen hundred Indians joined in the defense of Canada in 1759; even Dakotas from the Plains and Crees from the subarctic offered their services in the defense of Quebec. They would find, however, that Montcalm had little use for them, for he was resolved to conduct the war in as civilized and conventional a manner as possible, and that gave precious little scope to the kind of freewheeling frontier guerrilla war that had served New France so well for so long.

The withdrawal of Indian support left Vaudreuil's offensive in ruins. He had intended that Montcalm, having taken Fort William Henry, should proceed against Fort Edward; but Montcalm, having discovered the hard way that he could not command Indians as auxiliaries, found himself without the scouts he needed to carry on the campaign and so contented himself with destroying the works at Fort William Henry and returning to Canada. Each marquis condemned the other in angry letters to Versailles. Vaudreuil blamed Montcalm for having squandered the greatest military advantage New France had ever enjoyed; Montcalm blamed Vaudreuil's policies for the grisly events of August 10, suggesting that the early termination of the campaign was Vaudreuil's fault. Vaudreuil accurately foresaw that New France would now be forced onto the defensive, a position he dreaded because it so obviously favored the numerous British. Montcalm, on the other hand, welcomed the necessity of fighting a defensive campaign of phased withdrawal from the frontiers to the heartland, where he would concentrate his forces and pursue the kind of professional, honorable war he longed to fight. The two men went on campaigning against each other with increasing bitterness until the breach between them was open and public. Eventually the dispute, which threatened to cripple the French war effort in America, had to be resolved by the king himself.

PART THREE

TURNING POINT

CHAPTER ELEVEN

The Ascent of William Pitt

The year 1757 ended badly for the British on more counts than the loss of Fort William Henry. Lord Loudoun's Louisbourg expedition never got beyond Halifax, foiled by foul weather, delay in the arrival of a Royal Navy squadron, and the appearance at Louisbourg of eighteen ships of the line—the most powerful naval contingent France ever sent to American waters. Admiral Francis Holburne, unwilling to confront a superior force, advised Loudoun to abandon the intended campaign. Reluctantly, prudently, Loudoun agreed. In August he left most of his army to winter in Halifax so that it would at least be close to its objective in the coming year, and returned to New York. There he devoted his considerable reserves of energy to reversing the ill effects of Fort William Henry's fall. He soon discovered, however, that opposition was mounting to his methods, which colonial politicians had come to regard as high-handed, or even tyrannical.

As the fall of 1757 gave way to winter and planning for the coming campaigns began in earnest, it became obvious to Loudoun that the colonial governors—men whom he expected to obey him with as much alacrity, and as little protest, as his colonels—were not doing their jobs. That they lacked the will or the means to discipline their legislatures was no trivial matter, for unless something could be done to sway the uncooperative assemblymen, the North American war effort might founder altogether in 1758. William Shirley's cronies in the Massachusetts assembly,

Loudoun knew, led the opposition. They had protested, the previous fall, when he decided to retain several companies of Bay Colony provincials past their normal discharge date to guard the New York frontier. Later they had refused to raise the ranger units Loudoun needed for winter scouting duty. Finally they had had the effrontery to invite the other New England provinces to join them in appointing commissioners who would meet and determine, by negotiation, what their respective colonies would contribute to the coming campaigns. For the commander in chief, that was the last straw.

Incensed that the provinces would trespass so flagrantly on his authority, Loudoun summoned the governors of the four New England colonies, New York, and New Jersey to meet him at Hartford on February 20, 1758. There he dressed them down for allowing such impertinence to flourish in their assemblies and informed them of the numbers of men that each colony was to provide for the campaigns of 1758. When Governor Thomas Pownall of Massachusetts protested that his province's legislators would not submit to dictation, Loudoun marched off to Boston to show them who was commander in chief. He expected that they would submit once he showed his displeasure—he had bent other assemblies to his will in previous confrontations—and so was astonished and outraged when the assembled legislators stood fast, refusing to raise the 2,128 men he demanded. They debated the issue for more than a week, as Loudoun grew more and more chagrined at their insolence. Then, on the morning of March 10, Pownall received two letters that changed everything.

The letters came from Secretary of State William Pitt, the official in whom the crown vested the powers of appointment and supervision for all provincial governors and other royal officials in the colonies. They were in every sense extraordinary documents. The first contained news that Lord Loudoun had been recalled from his position as commander in chief and that his second-in-command, Major General James Abercromby, had been appointed to succeed him. The other letter directed Pownall, along with his fellow governors, to use "your utmost Endeavours, and Influence with the Council and Assembly of your Province, to induce them to raise, with all possible Dispatch, as large a Body of Men within your Government, as the Number of Its Inhabitants may allow." It also revealed that the officers of the provincial regiments to be raised would be considered as holding

William Pitt, First Earl of Chatham, **by Richard Houston, after William Hoare, c. 1754.** *This mezzotint after the artist William Hoare's 1754 portrait captures the British statesman and minister William Pitt on the eve of the Seven Years' War. Pitt's policies, crucial in reversing the early string of British defeats in the conflict with France, encouraged American colonists to view themselves less as the colonial subjects of a sovereign British authority than as partners in a great British imperial adventure.* (National Portrait Gallery, London)

rank junior only to regular officers of similar grades; colonial field officers and generals no longer would rank only as "eldest captains," but would be subject only to the commands of regular officers of their own ranks, or higher. This was a great salve to the pride of provincial officers, but the letter promised an even greater emollient for the provincial assemblies by announcing that the crown henceforth would pay for the equipment and provisions of all men to be raised, and would reimburse the colonies for other expenses, in proportion to "the active Vigour and strenuous Efforts of the respective Provinces." That evening Pownall laid the letters before the assembly. The next morning its members voted to raise seven thousand men. No documents record Loudoun's reactions, but they can be easily imagined. He departed immediately for New York, where he turned his official papers over to Abercromby and took the first available ship for Britain.

What had happened? Weeks would pass before it became clear to the colonists what had brought the British ministry to make such a remarkable reversal in policy. Pitt's letters to the colonial governors marked not only an abrupt change in direction but also his emergence as his nation's preeminent war leader. These alterations in turn flowed from the truly miserable start that Britain had made in the contest with France. The loss of Minorca had been bad enough, but when war broke out on the Continent, King George II had found his other realm, the Electorate of Hanover (the homeland he loved better by far than unruly Britain), exposed to invasion by the French. The duke of Cumberland hastened to Hanover and assumed command of its army, along with a large contingent of Hessian troops who served in British pay. He arrived just in time to face a powerful French advance and suffer defeat at the Battle of Hastenbeck on July 25, 1757. He retreated toward the mouth of the Elbe and called for help from the Royal Navy but the French moved quickly to trap his army in the northeastern quarter of the Electorate. Cut off from the sea and all hope of rescue, Cumberland held out as long as he could, then negotiated a surrender, the Convention of Kloster-Zeven (named for the village where it was signed), that spared his army from destruction but allowed the French to occupy virtually all of Hanover.

The surrender combined military defeat and diplomatic humiliation with a perfection that staggered George II. He summoned his son home and publicly disgraced him. Cumberland immediately resigned his position as captain-general of the British army, and indeed all his offices, and withdrew into virtual seclusion. The duke's sudden absence from the military and political arenas in which he had hitherto bulked so large positioned Britain's most brilliant orator, William Pitt, and the realm's virtuoso manipulator of patronage, the duke of Newcastle, to dominate the politics of Parliament and the court. Lacking alternatives, the king and the Commons acceded to their leadership, which resolved itself (not without difficulty, for the two men had been bitter enemies) into a partnership. Newcastle, as first lord of the treasury, assumed responsibility for financing and supplying the war effort. Pitt, as secretary of state for the Southern Department, took control of the army, navy, diplomatic corps, and the formulation of policy. In the absence of any effective opposition, Pitt was now free to implement what he called his "system," which was in fact a good deal less coherent than that word would suggest. It was instead a grab bag of strategies aimed at retrieving the military initiative and prosecuting the war against France, which Pitt regarded as Britain's only significant enemy.

Pitt's system boiled down to making the most of his nation's shaky position by building on its strengths wherever they existed, striking France at its weakest points whenever possible, and holding the line in Europe by subsidizing Frederick the Great and Prince Ferdinand of Brunswick, who had succeeded Cumberland as commander of Hanover's army.* If Frederick and Ferdinand could use British money to buy the German troops they needed to tie down the French army and hold the Austrians at bay, Britain could use its superior fleet to harass the French coast with "descents," or raids; to interdict French merchant shipping on the high seas; and to blockade the French navy in its Atlantic bases. Meanwhile Pitt intended to employ the more than twenty thousand regular troops already posted in North America to attack Canada and the French West Indies. Parliamentary promises of reimbursements would encourage colonial assemblies to mobilize tens of thousands of provincial troops and other

---

*By the Convention of Kloster-Zeven the Hanoverian army *should* have ceased to exist as a fighting force. On Pitt's advice, however, George II annulled the Convention on October 8, citing the technicality that the French had not permitted the troops of Hesse to return home unhindered. The French, believing that the Convention was secure, had already shifted their forces east to attack Prussia; there they remained fully occupied until Frederick defeated them with stunning thoroughness at the Battle of Rossbach (November 5, 1757). Prince Ferdinand thus had time to reorganize Hanover's forces and attack the weakened French in a winter campaign. By spring he had driven the French out of Hanover, into Westphalia.

colonists—civilian artificers, merchants and traders, bateaumen, teamsters, and the male and female camp followers who provided an array of crucial services to the troops—to support the regulars who would do most of the fighting.

Pitt backed up his reassurances to the political leaders of the colonies that he would neither bankrupt them nor destroy their liberties by substantially reducing the powers of the commander in chief. Abercromby's new commission as commander in chief denied him Loudoun's viceregal authority over the civil authorities of the colonies, while Pitt himself assumed responsibility for planning the campaigns. The raising of so many provincial soldiers would generate supply and clothing contracts and hundreds upon hundreds of commissions that the governors could use as the currency of patronage, increasing their leverage in the assemblies. Pitt could not have cared less that the incentives he offered the colonies overturned ten years' worth of efforts by metropolitan authorities to economize and tighten their administrative grasp on the colonies. A supreme egoist if not an outright megalomaniac, Pitt cared only about winning the war. He was content to leave Newcastle to do the sums and fret over the expenses; as for the colonial assemblies, they could be brought to heel once victory had been secured.

The colonists responded with a surge of support and patriotic sentiment. Loudoun had demanded fewer than seven thousand provincial soldiers of the northern colonies for his planned campaigns in 1758 and had been met by what he regarded as the mutiny of the assemblies. Within weeks of the arrival of the letters that announced Pitt's new policies, by contrast, those same colonial legislatures voted to raise more than twenty-three thousand provincials. Thanks to the handsome enlistment bounties the assemblies now felt secure enough to authorize an addition to the basic soldiers' pay; provincial regiments were recruited to full strength for the first time since the beginning of the war, and were manned overwhelmingly by volunteers. By the beginning of the campaign season roughly fifty thousand regulars and provincials were in service, together with tens of thousands more sailors and marines. Even without counting the thousands of civilians whom the military employed in support roles and the thousands of mariners who served on board privateers, the campaigns of 1758 began

English punch bowl, c. 1756–1763. *Britons throughout the Atlantic world toasted the victories of their land and sea forces, together with those of their European ally Prussia, with punch served in ceramic bowls like this example, inscribed "Success To the King of Prussia."* (Colonial Williamsburg Foundation)

with a number of men under arms in British North America that virtually equaled the population of New France.

With a speed that would be remarkable today and which was literally astonishing in the mid-eighteenth century, Pitt's policies mobilized whole colonial societies for war. Provincial legislators agreed to unprecedented levels of military spending; that spending in turn stimulated the colonial economies to a level of wartime prosperity never seen before. The patriotic fervor of North America's Britons, revived by a shared sense of purpose, surpassed every precedent in the history of the colonies. And all of it had been accomplished because Pitt had given the colonists free rein to imagine that they were not so much subjects of the British empire as partners in a great imperial endeavor.

The campaigns Pitt designed for 1758 were by no means as innovative as his policies, for his plans were essentially the ones Loudoun had already set in motion. That strategy should show so much continuity while policy showed so little was in fact unsurprising, for the geography of eastern

North America imposed strict constraints on Britain's strategic options. Given the loss of Oswego and the neutrality of the Iroquois, Canada could be invaded by one of two routes: either by a seaborne expedition up the Saint Lawrence River, or overland, via the Lake George–Lake Champlain–Richelieu River corridor. Loudoun had planned to do both in 1758. In New York he intended to make Forts Carillon and Saint Frédéric targets of a massive bateau-borne expedition. If they fell quickly, the invading force could move north to attack Forts Île-aux-Noix, Saint-Jean, and Chambly, which guarded the Richelieu from the foot of Lake Champlain to the very doorstep of Montreal. Meanwhile, according to Loudoun's plans, the regulars who had wintered at Halifax were to embark on naval vessels that would bypass Louisbourg, sail directly up the Saint Lawrence, and attack Quebec.

Fort Duquesne remained a lethal threat to the Pennsylvania and Virginia backcountry so long as Indian warriors could launch raids from it. Loudoun understood that the fort's weakest point was its long, tenuous supply line. The raiders needed supplies of arms, ammunition, and trade goods to continue operating against the frontier, and those could come only by way of Lake Ontario, Lake Erie, the Rivière aux Boeufs, and the Allegheny. Loudoun therefore intended to cripple Fort Duquesne by sending an expedition up the Mohawk and past Oswego to seize Fort Frontenac, the naval base on the north shore of Lake Ontario that functioned as the main supply depot for all of New France's western forts and trading posts. With Frontenac out of the way, he reasoned, it would be a straightforward matter to destroy Fort Duquesne by sending a force overland from Pennsylvania by a road cut more or less straight west from Carlisle.

Pitt modified these plans at the margins, but kept their essential goals in mind. He set aside Loudoun's design for a seaborne expedition directly against Quebec in favor of a more conservative approach that would seize Louisbourg first, and then proceed against the heartland. A forty-year-old colonel, Jeffery Amherst, newly promoted to the temporary rank of "major general in America," would command that expedition. Lieutenant General Sir John Ligonier, the amazingly dynamic septuagenarian who succeeded Cumberland as commander in chief of the British army, had recommended Amherst as a systematic officer with formidable administrative and logistical talents. He also proposed that Amherst's temperamental opposite, Lieutenant Colonel James Wolfe—a brilliant, high-strung field commander, bold to a fault—be promoted to acting brigadier general and made Amherst's second-in-command. Ligonier proposed a similar pairing of opposites for the expedition that was to proceed against Forts Carillon and Saint Frédéric. The fussy and not overactive Abercromby was to command this crucial campaign, but the man who would bear responsibility for battlefield leadership was his second-in-command, Brigadier General

Major General James Abercromby, **by Allan Ramsay, c. 1760.** *The Scottish officer James Abercromby (1706–1781) served as deputy to the earl of Loudoun as commander in chief during 1756–57. He replaced Lord Loudoun the following year, but was recalled to Britain following his disastrous attack on Fort Carillon. The Scottish portraitist Allan Ramsay painted this likeness shortly after his return, and it remained with his descendants until recently.* (Collection of the Fort Ticonderoga Museum)

George Augustus, Viscount Howe—a thirty-four-year-old officer whose charismatic courage had made him tremendously popular among regular and provincial troops alike.

Pitt opted to simplify Lord Loudoun's two-pronged approach to Fort Duquesne by setting aside the expedition against Fort Frontenac and launching a larger force across Pennsylvania directly against the Forks of the Ohio. That campaign was to be entrusted to one of Loudoun's colonels, a methodical fifty-year-old Scot named John Forbes, also promoted to the temporary rank of "brigadier-general in America." Like Amherst, Forbes had earned a reputation for great steadiness and organizational acumen. As a young man he had been trained as a physician, and hence was in a far better position than Ligonier or Pitt to know that this expedition was likely to be his last. Although Forbes did his best to conceal his symptoms, he was steadily declining in health, the victim of a tormenting inflammatory skin condition and an inveterate disorder of the bowels that may have been chronic dysentery or even the beginnings of colon cancer.

The campaigns of 1758 reflected conventional thinking insofar as they relied on regular soldiers to bear the brunt of the fighting, a disposition that reflected the dim view Lord Loudoun (and virtually every other professional officer in North America) took of provincial soldiers. Expensive and inefficient and amateurish as they were, however, provincials played a crucial role in the war effort from 1758 on. Pitt's visionary desire to encourage colonial participation regardless of expense meant that colonists would be available in huge numbers to perform the tedious tasks of garrison duty and the inglorious, heavy labor of road construction and fortbuilding that ensured that the regulars would in fact be free to fight when the time came to do it.

Meanwhile the efficiency, energy, and professionalism of Lord Loudoun had enabled the regulars to conduct combat operations in the woods with greater skill and effectiveness than ever before. Loudoun had greatly improved the army's supply system by instituting reforms in procurement, regulating the quality of provisions by strict inspections, improving storage, and establishing systems of inventory control. Thanks to these, regular and provincial soldiers alike were better fed, equipped, clothed, and sheltered in 1758 than in any previous year. Similarly Loudoun had invested in the transport system by improving roads and creating specialized units of armed wagoners and bateaumen to haul supplies from the warehouses of Albany to advanced posts. As a result goods and provisions could be moved in 1758 at only one-third the expense per mile of 1756—a drop in costs that reflected massive gains in efficiency, and translated into improvements in the morale and discipline of the troops.

For all the emphasis on system and order and professionalism that made the American war effort look more like a conventional European military enterprise, Loudoun had also done much that was unconventional in helping his soldiers adapt to American conditions. The loss of Mohawk allies after the Battle of Lake George in 1755 had deprived the Anglo-Americans of virtually all useful intelligence on the enemy's strength, position, and movements in New York. Shirley, in his typically ad hoc way, had tried to compensate by raising three companies of provincial rangers under the overall command of a New Hampshire frontiersman, Major Robert Rogers, to act as scouts and raiders. Loudoun, who found that he could work with Rogers even if he did not fully trust him, had trebled the number of ranger companies and put them on the regular army's payroll. He also paid close attention to the tactics that the rangers had devised to fight in the woods, and encouraged regular commanders to make similar adaptations. When the rangers proved hard to discipline, Loudoun authorized the creation of a separate battalion of light infantry made up of "active, young, strong, and healthy" men to perform duties similar to theirs, but in a more orderly and reliable way.

Brigadier General Howe, noting the usefulness of the uniforms and tactics of rangers and light infantrymen, urged Loudoun and Abercromby to generalize them among ordinary regiments. By 1758 regular infantrymen were being trained in "bush fighting" tactics, learning how to move through the woods in single file, fight in a spread-out single rank or in loose order as skirmishers, avoid bunching up when attacked, and take cover when the command "Tree all!" rang out on the march. Loudoun ordered rifles to be issued to the ten best marksmen in each regiment, explicitly sanctioning the ungentlemanly practice of picking off enemy officers in combat. Perhaps even more surprisingly, he also ordered that ordinary infantrymen be trained to aim their muskets at individual targets, rather than continuing to follow the European practice of leveling the barrels in the general direction of the enemy and firing volleys on order. As the campaigns of 1758 began, troops lopped the long tails off their coats to keep them from tangling in brush; discarded regimental lace; carried tomahawks in addition to bayonets and often in place of swords; carried spare powder in cow horns to supplement the cartridges in their cartouche boxes; trimmed back the brims on their hats and wore them slouched rather than cocked up in the familiar tricorner form; cut their hair short rather than wearing it in queues. All of these modifications took a toll on appearances ("You could not distinguish us from common plough men," one officer wrote ruefully to an English correspondent) but not on fighting effectiveness. The proficiency of British units in America was markedly higher at the end of Lord Loudoun's term than at any point since Braddock's arrival.

Another factor, too, favored the Anglo-American forces as the campaigns of 1758 began: the growing efficiency of the Royal Navy in pre-

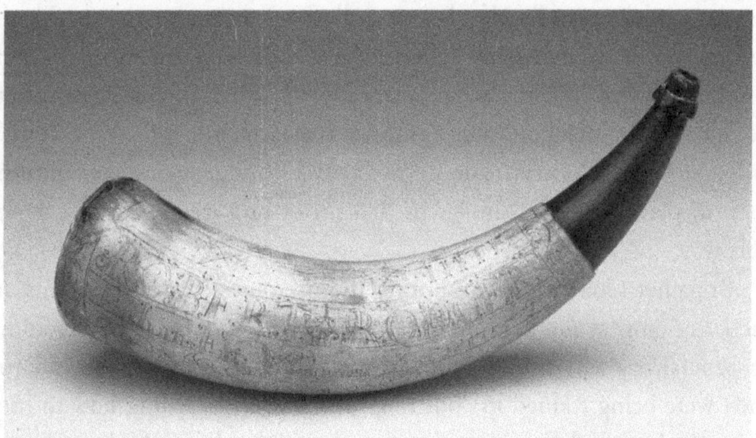

Powder horn, 1756. *Although born in Massachusetts, Robert Rogers (1731–1795) spent his formative years on the New Hampshire frontier. He achieved fame as a partisan leader in the Lake George region and trained regular British officers in irregular tactics. His powder horn, engraved by the African-American provincial soldier John Bush, was made at Fort William Henry in 1756.* (Collection of the Fort Ticonderoga Museum)

venting French ships from crossing the Atlantic. At the beginning of hostilities Britain had stepped up shipbuilding and naval recruitment at such a pace that by early 1758 it had 98 ships of the line in service, along with 141 frigates and smaller vessels. Forty-nine more men-of-war were under construction. By the fall of 1757 British warships effectively controlled the Strait of Gibraltar, limiting the ability of French ships to escape the Mediterranean. Although the navy's efforts to blockade the Atlantic ports were not yet seamless, the squadrons that patrolled the Channel and hovered off Brest and Rochefort were severely limiting France's ability to communicate with its colonies. In 1757 the French navy had dispatched eighteen line-of-battle ships to defend Louisbourg; in 1758, thanks to Admiral Edward Hawke's success in breaking up a big relief convoy off La Rochelle in April, only six men-of-war arrived safe in Louisbourg's harbor. Against this handful of vessels the British were able to assemble no fewer than twenty-three ships of the line, supported by sixteen frigates and smaller craft.

The increasing difficulty of Atlantic crossings created dramatic consequences for New France. Because the Royal Navy not only blockaded France's ports but patrolled the Gulf of Saint Lawrence and because Anglo-American privateers swarmed the Atlantic sea lanes, the only reliable way for the French to resupply Canada was by means of warships sailing *en flûte,* or stripped of most of their armament. In this configuration the more advanced French frigates and line-of-battle ships could outrun virtually any British man-of-war; but they carried only dispatches, reinforcements, and cargoes of arms, ammunition, and Indian trade goods. Welcome as those were, the *flûtes* brought no significant stores of provisions at a time when food supplies were growing critically short. Harvests in the Saint Lawrence Valley had failed in both 1756 and 1757, and the continuing diversion of men from agricultural labor to extended militia service made the outlook all the more foreboding. At the beginning of May 1758 the typical *habitant* of Quebec was subsisting on a weekly ration of fourteen ounces of bread, a half-pound of horsemeat, a half-pound of salt pork, and a quarter-pound of codfish. Only the arrival of a handful of supply ships on the twenty-second averted actual starvation in the district.

The prospects for New France at the beginning of the campaigning season in 1758 seemed dire indeed, but Pitt knew little about the actual conditions of Canadian life and remained far from optimistic about the year's prospects. Thus far Anglo-American commanders had shown no talent more consistent than their capacity to lose battles. It was still by no means certain that Pitt's radical policies would do more than allow Britain to snatch defeat from the jaws of victory at what now would be a truly ruinous cost.

CHAPTER TWELVE

The Red Cross of Carillon

The first battle of 1758 seemed to confirm what Pitt dreaded most. Following Loudoun's unceremonious departure in March, preparations for the campaigns had moved ahead quickly. Men came forward to enlist with an enthusiasm fueled in equal parts by patriotic feeling and the exceptionally generous bounties the provincial assemblies offered once they knew that Parliament would reimburse them in proportion to their participation in the war effort. By the beginning of July General Abercromby had established his headquarters next to the hulk of Fort William Henry, in the midst of the largest armed force ever assembled in North America, some sixteen thousand men. With sixteen heavy cannon, thirteen howitzers, eleven mortars, and eight thousand rounds of ammunition, the expedition's artillery train was sufficient to conduct sieges against every post from Fort Carillon to Montreal. A thousand boats had been built to transport men, guns, and baggage down the lake. When the army set out at dawn on July 5, the flotilla of sailing vessels, bateaux, and whaleboats moved in four parallel columns that stretched seven miles from end to end.

The marquis de Montcalm had arrived at Fort Carillon less than a week before. There he found eight understrength battalions of *troupes de terre,* one company of *troupes de la marine,* thirty-six Canadian militiamen, and fourteen Indians. Their food supply was sufficient for perhaps nine days. More men arrived thereafter, but by the morning of July 6, when members of the French advance guard came running with the unwelcome news that a British force large enough to cover the face of the lake was landing just four miles from the fort, Montcalm had only 3,526 men at his disposal. The provisions on hand, including every morsel the reinforcements had brought, would not sustain them for a single week. What made matters even worse was that Fort Carillon had been built in such haste following the Battle of Lake George that it was extremely difficult to defend. A seven-hundred-foot hill, now known as Mount Defiance, overlooked it from the west, less than a mile away, offering an ideal spot from which gunners could fire directly into the interior of the fort. To

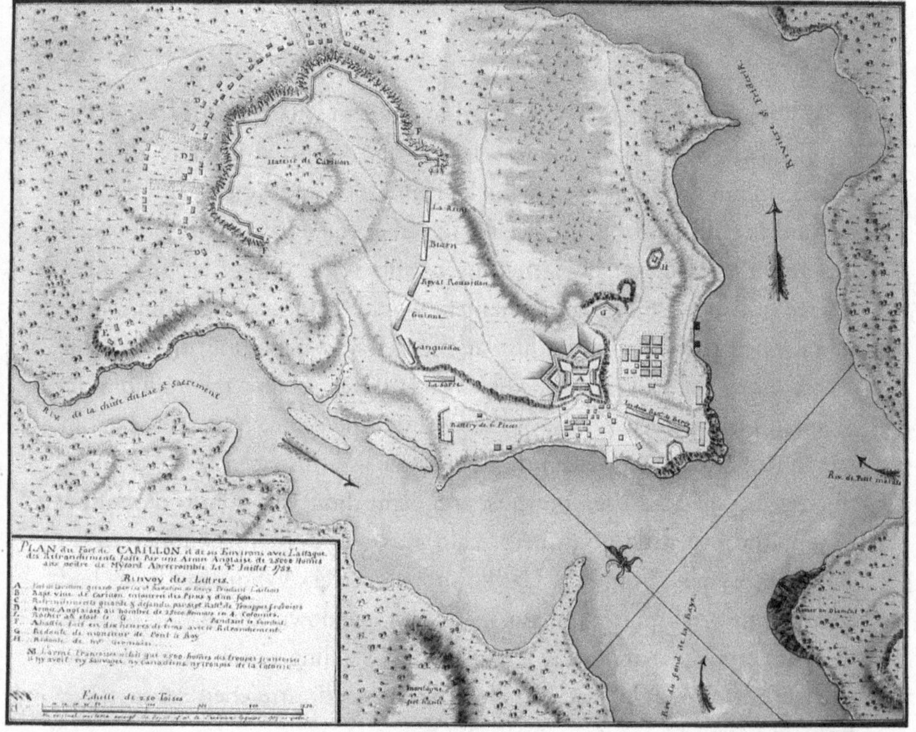

***"Plan du Fort de Carillon."** This contemporary plan illustrates the high ground north of Fort Carillon on which Montcalm's forces erected an irregularly shaped defensive wall and abatis. Montcalm's regular battalions encamped between the height of land and the fort, the locations marked here by rectangular icons.* (William L. Clements Library, University of Michigan)

A Map of the British and French Dominions in North America, by John Mitchell, cartographer, and Thomas Kitchen, engraver, London, 1755. *The Virginia native John Mitchell produced this influential map of eastern North America at a time of intensifying Anglo-French imperial rivalry. In contrast with French cartographers, who depicted the British colonies bounded by the Appalachian Mountains, Mitchell presented an expansive view of British North America. The map proved instantly popular in Britain and America, where copies were distributed to each of the colonial governors.* (Colonial Williamsburg Foundation)

Carte de la Nouvelle France, 1720. *This early eighteenth-century map illustrates French imperial ambitions in North America. British territory (green) is restricted to a narrow strip along the Atlantic seaboard and lands surrounding Hudson's Bay. The French colonies of Canada (pink) and Louisiana (yellow) encompass a broad swath of land stretching from the Saint Lawrence to the Mississippi Valley. At the time this map was made, the French population of this vast zone would not have exceeded twenty-five thousand men, women, and children.* (© National Maritime Museum, London)

The Capture of the Alcide *and* Lys, *June 8, 1755. Although the two countries were still officially at peace, a British fleet under Admiral Edward Boscawen tried to intercept French reinforcements headed for Canada in early 1755. The capture of the French ships* Alcide *and* Lys *off Newfoundland was the first naval engagement of the Seven Years' War.* (© National Maritime Museum, London)

Sir William Johnson, by John Wollaston (1736–1767), c. 1750–1752. *The Irish-born merchant William Johnson (1715–1774) emerged as an important intercultural diplomat and military leader in New York before the outbreak of the French and Indian War. In 1755, Major General Edward Braddock appointed Johnson to manage British relations with the Iroquois Confederacy and lead an expedition to capture the French Fort Saint Frédéric (Crown Point).* (Oil on canvas, Albany Institute of History & Art, Gift of Laura Munsell Tremaine in memory of her father, Joel Munsell, 1922.2)

General Gabriel Christie, artist unknown. *Gabriel Christie (1722–1799), a Scottish officer, arrived in North America as captain in the Forty-eighth Regiment, one of two British units that accompanied Braddock's expedition against Fort Duquesne. Like many British officers, Christie married an American and settled on land he received for service in the French and Indian War.* (Château Ramezay Museum Collection, Montreal)

John Campbell, Fourth Earl of Loudoun, by Allan Ramsay, c. 1754. *Commander in chief of British and American forces in North America from 1756 to 1758, Lord Loudoun was invested with extensive political and military authority to direct the war effort against New France. His efforts to use these formal powers to exert centralized control sparked considerable resistance, and his recall at the beginning of the 1758 campaign marked a decisive shift in the conduct of Britain's American war.* (Fort Ligonier, Ligonier, Pennsylvania)

General John Winslow, by Joseph Blackburn. *The veteran Massachusetts commander John Winslow (1703–1774) first led New England troops in the 1740s, and served briefly as a British officer during King George's War, before retiring on half-pay as a captain. In 1755 he commanded New England provincial troops in the siege of Fort Beauséjour and the subsequent expulsion of the Acadians. As commanding general of Massachusetts forces in 1756 he disagreed with Lord Loudoun over the terms on which provincial soldiers served; this was, as a result, his last campaign.* (Courtesy of Pilgrim Hall Museum, Plymouth, Massachusetts)

Pierre de Rigaud de Vaudreuil de Cavagnal, Marquis de Vaudreuil, unknown French artist, c. 1753–1755. *The marquis de Vaudreuil (1698–1778) was an experienced officer in the colonial regulars (*troupes de la marine*) and had been governor of Louisiana by the time he was appointed governor-general of New France in 1755. He was also the colony's last governor-general. A firm advocate of the traditional strategy of defending Canada through the use of Indian allies and spoiling raids against British colonial settlements, he was at loggerheads with the marquis de Montcalm for much of the war.* (Library and Archives Canada/C-147538)

Louis Joseph de Montcalm, Marquis de Montcalm de Saint-Véran, artist unknown. *As commander of the field forces in Canada, the marquis de Montcalm (1712–1759) abhorred the "barbarous" guerrilla warfare practiced by Canadians and native warriors, and clashed repeatedly with Governor-General Vaudreuil over strategy and tactics. Nonetheless, he was adaptable enough to lead mixed forces of regulars, Canadian militiamen, and Indian warriors with unbroken success through the defense of Fort Carillon in July 1758. Mortally wounded at the Battle of Quebec on September 13, 1759, he died the following day.*
(Library and Archives Canada/C-027665)

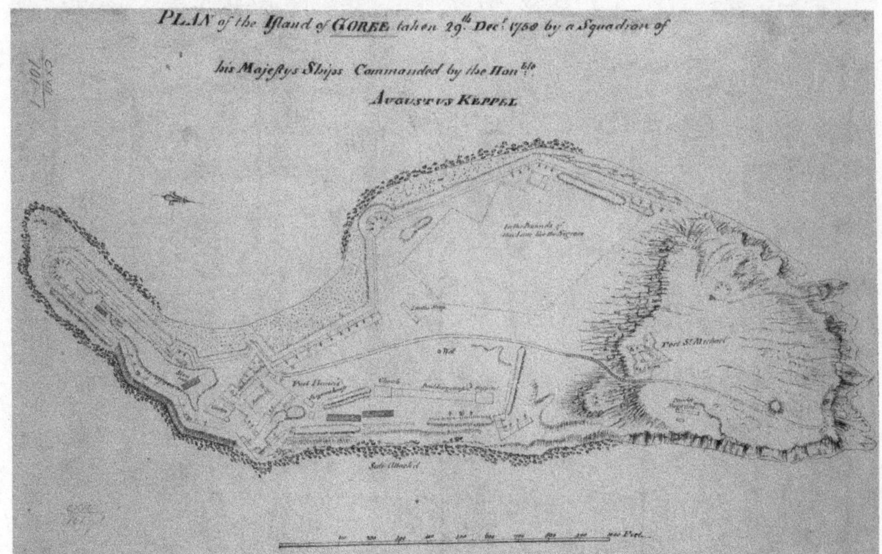

A Plan of the Island of Goree, 1758. *In December 1758, a British squadron under Admiral Augustus Keppel seized the French trading and slaving station at Goree off the coast of Senegal in Africa. The expedition reflected Willam Pitt's strategy of using Britain's superior navy to counter France's immense military strength in Europe by attacking vulnerable French possessions overseas. Most of all, by depriving West Indian planters of slaves, it struck the economies of the French sugar islands a devastating blow.* (By permission of the British Library; shelfmark Maps K.Top.117.101.1)

Scyacust Ukah (Ostenaco), by Sir Joshua Reynolds, 1762. *The Cherokee Nation, allied with the British through the government of South Carolina, sent large numbers of warriors north to fight the French and their Indian allies in the Ohio country at various points during 1756–1758. Misunderstandings and clashes with backcountry Virginians soured relations in 1758, leading to open conflict in 1759 and ultimately to a devastating Anglo-Cherokee war in 1760–1761. This portrait of leader Ostenaco (c. 1703–c. 1780) was painted in London in 1762 when he visited as a member of a peace delegation.* (Gilcrease Museum, Tulsa, Oklahoma)

***The Charity of General Amherst,* by Francis Hayman, 1761.** *This is an artist's study for one of the four monumental history paintings commemorating British victories in the Seven Years' War that were displayed at the fashionable Vauxhall Gardens near London. Amherst's magnanimity in feeding hungry Canadians after the capitulation of Montreal contrasted sharply with his (undepicted) willingness to "use every stratagem in our power"—including the spreading of smallpox among them—to "extirpate" the Indians who rose up against British power in 1763.* (Canadian War Museum)

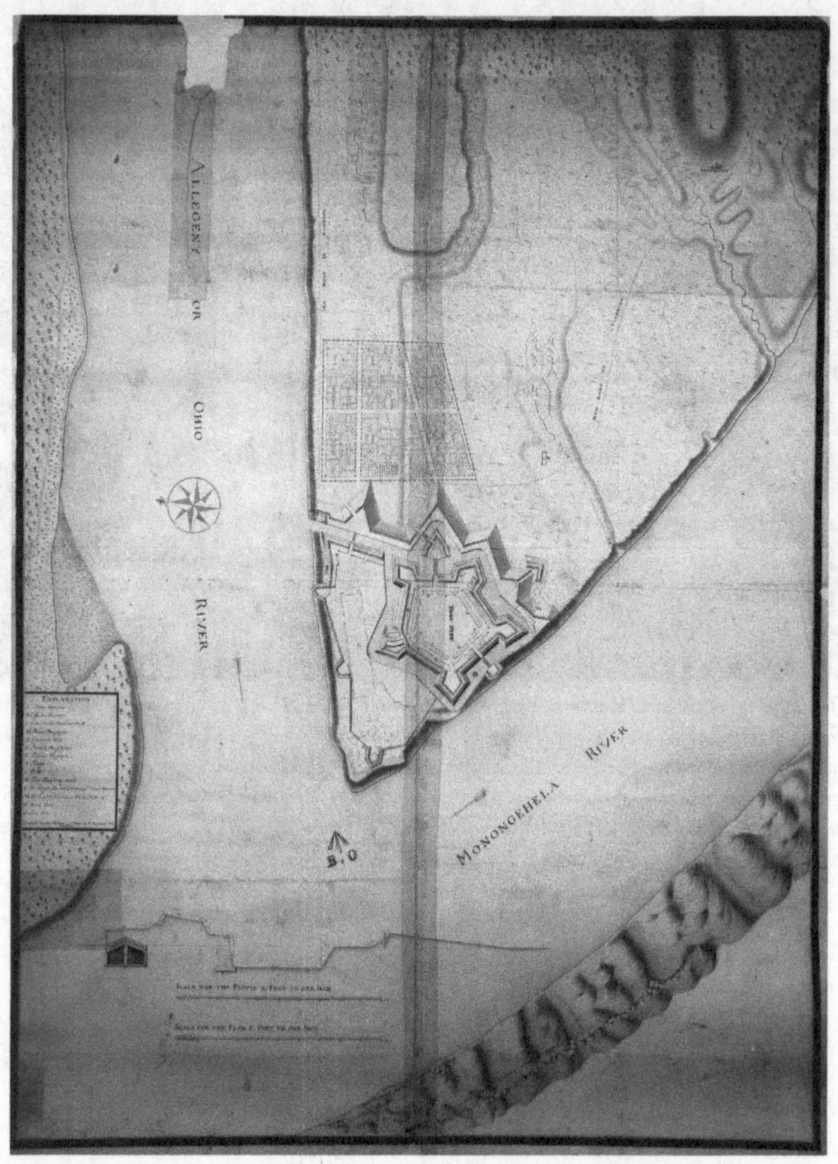

***Survey of the Environs of Fort Pitt*, ink and watercolor, surveyed by Lieutenant E. Meyer, c. 1761.** *British military engineer Elias Meyer produced this detailed survey of Fort Pitt and the Forks of the Ohio River after the fall of New France. The contrast between the massive earth and brick fortress and the comparatively tiny French Fort Duquesne (the faint outline of which appears at the point of land) struck many Ohio Indians as evidence of Britain's intention to seize their lands.* (The National Archives of the UK [PRO])

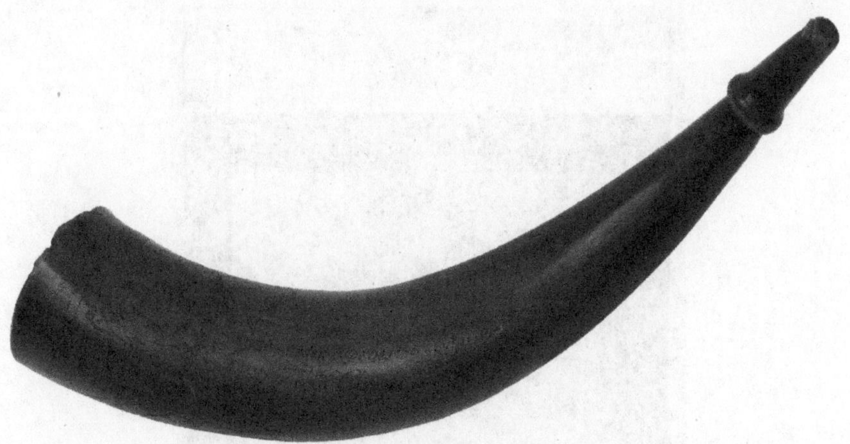

Powder horn, Fort Chartes, Illinois, 1767. *British troops took possession of French posts in the Illinois country only in the summer of 1765. Many French inhabitants moved their families and livestock across the Mississippi River to Spanish territory rather than live under British rule. This powder horn belonged to Captain Gordon Forbes (1738–1828), who commanded the British garrison of Fort Chartres until 1768.* (Courtesy of Jim and Carolyn Dresslar)

Powder horn, Saint Augustine, Florida, 1767. *This powder horn was owned by Captain Yelverton Peyton of the Ninth Regiment, a participant in the 1762 capture of Havana. The inscription commemorates the embarkation of British forces following the Peace of 1763, which returned Havana to Spanish control in exchange for Florida. The 1765 Stamp Act was designed to raise revenue to pay for garrisons in former French and Spanish territory.* (Courtesy of William H. Myers)

Sign of the General Wolfe Tavern, c. 1768. *Lieutenant Colonel Israel Putnam (1718–1790) returned to Pomfret, Connecticut, in 1765 after nine military campaigns, including the devastating siege of Havana. He opened a tavern and named it for General James Wolfe, whom he and most other Anglo-Americans lionized, and simultaneously led local opposition to the Stamp Act in eastern Connecticut. He went on to protest subsequent policies that treated colonists as anything less than full partners in the British empire; eventually he would serve as one of Washington's generals in the Revolutionary War.* (The Connecticut Historical Society Museum, Hartford, Connecticut)

George Washington in the Uniform of a British Colonial Colonel, by Charles Willson Peale, 1772. *George Washington chose to commemorate his military service during the French and Indian War when he sat for this, his first portrait, at Mount Vernon in 1772. He wears his uniform as colonel of the First Virginia Regiment; his gorget (a vestigial piece of armor worn around the neck by eighteenth-century officers) bears the engraved crest of the British crown. The faded crimson sash across his chest had belonged to General Braddock, who gave it to him before dying in July 1755. The folded paper marked "Order of March" in his pocket recalls his service as a brigade commander under General John Forbes in November 1758.*

(Washington-Custis-Lee Collection, Washington and Lee University, Lexington, Virginia)

George Washington, by Charles Willson Peale, 1776. *In May 1776 George Washington sat again for artist Charles Willson Peale, this time as commander in chief of the Continental Army in a uniform modeled on the Fairfax (Virginia) Independent Company that he had helped to equip and train in 1774–1775.* (Brooklyn Museum)

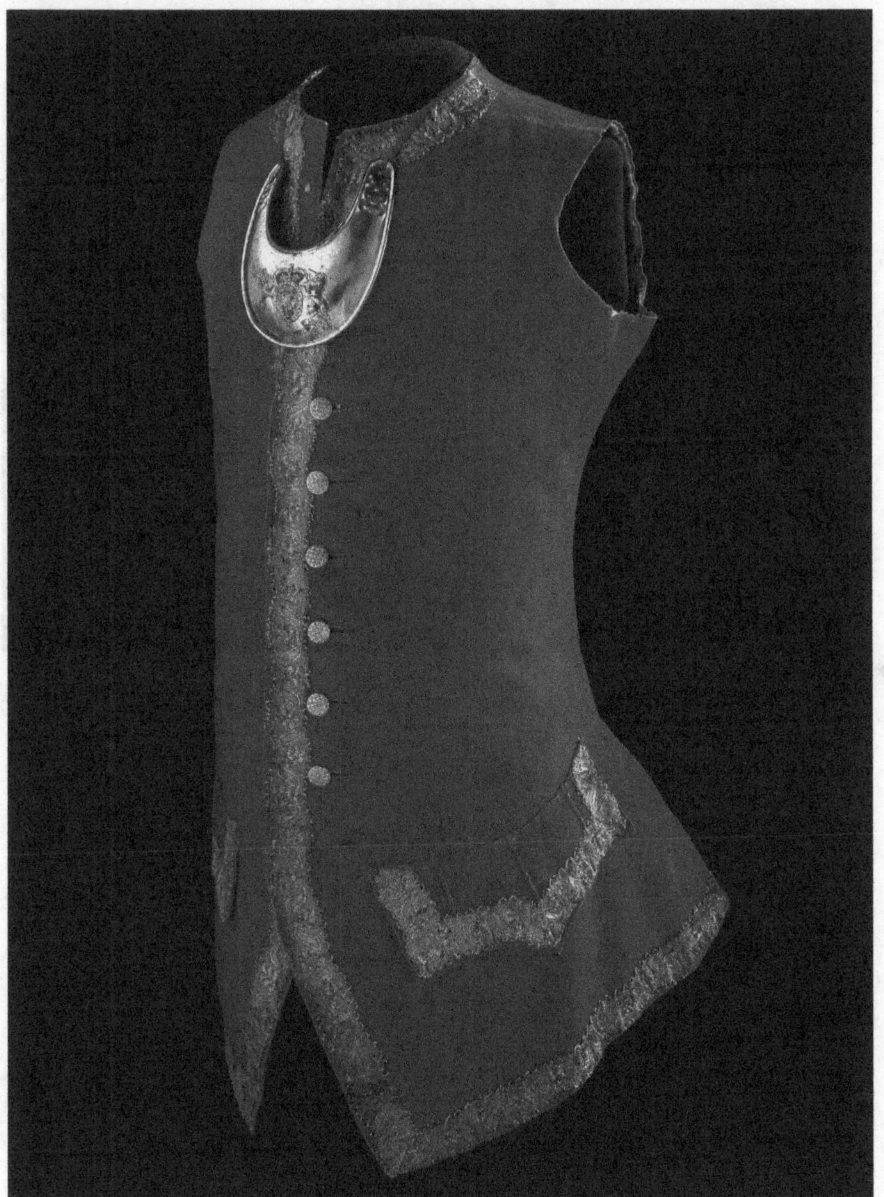

Uniform waistcoat and gorget, c. 1754–1755. *Adam Stephen (c. 1721–1791), a Scottish immigrant originally trained as a physician at the University of Edinburgh, led troops throughout the war in the First Virginia Regiment. He was present at Fort Necessity (1754) and Braddock's Defeat (1755); from 1756 through 1758 he acted as Washington's second-in-command, and succeeded him as the regiment's colonel. He went on to command Virginia forces in the Continental Army, where he rose to the rank of major general. Stephen's descendants preserved this uniform waistcoat and gilt gorget bearing the British royal arms as mementos of his French and Indian War service.* (Smithsonian Institution)

Washington Reviewing the Western Army at Fort Cumberland, Maryland**, attributed to Frederick Kemmelmeyer, after 1795.** *In 1794 President George Washington returned to Maryland's dilapidated Fort Cumberland, built after his defeat at Fort Necessity. On the cleared ground where Braddock's British regiments had mustered before the expedition against Fort Duquesne, Washington reviewed the American militia army preparing to suppress the Whiskey Rebellion in western Pennsylvania. It was the last act in a forty-year-long drama of imperial war and revolution in which Washington had played a central—and, given his youthful blunders of 1754, utterly unpredictable—role.* (The Metropolitan Museum of Art, Gift of Edgar William and Bernice Chrysler Garbisch, 1963 (63.201.2), Photograph © 1983 The Metropolitan Museum of Art)

the north, a quarter-mile from the north bastion, a low hill presented another advantageous location for an enemy battery. Captain Pontleroy, Montcalm's chief engineer, minced no words in describing the post's vulnerability. "Were I to be entrusted with the siege of it," he reported, "I should require only six mortars and two cannon."

Because Fort Carillon stood little chance of surviving a determined cannonade, Montcalm decided to oppose the invaders on the high ground to the north. On the evening of the sixth he laid out a line of entrenchments in a thousand-yard-long semicircle around the shoulder of the hill that commanded the only route to the fort from the land side. The next morning he and his fellow officers wielded axes to set an example for their men in felling trees and interweaving their sharpened branches to form a broad tangled barrier forty or fifty yards deep on the slopes below the trenches. The barrier of fallen trees, called an abatis, had a purpose identical to that of the rolls of concertina wire that enclose modern field fortifications: to arrest the progress of attackers and expose them to systematic destruction by the fire of small arms and field artillery. By sundown both the abatis and the entrenchment—now reinforced with a log breastwork topped by "wall pieces" (small-bore cannon mounted on swivels) and sandbags—stood ready.

Montcalm was grateful, if surprised, that he had been given time enough to complete this hasty fieldwork. Yet he knew that at most it could delay the British advance. Secure as it was against small arms fire, the log breastwork would become untenable as soon as the British brought even a few fieldpieces to bear on it; every cannonball that struck would dislodge a deadly hail of splinters that would soon drive the defenders back to the fort. Unless Abercromby proved so impetuous (or mad) as to order an infantry assault through the abatis, there was no realistic prospect that it would become the site of a decisive engagement.

Yet that, seemingly, was exactly what Abercromby did in the midday heat of Thursday, July 8. Two days before, near the army's landing place, Lord Howe had been killed while leading a detachment in pursuit of the French guards as they retreated through the woods. Abercromby, who reported to Pitt that he had "felt [Howe's death] most heavily," seems to have been at a loss for the rest of that Tuesday. While the French had worked feverishly to complete the trenches and abatis on Wednesday, Abercromby had recovered enough of his composure to march his men forward to within a mile and a half of the fort. A small party sent out to reconnoiter the French position brought word that the French were entrenching around a hill athwart the road to the fort, and speculated that the breastwork, which had not yet been completed, could be carried by storm. Abercromby, who did not go forward to see for himself, decided to make the attack the following day.

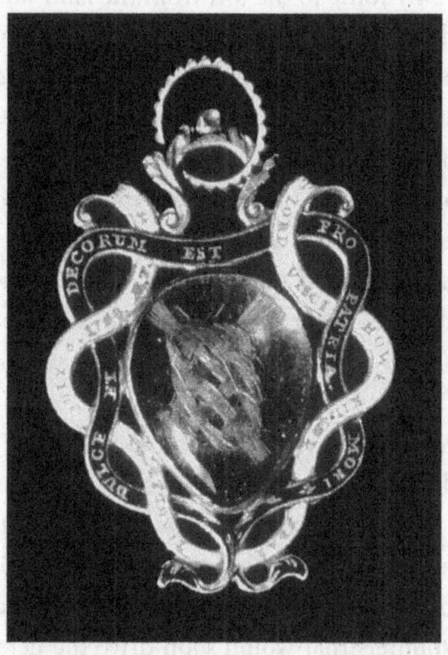

Mourning locket. *This mourning locket contains a lock of hair from George Augustus, Viscount Howe (c. 1725–1758), colonel of the British Fifty-fifth Regiment and Abercromby's deputy commander on the expedition against Fort Carillon. Howe's death in a confused skirmish shortly after the British landing at the foot of Lake George affected Abercromby deeply, and may have contributed to the failed attempt to storm Montcalm's defensive works on July 8, 1758.* (Collection of the Fort Ticonderoga Museum)

By noon on Thursday eight regular battalions—about seven thousand men—were drawn up opposite the breastwork in battle order and readied for a frontal assault. Six thousand provincials formed the reserve. The army's heavy siege artillery, which would have taken another day or more to move forward, remained parked near the landing place, four miles away. The assault, however, was not to be made without artillery support. Four field guns—three six-pounders and a howitzer—were loaded on rafts and towed down the Rivière de la Chûte, to be landed near the base of Mount Defiance. These were to be dragged up the hill, from which they could fire down on the rear of the French lines. The British infantry would attack when the battery opened fire.

Unfortunately for the men drawn up to make the attack, the planned cannonade never began. The towboat crews overshot the place where they should have landed, and drifted within range of the cannon on the southwest bastion of Fort Carillon. The fort's gunners, noticing what was afoot, fired on the British boats, sinking one of the rafts and so endangering the boats that the officers in charge ordered the remaining raft to be rowed back upstream to safety. The two remaining cannon were never landed or brought to bear on the French fieldworks.

In all likelihood it was the sound of French cannon shelling the rafts that caused the British troops to advance at about twelve-thirty. Abercromby, who stood on a rocky outcrop from which he could observe the battlefield, apparently did not give the order to charge. The attack, which began raggedly, gathered momentum as regiment after regiment, seeing its neighbor move ahead, advanced into the abatis. According to a lieutenant in the Highland (Forty-second) Regiment, once "the fire became general on both sides" it grew "exceedingly heavy," and continued "without any intermission; insomuch that the oldest soldiers present never saw so furious and so incessant a fire." The abatis, he reported, "was what gave them the fatal advantage over us." The entangled branches of its "monstrous large fir and oak trees . . . not only broke our ranks, and made it impossible for us to keep our order, but . . . put it entirely out of our power to advance briskly; which gave the enemy abundance of time to mow us down like a field of corn, with their wall pieces and small arms, before we fired a single shot."

Hopeless as they were without artillery support, the British attacks continued until seven o'clock that evening. At least 551 redcoats and provincials died and more than thirteen hundred were wounded trying to come to grips with the thirty-six hundred well-protected French and Canadian troops who methodically cut them to shreds. The Battle of Ticonderoga, as the Anglo-Americans called it, was the heaviest loss of life that His Majesty's forces sustained during the whole American war. It was, in fact, the bloodiest day the British army would see in North America until the Battle of New Orleans in 1815. The French, by contrast, suffered a total of 377 casualties.

Montcalm expected that the British would renew the attack the next morning, and was surprised when they did not. Suspecting that the enemy had feigned retreat in order to draw him out of his lines, he waited until Saturday before sending out a reconnaissance party to see what had become of his enemy. What they found—"wounded [men], provisions, abandoned equipment, shoes left in miry places, remains of barges and burned pontoons"—was evidence of the panic that had gripped Abercromby's defeated force late Thursday night. Following the battle, the men had withdrawn to their original staging area, a mile from the battlefield. Hours later, Abercromby had given the order to pull back to the landing place, three miles farther back. His intent was to reorganize his forces the following morning. The men, not knowing the reason for the withdrawal, believed that they were about to be attacked by the French and stampeded for the boats. By dawn the greatest army Britain had ever assembled in North America was rowing frantically for the other end of Lake George, fleeing an enemy that it still outnumbered by more than three to one—an enemy that at that moment was preoccupied with strengthening its fortifications against the British attack that would never come.

When Montcalm finally grasped what had happened, the only possible explanation that came to him was that God himself had intervened to preserve His Most Christian Majesty's dominions in North America. On July 12, he and his men sang a *Te Deum* for their deliverance. In late August he ordered a huge red cross to be raised on the hilltop above the abatis where Abercromby's troops had poured out their lives for nothing. On the cross Montcalm directed that a Latin couplet of his own composition be inscribed, along with its paraphrase:

Chretien! Ce ne fut point Montcalm et la prudence,
Ces arbres renversés, ce héros, leur exploits,
Qui des Anglais confus ont brisé l'espérance;
C'est le bras de ton Dieu, vainqueur sur cette croix.

Christian, behold! Not all the care that Montcalm took,
Nor this fearsome abatis, nor all our heroes' feats
Have stunned the English here, have shattered all their hopes;
Instead the arm of God prevailed, the victor of this cross.*

The Battle of Ticonderoga marked Montcalm's greatest victory—not only over the hapless Abercromby and his vastly superior army, but over Vaudreuil as well. In reports to the ministry he claimed the governor-general was responsible for the small numbers of troops on hand to defend against the British onslaught, and blamed him for the lack of Indian scouts and raiders. He similarly overstated the numbers of enemy casualties his men had inflicted, inflating Abercromby's numbers to twenty-five thousand and claiming that as many as five thousand of them had been killed in the battle. None of this was true; all of it supported Montcalm's plea to be given plenary control over the war effort in Canada. He sent his chief aide, Louis-Antoine de Bougainville, along with the reports, to make his case at Versailles. He must be free, he argued, to use his regulars to mount a concentrated, conventional defense of the capital and its surrounding settlements—a defense that would mimic, on a vastly larger scale, his hedgehog tactics of July 8.

Vaudreuil realized how vulnerable he had become, and quickly dispatched his own emissary with a set of proposals for the defense of Canada in the coming year. The governor-general advocated the renewal of guerrilla strategies and begged for resources to revive the Indian alliances that

---

*Or more literally:

Christian! It was not Montcalm and his prudence,
These felled trees, these heroes, their exploits,
That have confused the English and broken their hopes;
It was the arm of thy God, victor on this cross.

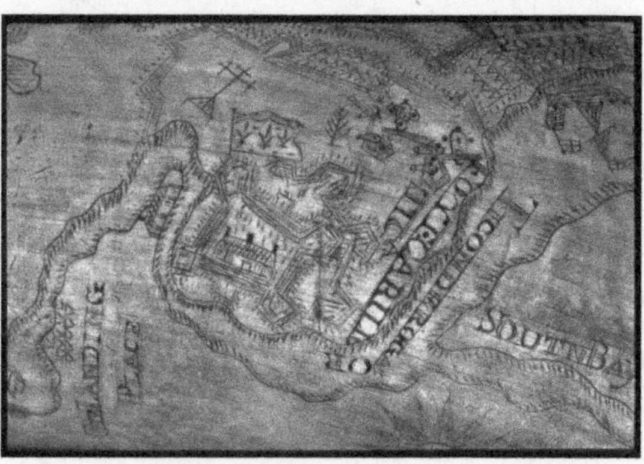

Detail of engraved powder horn, c. 1759. *When British forces under Major General Jeffery Amherst took Fort Carillon in 1759, a British or provincial soldier carefully inscribed this powder horn with a map of the territory between Lake George and Crown Point. This detail includes a unique depiction of the cross Montcalm's forces erected on the Height of Carillon.* (Courtesy of Jim and Carolyn Dresslar)

had flagged in the aftermath of Fort William Henry. His strategy remained the classic one of dispersed attacks against the Anglo-American frontiers. In the event of a British invasion of the Saint Lawrence, he proposed the evacuation of the civilian population from the lower valley to Trois Rivières. If Quebec became untenable, Canada's defenders could retreat to Montreal.

Bougainville returned in April 1759, carrying the decision of Louis XV in favor of Montcalm and a professionalized, Europeanized war. By then, however, the outcomes of the other campaigns of 1758 were known, and it was clear exactly how far the military balance in North America had shifted. Montcalm might have the power for which he had so ardently wished, but he would also face an enemy that would be as unstoppable in fact as Abercromby's army had seemed to be in appearance.

CHAPTER THIRTEEN

Louisbourg

It was only in early September that Montcalm learned that his triumph before the walls of Fort Carillon had been the exception to the rule of that summer's military events. On the sixth a courier brought him news of not one but two ominous defeats. Louisbourg had fallen to British and Anglo-American besiegers on July 26 after a six-week siege. A month to the day later, an Anglo-American force had besieged Fort Frontenac, the naval base that guarded the head of the Saint Lawrence on Lake Ontario and the depot from which all of France's interior forts were supplied. Its commandant had surrendered on the next day. Montcalm left Fort Carillon immediately to confer with Vaudreuil at Montreal. Little as he relished consulting a man whom he disdained as a provincial and feared as a rival, he had no choice: the position of New France suddenly seemed dire indeed.

As Montcalm's sloop skimmed northward on Lake Champlain, he could not have known that only an extraordinary stroke of luck on the day of the British landing had kept the attack on Louisbourg from becoming a failure as spectacular as Abercromby's attempt to storm his lines at Ticonderoga. Louisbourg's defenders had strongly fortified Gabarus Bay in the area where Jeffery Amherst hoped to land his forces, about four miles from the landward wall of the fortress. A twenty-foot-deep abatis lay before the trenches that lined the rockbound shore; no fewer than twenty-three hundred soldiers awaited the invaders, with thirty cannon well placed to blast their landing boats to splinters. To succeed, the British would have to fight their way ashore, form ranks under fire, and then penetrate the abatis: a formidable task in the best of circumstances. It was to all appearances an impossible one on the morning of June 8, when conditions were anything but favorable. Heavy swells kept the infantry-laden whaleboats wallowing offshore, well within cannon range, while the man charged with supervising the landings, Brigadier General James Wolfe, searched for a spot—any spot—where the boats could go ashore.

***Lieutenant General Jeffery Amherst,* by Joseph Blackburn, 1758.** *Joseph Blackburn painted Amherst in North America in 1758, the year that he, as "Major General in America," commanded British forces in the siege and capture of Louisbourg. Following that action, Amherst initiated another round of ethnic cleansing that caught up and deported thousands of French-speaking inhabitants from the region.* (Mead Art Museum, Amherst College, Amherst, Massachusetts, Gift of Mrs. Richard K. Webel, Acc. No. AC 1972.1)

None presented itself, and Wolfe was at the point of calling off the landing when he realized that three boatloads of soldiers had parted from his division without orders and were making for the shore near a "neck of rocks" that offered some degree of shelter from both the surf and French fire. Impulsively he signaled the division to follow them in. Once ashore he quickly formed a detachment and, armed only with a walking stick, led them in a bayonet charge against the nearest entrenchments. A short and brutal fight left Wolfe's men in control of the trench, with the French defenders fleeing down the line toward the city. It had been, in Wolfe's own words, "a rash and ill-advised" landing, and only "the greatest of good fortune" had prevented a catastrophe. Nevertheless, nightfall found most of the expedition's thirteen thousand redcoats safe ashore, hurriedly throwing up defenses around a siege camp near Fresh Water Brook, just a couple of miles from the walls of Louisbourg. The next day Amherst began methodically landing cannon and supplies in preparation for a *siège en forme.*

Provided that the men dug their trenches deep enough, and shored them well against collapse, sieges entailed comparatively little risk for the attacking force. Fewer than half of the 195 redcoats who died in the Louisbourg campaign lost their lives in five weeks of siege operations; the rest drowned or were cut down by cannon and musket fire during the landings of June 8. As the British entrenchments inched closer and closer to the objective, Amherst's gunners established batteries at successively shorter ranges in a textbook example of siege operations. By July 3 British cannon stood in batteries within six hundred yards of the King's Bastion, systematically pounding it to rubble. Mortars, too, joined in, lobbing fragmentation shells and incendiary shot over the walls into the heart of the town. Meanwhile the small French naval squadron, trapped in the harbor, came under increasingly effective fire from guns the invaders positioned opposite the town's harborside walls, on a strategic point of land and an island in the mouth of the harbor. Only a single frigate, Captain Jean Vauquelin's *Aréthuse,* escaped, creeping out through the fog on the night of July 14 and then outrunning its Royal Navy pursuers, all the way to France. One by one the rest of the French men-of-war in the harbor were sunk, blown up, or burned. Just two remained afloat on the foggy night of July 25, when Admiral Edward Boscawen ordered a daring boat raid that seized them both. Boscawen's men boarded the sixty-four-gun *Prudent* and set it ablaze before anyone on shore knew what was happening; it burned like a torch while the raiders towed the *Bienfaisant*, the squadron's flagship, across the harbor to safety.

Over the next twelve hours the British poured more than a thousand rounds of shot and shell into a virtually defenseless town. With Louisbourg's harborside indefensible and its landward defenses collapsing under fire from batteries that were now less than two hundred yards away, Governor Augustin de Drucour asked for a truce to discuss terms of surrender. The city's defense had been a gallant one. Much of the town had been burned, and scarcely a building within the walls remained undamaged. More than four hundred of Louisbourg's defenders lay dead, and nearly eighteen hundred more were either too badly wounded or too sick to stand. Fewer than a half-dozen cannon remained capable of firing. Drucour fully expected that Amherst would recognize such evident heroism by allowing the defenders to capitulate with the honors of war.

But the chevalier soon found, to his horror, that Amherst had no such intention. Louisbourg's four thousand civilians, Amherst informed him, would be allowed to retain their personal effects, but the fifty-six hundred surviving soldiers, sailors, and militiamen would be forced to surrender their colors and arms and would be made prisoners of war. To submit to such terms was to accept disgrace, but Drucour lacked any alternative, and Amherst believed that Montcalm's failure to restrain his Indian allies at Fort William Henry had deprived the French of all claim to honor. At eight o'clock on the morning of July 27, British detachments formally took control of the fortress. Men who had borne arms in the siege were sent to England until they could be exchanged for British prisoners whom the French held in Europe.

Amherst went on to exact an even higher price. He ordered the town's civilian inhabitants to be deported to France, then directed Wolfe to supervise the rounding up and deportation of the entire French population on the islands of Île Royale (Cape Breton Island) and Île Saint-Jean (Prince Edward Island), as well. These were largely Acadian refugees who had fled there to avoid capture in 1755. Now they were exiled to a country whose language they spoke, but which proved remarkably indifferent to their welfare once they arrived. In the end more than eight thousand men, women, and children were shipped out under Amherst's orders—a number exceeding that of the victims of Britain's original ethnic cleansing of Nova Scotia, three years before.

For the Mi'kmaq Indians of the region, the redcoats and rangers (mostly New Englanders eager to avenge the killings at Fort William Henry) adopted a policy of massacre: "We cut them to pieces wherever we found them," Wolfe reported to his uncle Walter, "in return for a thousand acts of cruelty and barbarity." The Mi'kmaqs fought back, however, drawing what support and aid they could from the single Acadian community that remained intact and unconquered, the refugees who had fled to the Saint John River Valley in what is now New Brunswick. Despite the relentless efforts of the British and Anglo-Americans who occupied the region to hunt them down, the Mi'kmaqs began to make peace only in 1760, when the British offered terms that recognized their traditional hunting and fishing rights; a few bands continued to resist until 1762.

CHAPTER FOURTEEN

Colonel Bradstreet's Coup

Oddly enough, it was a Nova Scotian of Acadian descent who engineered Britain's second victory of 1758, the taking of Fort Frontenac on August 27. Jean-Baptiste Bradstreet, born forty-four years earlier to an Acadian mother and a British army lieutenant, had literally grown up in his father's regiment, the Fortieth Foot, which he joined as an ensign in 1735. A chance meeting with William Shirley in 1744 helped persuade the governor of Louisbourg's vulnerability and led to Bradstreet's participation in the expedition of the following year. His organizational expertise and initiative so impressed the governor that Shirley sought him out a decade later when he needed someone to organize a transport service to carry supplies by bateau from Albany to Oswego. It was a testimony to Bradstreet's talents that Lord Loudoun left him in charge of transport notwithstanding his connection with Shirley, and even promoted him to the rank of lieutenant colonel. Loudoun's later decision to make Bradstreet his deputy quartermaster general testified to his willingness to reward the colonel's success, if not his virtue. Tireless as he was in improving the army's logistical position, Bradstreet (like many a quartermaster in history) was also committed to enhancing his own financial position, and ultimately made himself a rich man by exploiting his office for private advantage.

Welcome as it was, wealth did not quench Bradstreet's thirst for military glory, and he never ceased promoting a plan he had first conceived in

Northern Theater of Operations, 1754–1760: *New York, New England, New France, and the Lake Champlain–Richelieu River Corridor*

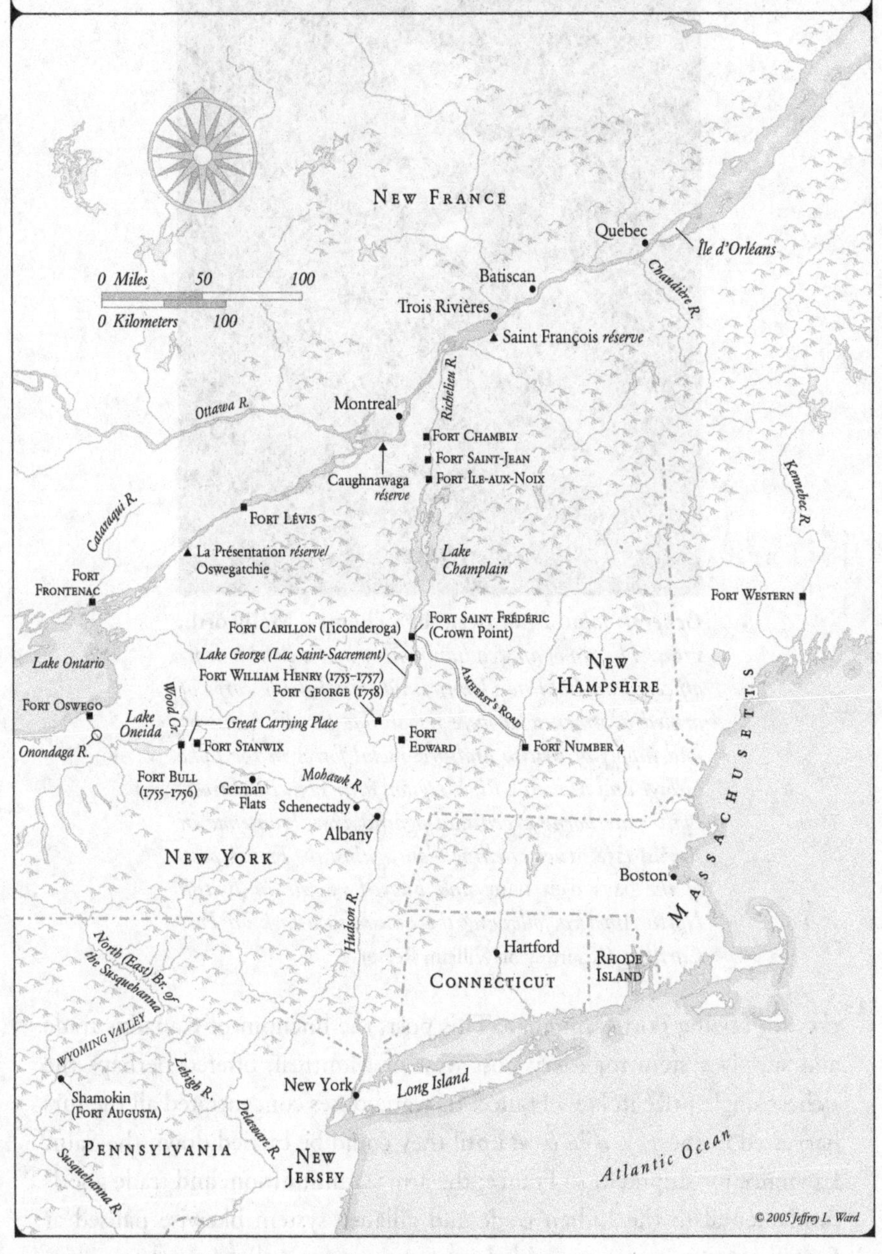

General John Bradstreet, **by Thomas McIlworth, 1764.** *The son of an Acadian mother and a British army officer, Jean-Baptiste (John) Bradstreet led the corps of armed boatmen who were responsible for the transport and supply of British and provincial forces in the Lake George and Mohawk River regions after 1755. Bradstreet's swift waterborne expedition against Fort Frontenac in August 1758 struck a telling blow against the French posts of the* pays d'en haut *and buoyed morale in British North America following the disastrous attack on Fort Carillon.* (Courtesy of William Reese)

1755 for seizing Fort Frontenac. This post, the linchpin of Canada's trade and supply system for every post west of Montreal, offered perhaps the richest single prize in New France. Its warehouses concentrated all the furs harvested in the *pays d'en haut* until they could be carried down the Saint Lawrence for shipment to France; the arms, ammunition, and trade goods fundamental to the Indian trade and alliance system likewise paused at Fort Frontenac to be assembled into cargoes for sailing vessels to carry west. To seize the post would destroy Canada's naval base on Lake Ontario and deprive every fort above it in the Great Lakes Basin of the supplies it needed to remain tenable. Most significantly for the inhabitants of Pennsylvania's and Virginia's battered frontiers, the cutoff in trade goods and ammunition to Fort Duquesne would weaken France's alliance with the Indians of the Ohio country.

Loudoun, impressed both by Bradstreet's announced willingness to pay for an expedition against Fort Frontenac out of his own pocket and by the strategic elegance of the plan, made it part of the projected New York campaign in 1758. Pitt, who lacked detailed knowledge of local circumstances in America, thought it superfluous, and omitted it from his list of approved operations when he sacked Loudoun. When James Abercromby succeeded to the post of commander in chief, he let the matter drop, but the catastrophe at Ticonderoga altered everything. Within hours of Abercromby's beaten army's arrival back at the head of Lake George, Bradstreet laid siege to the badly shaken commander in chief with requests for men and arms to attack the fort. Worn down no less by Bradstreet's badgering than by the humiliation of defeat, and desperate to salvage something from a ruined campaign, on July 13 Abercromby gave in. In two weeks' time Bradstreet had assembled a task force at Schenectady made up of 184 regulars, 70 Iroquois warriors, and more than 5,000 provincials from New England, New York, and New Jersey. In short order he equipped them with bateaux, supplies, and field artillery, and before the month was out they were rowing westward up the Mohawk.

Their destination, as Bradstreet elaborately explained to them (and to everyone else in earshot at Schenectady), was the Great Carrying Place, the portage between the headwaters of the Mohawk and those of Wood Creek, whose waters flowed west toward Lake Oneida and Lake Ontario. They would build a new fort here and reoccupy ground that the British had abandoned two years earlier, after the fall of Oswego. This was ostensibly a goodwill gesture, for the Six Nations had lacked access to trade goods in the heart of Iroquoia for two years; that was why the chiefs of the Onondaga and the Oneida provided warriors as an escort. It was also an elaborate ruse intended to deceive the French (whom the Iroquois could be counted on to inform) about the expedition's real intent, the seizure of Fort Frontenac. Only after the troops' arrival at the Carrying Place did Bradstreet and Brigadier General John Stanwix, the expedition's nominal commander, reveal their true mission. About half of the warriors left the expedition as soon as they learned its goal. Bradstreet kept the rest by promising them first claim on the booty that Fort Frontenac would be sure to yield.

Thus General Stanwix remained at the Carrying Place with two thousand men to build a fort while Bradstreet and the remaining three thousand lugged their boats and matériel, including eight cannon and more than five hundred rounds of ammunition, across the portage, then dropped down Wood Creek toward Lake Ontario. On August 21 they encamped by the ruins of Oswego; four days later, still undetected, they beached their boats on the Cataraqui promontory within a mile of Fort Frontenac. They threw up hasty defenses against the cannonballs the surprised French began to fire in their general direction, and waited for the next morning. At dawn they landed their field guns, mounted them on carriages, and hauled them to an improvised battery in a breastwork the French had abandoned, just 250 yards from the fort's western wall. That evening Bradstreet's men seized a hill even closer to the fort—150 yards from its northwest bastion—and erected a second battery. As day broke on August 27, all eight of Bradstreet's guns opened fire. In less than two hours a red flag of truce fluttered above the fort's battlements.

Bradstreet was astonished by the lack of effective opposition from the fort. He understood it better when he found that Frontenac's sixty-three-year-old commandant, Major Pierre-Jacques Payen de Noyan of the *troupes de la marine,* had only 110 men under his command, while the fort held many women and children, the dependents of garrison members who earlier had been sent to aid in the defense of Fort Carillon. Noyan had no shortage of supplies, guns, or ammunition, but could man fewer than a dozen of his fort's sixty cannon. Knowing that the post's aged walls could not withstand sustained bombardment, he had despaired of holding out for the week or more that it would take for reinforcements to arrive from Montreal, two hundred miles down the Saint Lawrence.*

---

*On August 25 Noyan dispatched a courier to Montreal, who reached Vaudreuil the following day. Militiamen, assembled from harvesters in the district, left for Fort Frontenac on the morning of the twenty-seventh. After what must have been an exhausting pull against the current, they arrived at the ruins of Cataraqui six days later to find an empty, shattered fort.

Bradstreet lost no time in accepting Noyan's surrender, for within the fort he had seen enough freshly baked bread to feed four thousand men, and he had no idea of how near a relief expedition might be. He therefore allowed the fort's troops and civilians to leave with their personal possessions in return for Noyan's promise that an equal number of Anglo-Americans held captive in Canada would be released; then he and his men set about plundering the richest post in the interior of North America. Bradstreet's troops were staggered by what they found in the fort's stores: hundreds of bales of cloth, laced and plain coats and shirts by the thousand, vast numbers of deerskins, beaver pelts, and other furs, great quantities of small arms and ammunition, and other "warlike Stores of all Sorts for the Endions." There was too much to carry off; in the end, however, Bradstreet's men succeeded in cramming booty worth £35,000 sterling in the holds of a brigantine and a schooner that lay at anchor in the harbor behind the fort. They destroyed what they could not carry, along with the remainder of the shipping (seven vessels, the whole of the Lake Ontario squadron), burned the buildings of the post, and used the great stocks of gunpowder in the fort's magazines to blast its walls to rubble.

With enormous satisfaction Bradstreet took stock of the destruction on the afternoon of August 28. Then he ordered his troops to board their boats and make for Oswego, knowing that he had broken the back of the French supply system in the Great Lakes Basin. And he had done it without the loss of a single man.

CHAPTER FIFTEEN

Makers of War, Makers of Peace

Britain's third victory of 1758, the taking of Fort Duquesne, came about in part because Bradstreet's seizure of Fort Frontenac weakened France's hold on the west. In even greater measure, however, Fort Duquesne became untenable, and the Franco-Indian war against the British frontiers unsustainable, because the commander of the Anglo-American expedition, Brigadier General John Forbes, attended more closely to Indian diplomacy than any other regular officer who served in North America. To do so he forged an unlikely alliance with Pennsylvania's governor, a group of Quaker philanthropists, a pacifist Moravian missionary, and several Indian leaders. The complex interactions within this amazingly diverse set of actors can best be understood by looking back to the fall of 1755, and the aftermath of Braddock's defeat.

The frontiers of the central colonies collapsed when the first parties of Delaware, Shawnee, and Mingo warriors left their Ohio villages in the company of *troupes de la marine* and French-allied Indians from the Great Lakes who had gathered at Fort Duquesne. Their descent on the frontiers of Pennsylvania and Virginia reflected a cold calculus of terror, for the goal was to bring anarchy to backwoods communities that even in time of peace were fragile, unstable, and intensely localist in orientation. The fifteen hundred frontier farmers whom the raiders killed and the additional thousand whom they took captive during the last months of 1755 served the strategic purpose of terrorizing hundreds of thousands of white settlers and creating a massive refugee crisis to which colonial governments were utterly unprepared to respond.

As the frontiers emptied of population, the raiders continued to probe eastward, deep into more densely settled areas, always in search of captives, scalps, and plunder. While a report from Fort Duquesne in August 1756 that the Ohio Indians had taken three thousand English prisoners almost certainly exaggerated the number, it is quite clear that by then every Indian town on the Allegheny, the Ohio, and their tributary waters housed substantial numbers of captives. (One reliable witness reported that Kittanning, a Delaware town on the Allegheny, had about a hundred white prisoners in residence in September 1756.) According to careful modern estimates, the frontier counties of Virginia, Maryland, and Pennsylvania lost between one-third to one-half of their populations between 1755 and 1758. During that time approximately 4 percent of the area's prewar inhabitants were either killed or taken captive.

Grown men seized in raids stood the best chance of being slain, for their captors regarded them as dangerous enough to kill as a precautionary measure, or as a warning to other prisoners of the fate that awaited them if they tried to resist or flee. Yet most adult male captives, troublesome

Prisoner halter, probably Kahnawake Mohawk, c. 1745–1746. *Strong, finely decorated cords and halters made of woven plant fiber or animal hair were used by the men from many eastern American Indian nations to secure captives when returning from raids and battles. Captive-taking and ritual adoption helped offset population losses to disease and wartime casualties in Indian nations. The practice also greatly contributed to Indian-hating among white settlers on the British colonial frontier.* (Photograph courtesy of the Pocumtuck Valley Memorial Association, Memorial Hall Museum, Deerfield, Massachusetts)

though they might be, were spared, for the simple reason that they had cash value. Delivered in good health to Detroit or Montreal, they were typically ransomed (i.e., bought) by the French, who desperately needed agricultural laborers and artisans, and so could justify what amounted to enslavement as the charitable Christian act of redeeming captives from *les sauvages*. The whites whom Indians tended to retain in the Ohio villages were the least troublesome sort: women and children. The majority seem to have adapted to their new lives, learning Indian languages and customs well enough to be incorporated into native families. Some underwent permanent transculturation. Mary Jemison, who was fifteen or sixteen when Shawnee raiders took her captive in Pennsylvania in 1758, married Sheninjee, a Delaware warrior, in 1759 and bore him two children, a daughter who died in infancy and a son. When Sheninjee died, she married another warrior—a Seneca named Hiokatoo (or Gardow)—with whom she had six more children. They remained man and wife for fifty years. Mary never forgot her origins and gave her children English names ("after my relatives, from whom I was parted") but became in every other sense a Seneca. She refused to leave her people when offered the chance to do so, as did many captives at the end of the war. Not all, of course, became "white Indians"; many, like James Smith, adopted native ways without losing their English identity. Smith, an eighteen-year-old laborer on Braddock's expedition when he was captured in 1755, became a trusted member of a Caughnawaga (Catholic Mohawk) family and a notable hunter. Even so, he never ceased looking for an opportunity to escape, and when his chance finally came in 1759, he fled without hesitation. Most captives, falling somewhere between these extremes, performed the functions and roles that were required of them and took life as it came. Those who returned often experienced difficulty readapting to white society, and commonly seemed "greatly dissatisfied" or "very restless & uneasy" to their puzzled, frustrated kin. Some had to be guarded to keep them from fleeing. More than a few succeeded in making their way back to the Indian families whom they had come to regard as their own.

At every level from the disordering of personal lives to the destruction of social order, war devastated the frontier. The taking of captives, without whom Indian societies and economies could not have continued to function, became for many whites the preeminent symbol of Indian barbarity. Because every abduction tore a hole in the life of a family and its community, those lucky enough not to have been taken were convinced that Indians were the worst kind of enemy; insofar as no one knew what happened to those who had been seized, colonists tended to assume the worst. That captive children, particularly, were known to be adopted and effectively made into Indians, exacerbated the grief of family members tortured by the knowledge that even if a loved one had not been killed, he or she might be lost forever. So much suffering and uncertainty created a volatile emotional climate that left frontier settlers not only bereft and grieving, but enraged and willing to contemplate drastic measures aimed at recovery or revenge. The conditions of backcountry warfare thus made Indian-hating a common cultural coin among whites, both on and off the frontier. Cabins could be rebuilt, lost farm animals replaced, the dead buried and mourned, but captive-taking inflicted wounds that refused to heal, and awakened implacable desires for vengeance.

Virginia's House of Burgesses had responded to the chaos of the frontier after the remnants of Braddock's force withdrew to Philadelphia by resurrecting its provincial regiment, placing George Washington once more at its head, and then appropriating far too little money to support it. In mid-September 1755 Washington established his headquarters at Winchester, the largest settlement in the Shenandoah Valley, and began trying to put the region as a whole in a posture of defense. He could do little, however, to staunch the flow of refugees, who by mid-October were crossing the Blue Ridge in such numbers that one of Washington's subordinates, arriving from Alexandria, reported "that it was with great difficulty he pass[e]d the Ridge for the Crowds of People who were flying [eastward], as if every moment was death." Those who did not flee were demoralized, confused, and so desperate that Washington found he had no effective authority over them. "No orders are obey'd," he reported, "but what a Party of Soldier's or my own drawn Sword Enforces." Some of the refugees, he wrote, replied to his attempts to organize them for self-defense with threats " 'to blow out my brains.' " For the next two years Washington and his men barely held their own against the raiders' destruction and the settlers' dread. It was only in 1758, after Pitt's promises of

***Colonel Edward Fell*, by John Hesselius, c. 1764.** *George Washington's drive to model his Virginia Regiment on the British army extended beyond discipline and training. Virginia officers embraced the dress and accoutrements of the regular army, including richly laced uniforms and silver-mounted swords of the sort shown here. Although traditionally identified as Colonel Edward Fell of Maryland, the officer may be Ensign Robert Fell, who held a Virginia commission in 1757.* (The Maryland Historical Society, Baltimore, Maryland)

reimbursement finally assuaged the burgesses' fear of bankrupting their province, that Virginia authorized a second regiment and increased soldiers' compensation to a level that allowed Washington, for the first time, to fill the ranks of his regiment with volunteers.

Ineffectual as it was, Virginia's response had at least a kind of rudimentary order to it. In Maryland the assembly and governor simply panicked, abandoning Fort Cumberland for Washington to defend and designating

Fort Frederick, forty-five miles west of Baltimore, as the limit of the province's frontier defenses. Pennsylvania was even worse off. Lacking a militia, it had no way to protect any of its settlements from attack. The slaughter of pacifist Moravian settlers at Gnadenhütten in November 1755 signified the impotence of political leadership in the province. In the factionalized legislature the leaders of the dominant Quaker party refused to violate the Peace Testimony by voting funds for defense; non-Quaker members, meanwhile, divided between an antiproprietary faction (previously allied with the Quaker party) that demanded the lands of the Penn family be taxed, and a proprietary party that defended the Penn family's sovereign immunity to taxation, even for purposes of defense. Only at the end of November did the antiproprietary leader Benjamin Franklin broker a deal by which the Penns agreed to make a £5,000 "gift" to match a legislative appropriation of £55,000 "for the King's use"—masterfully chosen euphemisms that enabled the proprietors to maintain that they had not surrendered their claims to immunity from taxation and allowed the Quaker legislators to believe that they had not voted funds for defense.

By then it was too late to save Gnadenhütten and dozens of other places (some lying within two days' travel of Philadelphia) that had been burned or abandoned in the face of Indian raids. The warriors who devastated the frontier came both from villages in the Ohio country and from a cluster of eastern Delaware settlements in a part of the Susquehanna Valley known as Wyoming (near modern Wilkes-Barre). The chief of the eastern Delawares, a complex, remarkable man in his mid-fifties, was called Teedyuscung among his people and Gideon by the Moravians who had baptized him in about 1750. In the aftermath of Braddock's defeat he had initially favored an alliance with the English, but when Pennsylvania's government refused to supply him and his people with arms and trade goods, he could not prevent the young men among his people from joining their Ohio kinsmen on the warpath. Rather than forfeit his position as chief, he joined in, leading raids against the frontier late in 1755.

Taking up the hatchet solidified Teedyuscung's leadership, but it placed his people in precarious circumstances, for once the traders who had lived among them fled to safety, the eastern Delawares had no access to arms and manufactured goods. For the time being the raiders supplied themselves with what they needed from the villages and farmsteads they looted, but this was at best a temporary expedient. When the harvest failed on the Susquehanna in 1755, crisis struck: by mid-winter Teedyuscung's people were starving. By the time the Pennsylvania assembly formally declared war in April 1756, Teedyuscung had already led his band and their captives up the Susquehanna to Tioga, on the New York border, where they hoped to obtain food from the Six Nations and believed they would be safe from retaliation by scalp-hunting Pennsylvanians. Once on the southern edge of Iroquoia, however, Teedyuscung found himself under increasing pressure to cease raiding, and began to veer in the opposite direction, toward peace.

He did so not only because chiefs of the Six Nations, acting at Sir William Johnson's behest, instructed him to desist, but because he began to see advantages in the role of peacemaker. Pennsylvania's government, reeling under the blows of frontier raiders, might be willing to offer concessions in return for peace, particularly if he could represent himself as an intermediary in negotiating a larger ceasefire with his kinsmen, the Ohio Delawares. He realized that he could exploit his position to gain guarantees of security for him and his people, and even more. If he played his hand well, he might induce Pennsylvania's government to create a permanent reservation in the Wyoming Valley as a means of compensating his people for the land they had lost in the Walking Purchase fraud of 1737. In the meantime the negotiations themselves would give him leverage to demand subsidies and aid for his people.

Fortuitously, despite Pennsylvania's declaration of war—or, more accurately, because of it—Teedyuscung soon found allies in Philadelphia's Quaker community. The Quaker mercantile elite that had dominated the Pennsylvania assembly for seventy years divided rancorously over appropriating monies for military purposes. When the provincial government declared war in April, the more conscientious of the Quaker leaders withdrew from politics rather than risk "disownment" for abandoning the Peace Testimony. The more pragmatic ones remained active and found themselves duly disowned by the Philadelphia Monthly Meeting. As a result, the long political era in which an assembly under the control of Quaker grandees had dueled with the Penn family over control of the province drew to an abrupt close. The leadership of the antiproprietary forces in the assembly passed to two non-Quakers, Benjamin Franklin and Joseph Galloway.

Unencumbered by pacifist scruples, the new antiproprietary leaders now continued to challenge the Penn family's prerogatives, even as they raised troops, built forts, and encouraged backwoods residents to wage freelance warfare against Indian villages. Most of all it was the assembly's decision to offer bounties for Indians, alive or dead—150 Spanish dollars for each Delaware man and 130 dollars for each woman or child taken prisoner, 130 dollars for the scalp of a Delaware male above ten years of age and 50 for the scalp of a woman—that drove the former assemblyman

Friendly Association gorget, by Joseph Richardson, c. 1757–1758. *Pennsylvania Quakers formed the Friendly Association for Regaining and Preserving Peace with the Indians by Pacific Measures in 1756 in order to finance and otherwise support diplomacy to end the conflict. These efforts included the production of diplomatic gifts such as this engraved gorget, made by the Philadelphia silversmith Joseph Richardson. It depicts a colonial figure passing a calumet to an Indian across a council fire, the emblematic act of peacemaking between peoples.* (Courtesy of The Historical Society of Pennsylvania Collection, Atwater Kent Museum of Philadelphia)

Israel Pemberton and his fellow Quakers to organize the Friendly Association for Regaining and Preserving Peace with the Indians by Pacific Measures, pledging their private fortunes to ending the war by diplomatic means. They had no official standing to do so; yet by working through the refugee Half King Scarouady, and the province's veteran Indian diplomat Conrad Weiser, they contacted Teedyuscung and urged him to meet with Pennsylvania's governor at Easton in July.

Teedyuscung and Pennsylvania's representatives met, on and off, until November in conferences that opened the way to treaty meetings in 1757 and 1758. Pemberton and the Friendly Association were active throughout, offering Teedyuscung advice and financial support to aid in the quest for peace. Most importantly, the Quakers could also provide a stenographer to keep minutes of the speeches made in council, thus creating an independent record of proceedings that would otherwise have been recorded entirely by the province secretary—a proprietary appointee whose dedication to accurate transcription did not exceed his devotion to the Penn family's interests. With this support, Teedyuscung felt secure enough to confront the governor over the Walking Purchase, demanding an investigation into the fraud as the price of peace, and insisting that his people deserved an adequate compensation for what they had lost.

Governor William Denny, an army officer who recently had been ap-

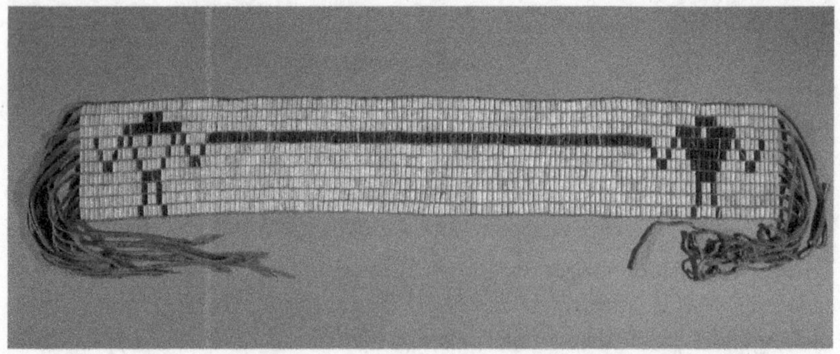

Wampum belt reproduction, 2003. *During his second trip to the Ohio country in November 1758, the Moravian missionary Christian Frederick Post presented "A large white belt, with the figure of a man, at each end, and streaks of black, representing the road from the Ohio to Philadelphia" as an invitation for the Ohio Indian nations to meet with British and provincial officials to establish peace.* (Courtesy of R. S. Stephenson)

pointed to his post by the Penn family, had no personal knowledge of the Walking Purchase and was alarmed at the thought that a twenty-year-old land fraud might in some way have led to the present war. He had no desire to embarrass his employers, much less expose them to an inquiry that might result in a royal order to compensate the Delawares for their losses; yet most of all he needed to restore peace and order to a province in chaos. Thus, with generous financial support from the Friendly Association, he presented the necessary diplomatic gifts to Teedyuscung and agreed to convene a peace conference in the coming year. Teedyuscung, in turn, agreed to bring in captives and to open a channel of communication with the Ohio Delawares.

To Denny's irritation, Teedyuscung's Quaker allies played an even more prominent role in the negotiations surrounding the 1757 Treaty of Easton. This conference, however, which was held near the center of lands taken in the Walking Purchase, offered a great deal for Pennsylvania and the Delawares alike. It almost certainly would not have reached the conclusion it did without the aid of Pemberton and his friends. At it Teedyuscung formally concluded peace between his people and the province, promised to continue pursuing negotiations with the Ohio Delawares, and offered to act as Pennsylvania's ally against the French. Denny, in return, pledged an official examination of the Walking Purchase, offered subsidies for the eastern Delawares (quietly underwritten by the Friendly Association), and agreed to the creation of a reservation for the Delawares in the Wyoming Valley.

The political costs of these promises were bearable for Denny because any formal investigation of the Walking Purchase would have to be conducted by the crown's northern Indian superintendent, Sir William Johnson. Given Johnson's ties to the Six Nations, it seemed improbable that the full extent of Iroquois collusion with the Penn family would ever be made public; this, Denny must have hoped, would mollify his masters. The costs were potentially much higher for Teedyuscung, for fundamentally the same reason. His independence as a diplomat acting on his own people's behalf was sure to arouse the notice of the Six Nations, and expose him to their wrath for proceeding without their permission. Thus, while he had earned potentially great benefits for his people at Easton, seeing them realized would depend on how much support he received from

Denny. Unless the governor recognized him as an independent Delaware spokesman, he would be helpless to resist the power of the League. Much therefore depended on Teedyuscung's ability to deliver the peace with the Ohio Delawares in the coming year. If he returned empty-handed to Easton in 1758, he would surely pay for his boldness—perhaps with his life.

CHAPTER SIXTEEN

General Forbes's Last Campaign

Teedyuscung's venture, bold as it was, would in all likelihood have failed before the Easton negotiations of 1758 could have begun had it not been for the intervention of General John Forbes. The resolute Scot was determined to use every means necessary to accomplish his mission of dislodging the French from Fort Duquesne and restoring peace to the central colonial frontier. A man of great perception and intelligence, Forbes knew that to succeed he would have to skirt the two great pitfalls that had doomed Braddock three years before. The first, overextension in the hope of a speedy victory, was solely military and consequently easy—if expensive and time-consuming—to avoid. He planned to build a new road to Fort Duquesne through the center of Pennsylvania, with substantial forts every forty or fifty miles and blockhouses between them at intervals of a day's march. These would stabilize the army's supply system, secure its communications with the east, and provide defensible positions to fall back to in case the enemy launched an attack like the one that had destroyed Braddock.

Braddock's second trap, the lack of Indian allies, was harder to avoid. Unlike the building of a well-secured wagon road, Indian diplomacy depended on factors Forbes could not control. The willingness of the Indians themselves to cooperate was of course the greatest of these variables, and—insofar as it depended on the natives' own calculations of self-interest and advantage—the least tractable. But there was an administrative hurdle to overcome as well: Sir William Johnson, the sole officer of the crown authorized to conduct Indian diplomacy in the northern colonies, had deep personal and economic ties to the Six Nations and was unlikely to do anything inimical to Iroqouis interests. The treaty Denny had negotiated with Teedyuscung in 1757 was, technically speaking, of dubious legitimacy because Johnson and the Iroquois (whom the crown, as well as the Penns, recognized as the Delawares' suzerain) had not taken part in the negotiations. It was only the manifest advantage of securing peace with the eastern Delawares and the potential benefit of using Teedyuscung to reach a similar accommodation with the Ohio Indians that had made London willing to look the other way. General Forbes, sizing up the situation after his arrival in Philadelphia, understood the advantages of developing ties with Denny, Teedyuscung, and Pemberton, and set out to cultivate them all, irrespective of Johnson and the Iroquois.

That May, Pemberton and the Friendly Association responded to Forbes's interest in their efforts by dispatching an agent, the Delaware-speaking Moravian preacher Christian Frederick Post, to the Wyoming Valley. Their intent was merely to press Teedyuscung to make further contacts with the Ohio Delawares. Post, however, discovered that the contacts he had hoped to promote were well advanced: an eminent western Delaware chief, Pisquetomen, had come to Wyoming at Teedyuscung's invitation, and was professing an interest in negotiating peace with the English. When Post returned to Philadelphia together with Teedyuscung and Pisquetomen, Forbes immediately pressed Denny to undertake negotiations, with or without Johnson. After some hesitation Denny agreed, sending Post and Pisquetomen back to the Ohio country with an offer of peace and an invitation to negotiate directly with Pennsylvania at a treaty conference to be held in Easton, in October.

Johnson did not take being circumvented lightly, but Forbes foiled his efforts to fight back by appealing to General Abercromby (who as commander in chief was Johnson's superior as well as Forbes's) for authorization to proceed without Johnson's participation. Abercromby, desperate for successes anywhere following the bloody fiasco of Fort Carillon, agreed on July 23, just days after authorizing Bradstreet's expedition against Fort

Frontenac. By that time Post and Pisquetomen were halfway to the Ohio country, and Forbes's principal commander, Colonel Henry Bouquet, was well along with the construction of the new road; yet Abercromby's permission to proceed was vital because it deprived Johnson of any grounds for protest.

Thus while Forbes's men hewed and sawed and graded and leveled their way slowly west through Penn's woods, Pisquetomen and Post advanced the most powerful arguments they could think of for peace around council fires in villages along the Allegheny, the Ohio, and their tributaries. The various Indian groups were divided in their councils, with some of the Delawares favoring peace strongly enough to suspend raids on the Anglo-American frontier, while a majority of the Shawnees continued to accompany parties sent out to harass Forbes's expeditionary force on the road. Even so, Fort Duquesne's commander could no longer conceal his waning stock of trade goods—a weakening of his position that increased the influence of chiefs who advocated abandoning the French and making peace. Six weeks of intense parleys convinced Pisquetomen that he could return to Easton and negotiate for peace with some confidence that the Ohio peoples would abandon the French alliance—provided that the English would open a trading post at the Forks on fair terms, while prohibiting permanent white settlement in the region. If the English were willing to promise those things to Pisquetomen, the Ohio Indians could look forward to the independence they had longed for decades to establish.

On September 8 Post and Pisquetomen left the Ohio country for Shamokin, where Teedyuscung's band had located near a new Pennsylvania provincial post, Fort Augusta. From there Pisquetomen headed for Easton, while Post made his way to General Forbes's headquarters at Fort Bedford. By this time Colonel Bouquet's advance force had cut the road nearly fifty miles farther west to Fort Ligonier, which lay at the foot of Laurel Ridge, the last great obstacle before Fort Duquesne. With so much progress made, Forbes should have been a happy man, but Post found him distressed, doubtful, and sadly debilitated. The three hundred or so Cherokee Indian allies whom the governor of South Carolina had procured for him had abandoned the expedition several weeks earlier, leaving him without scouts, and hence without intelligence of French movements.*

Forbes had lately encountered another kind of opposition, as well, in the form of a campaign by the colonels of the two Virginia provincial regiments to persuade him to redirect the road-building south to link up with the old Braddock Road. George Washington and William Byrd had both argued that, given the topography of the Pennsylvania route, the campaign might not reach Fort Duquesne before winter would bring a halt to all operations. Forbes suspected their real interest was to keep Pennsylvanian speculators and settlers from horning in on an Ohio Valley that they wanted to make Virginia's private preserve, and had upbraided them for valuing "their attachment to the province they belong to" above "the good of the service." But delays owing to bad weather and a major setback on September 14 made him wonder if perhaps Byrd and Washington had a point; perhaps the campaign would have to be postponed until the following year after all. In that case he had reason to doubt that he would see the completion of his mission, for his bowel disorder, weakness, and pain were now such that he could barely do more than walk from his bed to his desk and write letters.

Not long after Post arrived, Forbes learned that Bouquet had detached a 750-man party on September 9, to make a reconnaissance-in-force of Fort Duquesne. Astonishingly, this body, largely made up of Highlanders and other regulars under Major James Grant, reached the fort undetected, only to become dispersed in the woods on the night of September 13. Early the next morning Grant ordered a piper to play, summoning them to assemble. Even as they responded, however, Indian warriors streamed from the fort and attacked. In the uneven battle that followed, Grant was taken prisoner and three hundred of his men were killed, wounded, or captured. Because the troops who escaped could fall back to a secure haven at Fort

*Their departure had been Forbes's own fault. Unfamiliar with Indian warfare, he had attempted to reduce them to auxiliaries, offending warriors who understood themselves as independent actors and who responded to his attempts to give them orders by refusing to obey or leaving the expedition. As his Indian force had dwindled, Forbes's response had been to imprison their chief, Attakullakulla (Little Carpenter), a severe miscalculation. By the time Forbes realized his mistake and freed Attakullakulla, the Cherokees had been completely alienated, and withdrew en masse from the campaign.

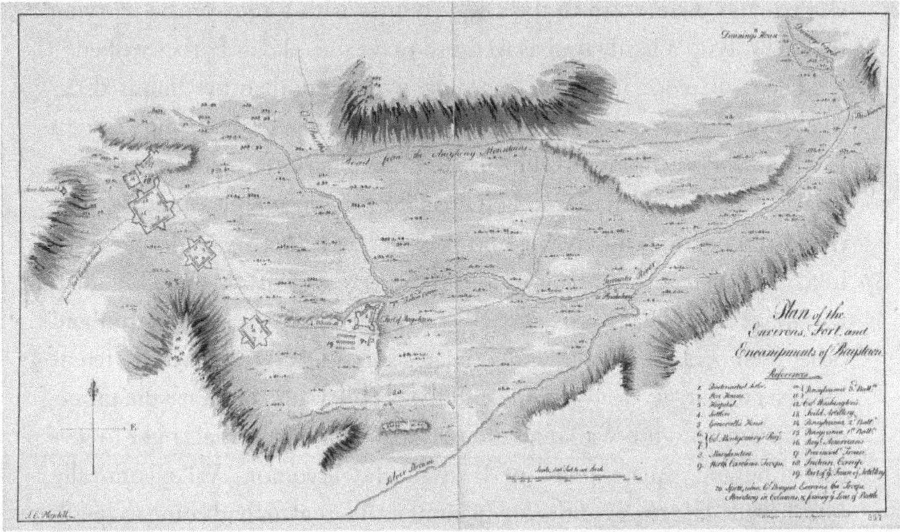

A Plan of the Environs, Fort, and Encampments of Raystown, 1758. *Following his journey to the Ohio with the Delaware chief Pisquetomen, Christian Frederick Post conferred with the British commander John Forbes at the commander's advance headquarters at Raystown. This plan by the British military draftsman John Cleve Pleydell shows Fort Bedford and encampments of British, American, and Cherokee forces near Juniata Creek, a tributary of the Susquehanna.* (The Royal Collection © 2005, Her Majesty Queen Elizabeth II)

Ligonier, Grant's defeat amounted only to a humiliating setback, not a fiasco on the scale of Braddock's. Forbes, however, took little comfort in this demonstration of the fundamental soundness of his approach. The campaigning season was growing late, and he feared the worst.

Post's arrival with news that a diplomatic breakthrough might yet bring the campaign to a successful end revived Forbes's flagging hopes. He quickly wrote to the Pennsylvania delegation at Easton, instructing them to lose no time in making peace. Pisquetomen's demands, he thought, were reasonable, and "giving up sometimes a little in the beginning will procure you a great deal in the end." He directed that Pemberton and the Friendly Association, who had "the publick good and the preservation of these provinces" at heart, should be allowed to participate as well—a move by which he intended to benefit Teedyuscung, and ensure that the integrity of the proceedings would be as high as possible. Then he asked Post to carry these instructions to Easton, remain there until peace had been concluded, and then return to the Ohio country with Pisquetomen, carrying the news. Post, a hardy soul as well as a brave one, did as Forbes wished.

The conference at Easton was large, with more than five hundred natives from thirteen nations in attendance, including Teedyuscung's eastern Delawares, Pisquetomen's Ohioans, all of the Six Nations, and a variety of smaller Iroquois clients. Among the Anglo-American representatives were the governors of Pennsylvania and New Jersey (sponsors of the proceedings), as well as other officials from their governments, George Croghan (acting as Sir William Johnson's chief deputy), and Israel Pemberton and other members from the Friendly Association. All had come with different interests to pursue. Teedyuscung and his people wanted to have the promised inquiry into the Walking Purchase begun, and have their right to several thousand square miles of land in the Wyoming Valley officially established. The chiefs of the Six Nations and Croghan had come to quash the inquiry, to reassert control over Teedyuscung, and if possible to renew Iroquois claims to sovereignty over the Ohio country. Pemberton and his associates wanted to protect Teedyuscung and to see to it that the Penns allocated sufficient lands to compensate his people for their Walking Purchase losses. Governor Denny had come to preserve the lands and interests of the Penn family, as well as to negotiate a peace settlement with Pisquetomen and the Ohio Indians. Prior to Post's arrival on October 20, the maneuvering among these groups and their interests had been intense but inconclusive. Forbes's letters clarified matters by informing Governor Denny, in no uncertain terms, the his highest priority must be to make peace with the Ohio Indians.

So illuminating indeed were Forbes's instructions that it took less than four days from the time Post arrived for Denny to conclude peace with the Ohio Indians. The agreement was based on Pisquetomen's pledge that English captives would be returned and secured by the governor's solemn promise, on behalf of the Penns and the province, that they would henceforth deal directly with the Delawares by "kindl[ing] up again" William Penn's "Old Council Fire" at Philadelphia. Pennsylvania traders would open a trading post at the Forks, Denny promised; he also agreed, on behalf of the crown, that white farmers would be forbidden to settle on lands west of the Alleghenies after the war.

This great result, for which Forbes had so fervently prayed, also had the effect of undercutting Teedyuscung's bargaining position. Forbes seems not to have intended that it should have been so, but once Pisquetomen spoke on behalf of his people, Teedyuscung (who had already made peace) forfeited all leverage as an intermediary. This gave the chiefs of the Six Nations all the opening they needed to reassert control over the upstart Teedyuscung by claiming jurisdiction over his band on the Susquehanna, a claim that Croghan supported, Pisquetomen and Pemberton did not oppose, and Denny promptly recognized.* The leading Iroquois councillor then instructed Teedyuscung to return to the Wyoming Valley, without offering any guarantee that the League would ratify the creation of a permanent reservation there. Isolated and impotent, Teedyuscung went home knowing that he had lost most of what he had hoped to gain, and that what remained was no longer under his control. In the following year the Privy Council would respond to the allegations of fraud in the Walking Purchase by referring the case to Sir William Johnson for review, and would assign the decision on establishing a Wyoming Valley reservation for the Delawares to the Grand Council of the Iroquois League.

There was nothing that the Iroquois could do, at least for the time being, to assert control over the Ohio Indians. Governor Denny had recognized Pisquetomen as their spokesman and promised to deal with the Delawares directly in the future. Nonetheless, the Penn family's personal representatives at the conference cannily agreed to rescind an irregular cession of Iroquois rights to all lands within Pennsylvania's limits that a Mohawk diplomat had made to Conrad Weiser at the Albany Congress of 1754. This resumption of title by the Iroquois, together with a deed of release that established a boundary between the lands of the League and those of the Penns within the province, effectively returned the lands of

*Pisquetomen kept silent because he had no interest in seeing Teedyuscung recognized (as Teedyuscung himself wished to be) as a spokesman for the Delawares generally. Pemberton, who genuinely sympathized with Teedyuscung, had no standing to make an official objection because he was an observer, not a delegate, to the conference. Pemberton, moreover, had no interest in impeding the progress of the conference toward reestablishing peace on the frontier by insisting on Teedyuscung's claims at this particular, critical moment.

the upper Ohio to the League's control. Given Denny's agreement to deal directly with the western Delawares and the fact that only a relatively small part of the upper Ohio Valley lay within Pennsylvania's limits, the native peoples of the region could believe that this act did not make them once more into wards of the League. Yet the Penn family's retrocession of title to the upper Ohio gave the League a foundation on which it could hope to rebuild its claims to sovereignty over the whole valley and its inhabitants.

The Treaty of Easton, concluded on October 25 and 26 with the customary ceremonies of feasting and gift-giving, was the most important diplomatic agreement in North America since the Grand Settlement of 1701. Forbes could now proceed with confidence—provided that word of peace could be relayed to the peoples of the Ohio and his army could cross the last miles to Fort Duquesne before winter weather brought the campaigning season to a close. Post and Pisquetomen hastened to his headquarters to deliver the news. They found him at Fort Ligonier on November 7. There the emissaries paused only long enough for the general to write letters to the Ohio chiefs, embracing them as friends and inviting them to stand aside while his army dealt with the French. Then Pisquetomen and Post made the last, most perilous leg of their journey, arriving just as warriors were returning from a November 12 raid on Forbes's army that had inflicted numerous casualties and destroyed more than two hundred draft animals, but had failed to dislodge the Anglo-Americans from Fort Ligonier. To Post it was clear that "the people who came from the slaughter . . . were possessed with a murdering spirit," to such a degree that he feared they would act on the entreaties of the French officers at Fort Duquesne "to knock every one of us messengers on the head."

In the end, however, it was clear to the Ohio chiefs that the British had offered peace on terms that seemed to guarantee their political autonomy, an acceptable supply of trade goods, and a prohibition on settlement in the region by white farmers. The French, by contrast, were too weak to defend Fort Duquesne themselves and could no longer provide trade goods sufficient to sustain their alliances. They had no hope of surviving a confrontation with the great British force that was now bearing inexorably down on the Forks. Lacking any strategic or political reason to cling to a French alliance, the native peoples of the upper Ohio Valley stood aside.

Fort Duquesne cannon breech. *This iron breech section from an eighteenth-century cannon was found at Pittsburgh near the site of Fort Duquesne during construction activity in the nineteenth century. It was probably incapacitated and abandoned by French forces during the evacuation of Fort Duquesne in November 1758.* (Courtesy of the Historical Society of Western Pennsylvania)

The commandant of Fort Duquesne, Captain François-Marie Le Marchand de Lignery, had lost essentially all of his Indian allies from the Great Lakes and the west in September. Following the defeat of Major Grant's force, the Indians had taken their captives, plunder, and trophies and returned home to hunt for their families' winter provisions. Without support from the resident Indian groups, Lignery had only a weak garrison—three hundred militiamen and *troupes de la marine,* the majority of whom were sick or otherwise unfit for combat—to stand off Forbes's army of five thousand well-equipped, well-supplied men. Faced with an impossible situation, Lignery ordered the fort's cannon loaded on bateaux to be rowed downstream to the Illinois settlements. On November 23, he and his remaining soldiers set Fort Duquesne's buildings ablaze and exploded a gunpowder mine to level the walls. Then, waiting just long enough for Lignery to be sure that "the fort was entirely reduced to ashes," they paddled up the Allegheny to Fort Machault. There Lignery kept his hundred healthiest men for the winter, to await reinforcements and retake the Forks in the spring. The English, he knew, would be able to leave only a small winter garrison behind. With even modest numbers of Canadian militia, *troupes de la marine,* and Indian allies, Lignery stood an excellent chance of regaining what he had lost.

Forbes's army was ten miles away when Lignery detonated the charge that flattened Fort Duquesne. On the evening of November 24, Anglo-American scouts reported that they had seen "a very thick smoak from the Fort extending in the bottom along the Ohio." The next day Forbes and his men took control of the Forks. After four years of suffering and destruction, the war on the Pennsylvania and Virginia frontiers was over—at least for the time being.

CHAPTER SEVENTEEN

Reckonings

Many changes followed upon the revival of English fortunes in 1758. James Abercromby, the least competent officer ever to serve as British commander in chief in America, was recalled to Britain and promoted to the rank of lieutenant general. Jeffery Amherst, having proven himself both competent and cautious, was named as the new commander in chief of His Majesty's forces in North America. James Wolfe, the rash but lucky hero of Louisbourg, so disliked the prospect of serving under Amherst that he took leave to go back to London, where he used his reputation as a hero and every political string he could pull to gain himself an independent command in the coming year's campaigns. John Bradstreet, arguably the sole military genius the war in America had produced, published an anonymous pamphlet extolling his role in the destruction of Fort Frontenac and excoriating Abercromby for failing to follow up on the victory by launching an expedition (with Bradstreet, of course, in command) to seize the remaining French forts on the Great Lakes. Promoted to colonel in reward for his success at Fort Frontenac, Bradstreet found he could not escape the post of deputy quartermaster general for the more glorious commands he coveted. Thus he remained at Albany, longing for the recognition and reward he feared would never be his, his health decaying under the combined stress of drink, thwarted ambition, and the unremitting demands of complex and burdensome duties.

Teedyuscung, who returned to the Wyoming Valley after the Treaty of

Easton, never received the reservation that was supposed to compensate his people for the fraud of the Walking Purchase, because Sir William Johnson's inquiry into that transaction (unsurprisingly) exonerated both the Penn family and the Iroquois of wrongdoing. He had always been a heavy drinker; now, despondent, he spiraled ever more steeply into alcoholism. In the spring of 1763 he would die at the hands of an arsonist who torched the house in which he slept. Not long thereafter large numbers of white settlers began to move into the valley, displacing the Indian population.

Israel Pemberton opened a store at Britain's new post at the Forks of the Ohio, Fort Pitt, as soon as possible in the spring of 1759, in order to supply the region's Indians with trade goods at fair prices. This was less a venture aimed at realizing profits than an aspect of his larger philanthropic concerns. He would watch with growing apprehension as native leaders, including Pisquetomen, grew more and more alienated by the surge of white settlers into the Ohio country, unrestrained by a British crown that seemed heedless of the promises that had been made in its name at Easton. Pemberton's steadfast commitment to the welfare of native peoples earned him the enmity of thousands of Indian-hating frontiersmen of the sort who almost certainly murdered Teedyuscung. By 1763 Pemberton was the most reviled public figure in the province.

George Washington, who led the First Virginia Regiment as the advance element of Forbes's army from Fort Ligonier to Fort Duquesne, resigned his commission at Christmas 1758 and returned to Mount Vernon, looking forward to life with Martha Custis, the rich and handsome young widow who had recently accepted his proposal of marriage. He had, he believed, fulfilled his duty to the colony. In gratitude, the electors of Frederick County, perhaps including some of those who had threatened to blow his brains out in 1755, elected him to the House of Burgesses. Washington now had two goals: to establish himself as a gentleman tobacco planter and to regain his health. The former he believed he could accomplish, as he had accomplished so much already, by diligence and self-discipline. The latter worried him more: the dysentery that had plagued him at least since Braddock's expedition had grown worse late in the campaign, weakening him until he feared he might never recover. Yet the very fact that his life had repeatedly been spared—most recently in the last days of Forbes's expedition, when part of the First Virginia Regiment had mistaken members of the Second Virginia Regiment for the enemy at dusk and the two had opened fire on each other, with Washington between them, shouting the order to cease fire—may have given him hope that the Providence he believed had preserved him might yet have some purpose for him to fulfill.

John Forbes, on the other hand, knew at the end of the campaign that his own health was broken beyond recovery. He had been so weak and in such physical distress during the last phases of the march that he could neither walk nor ride; he had been able to move forward only on a litter slung between two horses, his pain dulled by drugs. Once the army had reached its objective, he remained only long enough to give the desolated site of Fort Duquesne the new name of Pittsburgh, to order the construction of a small fort to shelter a two-hundred-man winter garrison there, and to invite the local Indian leaders to a conference to cement their new alliance with Britain. On November 26, "being seized with an inflammation in my stomach, Midriff and Liver, the sharpest and most severe of all distempers," he turned the command over to Bouquet, who evacuated him to Philadelphia. That Forbes survived the six weeks' journey across Pennsylvania with winter coming on testified to the toughness of spirit that had brought him through the campaign. That he survived six weeks more after his arrival in Philadelphia attested, at least in part, to his determination to inform the new commander in chief about what was at stake in Pennsylvania and the west.

Relations with native peoples were critical, he wrote: Amherst must not "think trifflingly of the Indians or their friendship," for Britain's hold in the Ohio depended upon having Indian relations "settled on some solid footing." Indian affairs had almost always been misunderstood, "or if understood, perverted to purposes serving particular ends." Among those who understood Indians but sought to exploit them in a self-interested way, two offenders stood out: "Sir William Johnstone [Johnson] and his Myrmidons" on one hand, and "the Virginians & Pensilvanians" on the other, "as both are aiming at engrossing the commerce and Barter with the Indians, and of settling and appropriating the immense tract of fine country" around Pittsburgh. Amherst, Forbes stressed, must take a strong hand in dealing with all these potential sources of disorder. If Amherst neglected to protect the Indians' interests, and particularly if uncontrolled white settlement occurred west of the Alleghenies, chaos could easily engulf the region, and the interior of North America would be lost to the crown.

There is nothing to indicate that the commander in chief paid any attention to the concerns that the dying Forbes voiced with such clarity and fervor. In the early months of 1759 Jeffery Amherst was coming to terms with his new responsibilities, concentrating on plans to sustain the momentum Britain had achieved in the recent campaigns and carry on to conquer Canada. To a greater degree than he ever understood, a shift in Indian alliances that grew out of Forbes's campaign of 1758 would make that goal attainable. But Amherst knew little of Indians, and cared less. One day he would pay a heavy price for those attitudes, but the day of reckoning would not come until 1763. When it did, no one in America would be more astonished than he.

PART FOUR

CONQUESTS AND CONSEQUENCES

CHAPTER EIGHTEEN

A Shift in the Balance

Of all the groups that reckoned their positions anew in the months after the fall of Fort Duquesne and the cessation of hostilities on the Pennsylvania-Virginia frontier, none made a closer calculation of interests and priorities than the chiefs of the Iroquois Confederacy. This seems to have occurred in a meeting of the League council at Onondaga sometime in the waning days of 1758. No written record survives to confirm it, because none would have been made at a gathering attended only by the chiefs of the council. Two events, however, in the early days of 1759 make it clear that the leaders of the Six Nations realized that it was no longer in their interest to maintain the neutrality they had observed more or less consistently since the fall of 1755.

The first was in January, when a delegation of Iroquois chiefs arrived at Pittsburgh and took aside Lieutenant Colonel Hugh Mercer, commandant of the winter garrison holding the Forks, to warn him not to trust the Shawnees and Delawares. Chiefs of both peoples (they said) were planning to unite against the Six Nations, and had not fully severed relations with the French. If, however, "a very powerfull aid is afforded them [the Iroquois] by the English," Mercer reported, they could prevent the Shawnee-Delaware conspiracy from succeeding, hence preserving the Ohio country in English—and, presumably, Iroquois—control. The second event took place in February, when Iroquois emissaries arrived at Sir William Johnson's headquarters (Fort Johnson, on the Mohawk River) and made similar overtures, along with an offer they knew Johnson could not refuse: military aid. On February 16 Johnson wrote to inform Amherst that if "a large Augmentation" could be made to the gifts he was authorized to distribute, he could procure Iroquois support for an expedition against the last great French stronghold on Lake Ontario, Fort Niagara.

These nearly simultaneous approaches to Mercer and Johnson signaled an abrupt reversal in policy, driven by the desire to reestablish the League's influence in the Ohio country after a long, dangerous hiatus. Control (or at least the plausible illusion of control) over the Ohio Valley had long been the fulcrum on which Iroquois spokesmen had based their efforts to play the French and British empires off against each other. The inability of the Iroquois to influence developments on the Ohio in the early 1750s, when the Delawares, Shawnees, and Mingos had begun trying to deal independently with the British and the French, had brought about the confrontation that triggered the war. The expulsion of the French from the Forks now offered the Iroquois a chance to reassert their claims and subordinate the independence-minded Ohio Indians to their control. That would have made sense to Sir William Johnson, whose understanding of Iroquois culture and diplomacy was second to none. What even Johnson could not have known, however, was that the Six Nations had reason to fear that if they did not reclaim their influence soon, and with substantial support from the British, they might never again be able to do so.

The Iroquois chiefs' unease arose from a prophetic spiritual movement that had begun taking shape among the displaced Delawares of the Susquehanna Valley a decade or so before, a movement that the war's stresses and disorders had helped to spread into the Ohio country, where other groups beyond the Delawares began to respond to it. Although by 1758 the movement had not yet achieved the coherence it would gain in the early 1760s, when a Delaware prophet known as Neolin began to preach, its rudiments were evident in the spreading belief that the Master of Life had created Indian, black, and white people as separate races, each with its own way to paradise. Indians who had grown too close to whites had been corrupted by white ways, which would prevent them from reaching heaven. The worst of these corruptions was alcohol, but at some level everything associated with whites—cattle, gunpowder weapons, trade goods of all sorts—was inimical to Indian well-being, Indian spiritual power.

These "nativist" beliefs provided a foundation for a pan-Indian revival movement based on the novel notions that native peoples had more in common with one another than with whites, and that they could regain the full measure of power only by recovering the old, uncontaminated ways of life that had prevailed before the coming of the whites. The Six Nations and other groups closely bound to the Euro-Americans had become corrupted to a degree that justified withdrawing from contact with them until they, too, chose to follow this path back to undiminished spiritual power. The emerging religious climate on the Ohio, in other words, not only portended resistance to the whites, but a wholesale denial of the legitimacy of Iroquois influence as well. With a religious justification and a principle for cooperation among themselves, the Delawares, Shawnees, Mingos, and others who had initially sought independence by moving west might well achieve it. Unless the League moved quickly to assert supremacy over the Ohio peoples, and unless it did so with substantial material support from the English, a great deal more than just their ancient claim to the Ohio might be lost. In this context moving from neutrality to alliance with the Anglo-Americans was not only a reasonable choice, but a necessary one, for only by harnessing British material wealth and military power to Iroquois ends would the Six Nations secure their ascendancy.

Neither the chiefs of the Six Nations nor Amherst and the other British commanders in America could have appreciated fully what adding the weight of the Iroquois into the balance of the war at this particular moment would do to influence its outcome. Thanks to Pitt's reimbursement policy and his demotion of the commander in chief from virtual viceroy to superintending military commander, the northern British colonies had reached an unprecedented level of mobilization in aid of the war effort. The assemblies of provinces that raised more than twenty thousand troops for the campaigns of 1758 did so in the expectation that overwhelming force would bring a quick end to the war. They had done their utmost for king and country—so much so that they quailed when Pitt asked them to duplicate those efforts in 1759. Nevertheless they pledged to do their best and in the end came close to meeting his request. Pennsylvania and

Virginia, having been delivered from the evil of guerrilla war, initially made cuts in recruiting for 1759, but the New England provinces, New York, and New Jersey together enlisted seventeen thousand men to support approximately twenty thousand of His Majesty's regular troops in what was expected to be a final, great push into the Canadian heartland.

As spring came on and the campaigns moved toward their start, the British and their colonists were poised to exert overwhelming pressure on French Canada. It is important to realize, however, that without Iroquois support even this extraordinary level of force might not have been enough to conquer New France. Two of the three possible avenues by which Canada could be invaded passed through Iroquois territory: the Lake George–Lake Champlain–Richelieu River corridor and the Mohawk–Oswego–Lake Ontario–Saint Lawrence route. Without Iroquois cooperation, no expeditionary force could pass through to get at the French. Moreover, the power of the Six Nations had always depended upon their ability to control the flow of information between the French and British authorities; in at least one previous instance they had foiled a projected Anglo-American invasion by covertly passing intelligence to the French. The new alliance with the British not only opened Iroquoia to Anglo-American military movements, but also denied the French advance warning.

Had these factors not entered into play, even the vast numerical superiority of the Anglo-Americans would scarcely have been adequate to conquer Canada, for the Saint Lawrence (the only remaining invasion route) was reliably open to navigation only seven months a year. Britain's hold on Louisbourg, of course, gave it the best chance yet to mount a successful attack by the Saint Lawrence route, because a properly organized expeditionary force could ascend the river as soon as the ice had broken up. Even so, success would depend on the ability of the invaders to make a decisive stroke against the well-fortified city of Quebec, and then to hold it over the long period between the freezing of the river and the next spring's thaw. Without overland communications with New York—a factor completely under Iroquois control—there was simply no reliable way to secure the conquest of Canada even after Quebec came under British occupation.

And there was another factor as well, which Sir William Johnson and other experienced Indian diplomats understood as the most important element of all. If the traditional Indian allies of New France—the Algonquian and Iroquoian converts of the Saint Lawrence *réserves* and the Ottawas, Ojibwas, Chippewas, and other peoples who lived around the Great Lakes—rallied to defend their French father, the British might well find themselves at the end of a long and tenuous supply line, embroiled in an unwinnable guerrilla conflict. The Iroquois alliance was crucial to avoiding that nightmare scenario. The ability of Six Nations diplomats to persuade the allies of New France to withdraw from the conflict gave them an importance precisely parallel to that of Teedyuscung in the Ohio campaign of 1758. Forbes's road had reached its victorious destination only because Teedyuscung had been able to contact Pisquetomen and other peace-minded Delawares, who in turn worked to ensure that when the Anglo-Americans finally reached the Forks, they would be greeted by leaders willing to build a working relationship with a new, British father. Just so, the extraordinarily experienced diplomats of the Six Nations, armed with British gifts and operating in advance of the invading Anglo-Americans, could persuade their fellow natives not to spill their blood in support of a New France that could offer them none of the advantages that a cooperative relationship with the British promised.

There is no indication that General Jeffery Amherst understood how much he would gain from the alliance that the Iroquois held out to him. In a crucial sense, however, he did not need to understand it. Sir William Johnson grasped the idea with perfect clarity, clung to it with all his might, and used his considerable influence to make sure the Iroquois received generous gifts of weapons, trade goods, and money. Exactly how much advantage the British enjoyed as a result of Johnson's activity, and to what purpose that diplomatic advantage could be put militarily, made itself clear in the first great campaign of 1759—the expedition against Fort Niagara.

CHAPTER NINETEEN

Incident at La Belle Famille

The Niagara campaign was one of three designed to bring about the conquest of New France in 1759. In the spring General Wolfe, having secured from Pitt the independent command he coveted, returned to Louisbourg and prepared to ascend the Saint Lawrence with more than eight thousand troops and a powerful naval squadron, to take Quebec. Pitt's plans called for Amherst, with approximately eleven thousand men, to seize Forts Carillon (Ticonderoga) and Saint Frédéric (Crown Point), then descend Lake Champlain and the Richelieu, rolling up the remaining forts at Île-aux-Noix, Saint-Jean, and Chambly on his way to Montreal. Brigadier General John Prideaux and his five thousand men had by far the most complex set of tasks to perform. From Fort Stanwix at the Great Carrying Place, they were to proceed by bateaux to Lake Ontario via Wood Creek, Oneida Lake, and the Oswego River. A detachment was to rebuild Fort Oswego while Prideaux took four thousand or so men, together with all the Iroquois warriors Sir William Johnson could muster, westward up the lake to besiege Niagara. With that critical point and its storehouses of trade goods and munitions in British control, the more distant French posts of the interior—Forts Presque Isle, Detroit, Michilimackinac, La Baye, and the rest—would be cut off, ending any French plans to reinvade the Ohio country. Having accomplished all this, Prideaux was to return to Oswego with the bulk of his command, then descend the Saint Lawrence, bearing down on Montreal from the west as Amherst approached it from the south.

This impossibly ambitious campaign plan was the only one of the three that placed much emphasis on Indian support. Wolfe had rangers with him to perform the scouting functions that Indian allies would have provided. Amherst also intended to rely on rangers as scouts, but needed Onondaga's cooperation insofar as he could attack Forts Carillon and Saint Frédéric only by passing through Iroquois lands. Prideaux, with the smallest number of men and the largest, most complicated array of tasks to perform, could hope to succeed at any of them only with large amounts of direct, active Iroquois aid. For this reason, and certainly not because anyone thought of him as a competent field commander, Amherst assigned Sir William Johnson as second-in-command of the Niagara expedition. For this reason, too, Prideaux was undoubtedly delighted in mid-June to find Johnson waiting for him at Fort Stanwix with five hundred warriors. More would appear as the campaign progressed. Eventually their numbers would swell to nearly a thousand—perhaps four-fifths of the fighting strength of the Six Nations—giving the most reliable indication of all that the Iroquois were fully committed to their new alliance.

The eminently capable commandant of Fort Niagara, Captain Pierre Pouchot of *la marine,* not knowing that the Iroquois had shifted from neutrality to support for the British, assumed from the lack of intelligence brought in by the nearby (and normally quite reliable) Senecas that his fort was under no threat of attack. At the beginning of the summer, therefore, he had sent the bulk of his command westward, along Lake Erie, to the Allegheny posts, where they could join Lignery in an attempt to regain the Forks of the Ohio. Pouchot was therefore stunned to learn, on July 6, that Prideaux's force had landed less than four miles down the lake. He had fewer than five hundred men on hand to defend the fort and its extensive outworks against twenty-four hundred regulars and Anglo-American provincials, as well as about nine hundred Iroquois warriors. Pouchot sent an urgent plea to Lignery for help, but knew that it had to come very soon if he was to avoid disaster. On July 10 he watched from Niagara's eastern wall as Prideaux's forces opened siege trenches at the edge of the woods about twelve hundred yards away. He knew only too well that once the British began their cannonade Niagara's days would be few.

Pouchot needed to delay the beginning of the bombardment as long as possible in the hope that the walls could remain intact until Lignery's relief force arrived. He bought some of that time by calling a three-day truce to allow the hundred or so local Senecas who had taken refuge in the fort to parley with their kinsmen in Prideaux's force. The chief of the Niagara band, Kaendaé, was baffled and outraged by what seemed to him an inexplicable shift from neutrality to alliance, and did his best to argue to the Iroquois war chiefs and Sir William Johnson that all of the Indians should withdraw and let the whites fight between themselves. On July 14 Kaendaé and his people retreated under a flag of truce to La Belle Famille, a spot about two miles up the Niagara River from the fort; Johnson's Iroquois did not accompany them, though they took little part in the siege operations that resumed shortly thereafter. Meanwhile Prideaux's sappers had driven their trenches rapidly forward during the cease-fire, so that when the fighting began again, the nearest approach lay only 250 yards or so from the fort's defenses.

Prideaux was inexperienced in siege warfare and lacked senior engineers who could manage operations for him, but his men persevered in digging until by the evening of July 20 they were able to position cannon in a "breaching battery" just eighty yards from Niagara's curtain wall. Prideaux's own death that night—his head was blown apart when he stepped in front of a mortar just as it was being fired—barely slowed the progress of the siege. Undistinguished though he was as a soldier, Johnson assumed the command and superintended the bombardment until the fort's defenses were at the point of collapse. Then, on July 23, the reinforcements Pouchot had prayed for suddenly appeared on the Niagara River above the falls, in such numbers that the river seemed "black . . . with bateaux and canoes."

As many as sixteen hundred Canadians, French regulars, and Indians accompanied Captain Lignery from Fort Machault—more than enough to make Johnson's position in the trenches before Niagara untenable. Johnson quickly detached about 450 men with orders to construct a log breastwork and abatis across the road from the falls to the fort, near La Belle Famille. Even more importantly, he also dispatched a delegation of Iroquois spokesmen to convince Lignery's Indian allies not to participate in the coming battle.

***General Johnson Saving a Wounded French Officer from the Tomahawk of a North American Indian*, by Benjamin West (1738–1820), c. 1764–1768.** *This painting, one of the Pennsylvania-born artist Benjamin West's earliest historical works, commemorates the action at La Belle Famille during the 1759 British siege of French Fort Niagara. On July 24, 1759, British, provincial, and Iroquois fighters intercepted and decisively defeated a force attempting to relieve the besieged French garrison.* (Derby Museums and Art Gallery)

The next morning at about eight o'clock Lignery's force appeared on the road before the breastwork. It was immediately clear that the Iroquois negotiators had succeeded, for almost no warriors accompanied the eight hundred or so regulars, militiamen, and *troupes de la marine* who marched up in columns and began to deploy into a line of attack. Under fire from the defenders, and from Iroquois warriors who had arrayed themselves in the woods to the right of their line, the French charged before they had finished deploying into battle order. The redcoats behind the barrier held their fire until the ragged line of militiamen and soldiers had almost reached the abatis, then poured volleys into them with devastating effect. When the smoke of battle cleared, perhaps 200 French and Canadian soldiers lay dead. Another 150 or so, mostly wounded, were taken prisoner; the remainder, who broke and ran, were for the most part either captured or killed by the Iroquois warriors who had filled the woods on the east side of the road. Johnson, who understood perfectly well what would happen to them, made no effort to interfere with the Iroquois warriors' taking of captives.

The brief engagement at La Belle Famille sealed the doom of Fort Niagara, and with it, the fate of French efforts to regain the Ohio country. Pouchot held out as long as he could, but when Johnson offered him and his garrison a personal guarantee of safety, if not the honors of war, he surrendered on July 26. Johnson could make such a promise with confidence because his Six Nations allies had already taken as many captives as they needed, and he allowed them to take what they wished in plunder from Niagara's large stores of trade goods, pelts, and weapons. Pouchot and his men thus surrendered and became prisoners of war; Pouchot himself would later be exchanged and return to fight once again in the defense of Canada. Johnson then set about establishing friendly diplomatic relations with the local Indians, intending (as he reported to Amherst) to settle "an Alliance between us & them distant Nations" north of Lake Ontario, as well.

What Johnson did not do was attempt to carry out the remainder of the campaign plan by turning back east and attacking Montreal. Even so, the Niagara campaign was a success. The loss of this crucial post and the establishment of a new British stronghold, Fort Ontario, on the site of Oswego effectively cut off France's interior forts from contact with Canada. Deprived of trade goods, these posts on the Lakes and in the *pays des Illinois* would remain a while longer in French hands, but they could no longer contribute significantly to the war. By early August the effective western limit of Canada's defenses lay at the mission of La Présentation (or Oswegatchie) and the fort of La Galette on the Saint Lawrence, just 115 miles upriver from Montreal.

CHAPTER TWENTY

General Amherst Hesitates

Word of Niagara's fall reached Jeffery Amherst as he surveyed the ruins of Fort Saint Frédéric at Crown Point on the evening of August 4. His campaign, the most powerful of the year in the number of troops engaged, had been remarkably easy—a fact that only magnified his sense of unease. After a start delayed by a shortage of matériel and the tardy appearance of the provincials from New England, he arrived before the walls of Fort Carillon on July 22, resolved to avoid Abercromby's mistake by conducting a siege in the most systematic possible way. To his surprise—almost, one imagines, to his disappointment—the twenty-three-hundred-man garrison held out only four days, barely giving his gunners a chance to open fire before taking to their boats, detonating the fort's powder magazine, and retreating down Lake Champlain. Amherst, puzzled and cautious, ordered rangers to scout northward to Crown Point, where he expected the withdrawn garrison to add its strength to the troops at Fort Saint Frédéric and make a stand. He was astonished when they returned on August 1 and reported that the French had blown up that fort, too, and withdrawn north toward the fortified island that guarded the Richelieu River, Île-aux-Noix.

Amherst had therefore detached a thousand men to rebuild and garrison the shattered post he renamed Fort Ticonderoga and moved on to Crown Point, which he found in such ruins that he determined it would be necessary to build an entirely new fort on the site. The news from Niagara, encouraging as it was, did not settle his mind as he contemplated his next move. Amherst had begun the campaign with seven battalions of redcoats and nine of New England provincials, plus nine companies of rangers and a train of artillery, about eleven thousand men in all. He had detached a thousand men at the head of Lake George to construct and man a new post, Fort George, on the site of William Henry, and had left even more at Ticonderoga. If he detached still more to start work on a new Crown Point fort, he would be pursuing a retreating French army of unknown strength with a severely diminished force of his own, perhaps consisting of only four or five thousand men.

Amherst did not know the enemy's destination with any certainty, but if

"A View of the Lines and Fort of Ticonderoga," **by Thomas Davies, 1759.** *An artillery officer produced this elegant view of Ticonderoga as seen from Mount Defiance in the summer of 1759. On the promontory stand the "ruins of the fort after being blown up and deserted by the French." Zigzagging across the peninsula to the left are "the Lines at which . . . General Abercrombie was defeated in 1758." Masses of white tents indicate the position of three Anglo-American encampments. Also note the foreground, where an Indian hunter (lower right) draws a bead on a very large porcupine.* (Accession number 1954.1, negative number 38262a. The New-York Historical Society)

as he suspected they were awaiting him at the foot of the lake, he would have to navigate eighty miles of water to reach them. That was a very long way from any secure base of supply, and he had only bateaux to transport his men and their artillery down the lake. Meanwhile, he knew that the French retained a small but potent squadron of sailing vessels—a schooner and three xebecs that between them mounted thirty-two cannon—that could turn his bateaux to matchwood in short order. Amherst did not dare to move forward, then, until he had armed sailing ships to defend his boats. He had earlier directed his shipwrights, back at Ticonderoga, to construct two powerful vessels—a twenty-gun brigantine and a radeau (an eighty-four-foot floating battery that mounted six twenty-four-pound cannon); now he ordered them to build an additional sixteen-gun sloop. To build, rig, and arm them all took until the second week of October. In the meantime Amherst ordered his men to press ahead not only with the construction of the forts at Ticonderoga and Crown Point, but a new road as well, to run the seventy-seven miles from Crown Point to Fort Number 4 on the upper Connecticut River (the site of modern Charleston, New Hampshire), in order to secure access to supplies and reinforcements from New England.

Amherst's desire not to be lured into a trap proceeded not only from his native caution but also from his utter ignorance of Wolfe's progress at Quebec. He had tried to make contact with Wolfe by sending a couple of bold regular officers overland with a small escort of Mahican Indian rangers, but these had been taken captive by the Abenakis of the Saint François *réserve,* midway between Montreal and Quebec. Amherst knew this because Montcalm reported it to him, with elaborate politesse, in a letter sent under a flag of truce. The letter, written at Quebec on August 30, told Amherst nothing of the state of affairs on the Saint Lawrence other than that, at least by that time, Wolfe had not succeeded. There was no word from a third messenger, who had taken a more circuitous route. In the absence of intelligence, Amherst's sense that Wolfe would fail to take Quebec took on the force of conviction. And if Wolfe had failed, Amherst knew, Montcalm would be sure to shift troops from the Saint Lawrence to Île-aux-Noix. Montcalm might even try to launch a late-season attack on Crown Point. In view of so many unknowns, Amherst felt he could not be too cautious.

He therefore took pains to secure his position on Lake Champlain while investing no great energy in speeding the attack on Île-aux-Noix. Instead he contented himself with the construction projects at which he excelled, sent a large detachment of rangers under Major Robert Rogers to attack the Abenakis at Saint François, and waited for his vessels to arrive from the shipyard at Ticonderoga. It would be October 11 before he felt ready to order his men on board their bateaux and ships to move against Île-aux-Noix. Within a week the weather, turning cold and stormy, put an end to his resolve to proceed. On the nineteenth dispatches arrived to inform him that Quebec had indeed fallen, but by then it was too late in the season to do anything but suspend operations. By the twenty-first Amherst and his men were back at Crown Point, where he made preparations to send the regulars into winter quarters and to allow the provincials to return home. A month later he left for New York, to begin laying plans for a final thrust into the heart of Canada.

CHAPTER TWENTY-ONE

The Plains of Abraham

As Amherst would learn when he read the reports and spoke to officers who had accompanied Wolfe's expedition, the conquest of Quebec was anything but easy, its outcome anything but certain. Wolfe's troubles had started even before he arrived on June 28 with eleven infantry battalions aboard some 150 transports, escorted by "the finest squadron of His Majesty's Ships that had ever yet appeared in North-America"—forty-nine men-of-war, including twenty-two line-of-battle ships, the largest of which carried ninety guns. Those troubles had come in the form of just two French frigates and approximately two dozen supply ships that made it to Quebec in May, while Wolfe was still preparing to leave Louisbourg. This handful of vessels had brought between four and five hundred replacement soldiers, who were welcome enough, but also three commodities that Montcalm needed even more: provisions, intelligence, and instructions from the crown.

Because the Canadian harvest had failed once again in 1758 and the winter had been uncommonly severe, the civil and military population of Quebec was surviving on short rations when the relief vessels arrived. The food shortage was so extreme that the intelligence the ships carried—that Wolfe had orders to invade via the Saint Lawrence with Quebec as his target—would have been a signal for Montcalm to prepare to surrender, had not the holds of the vessels also been crammed with provisions. These were sufficient for Montcalm to contemplate a defensive campaign; thus

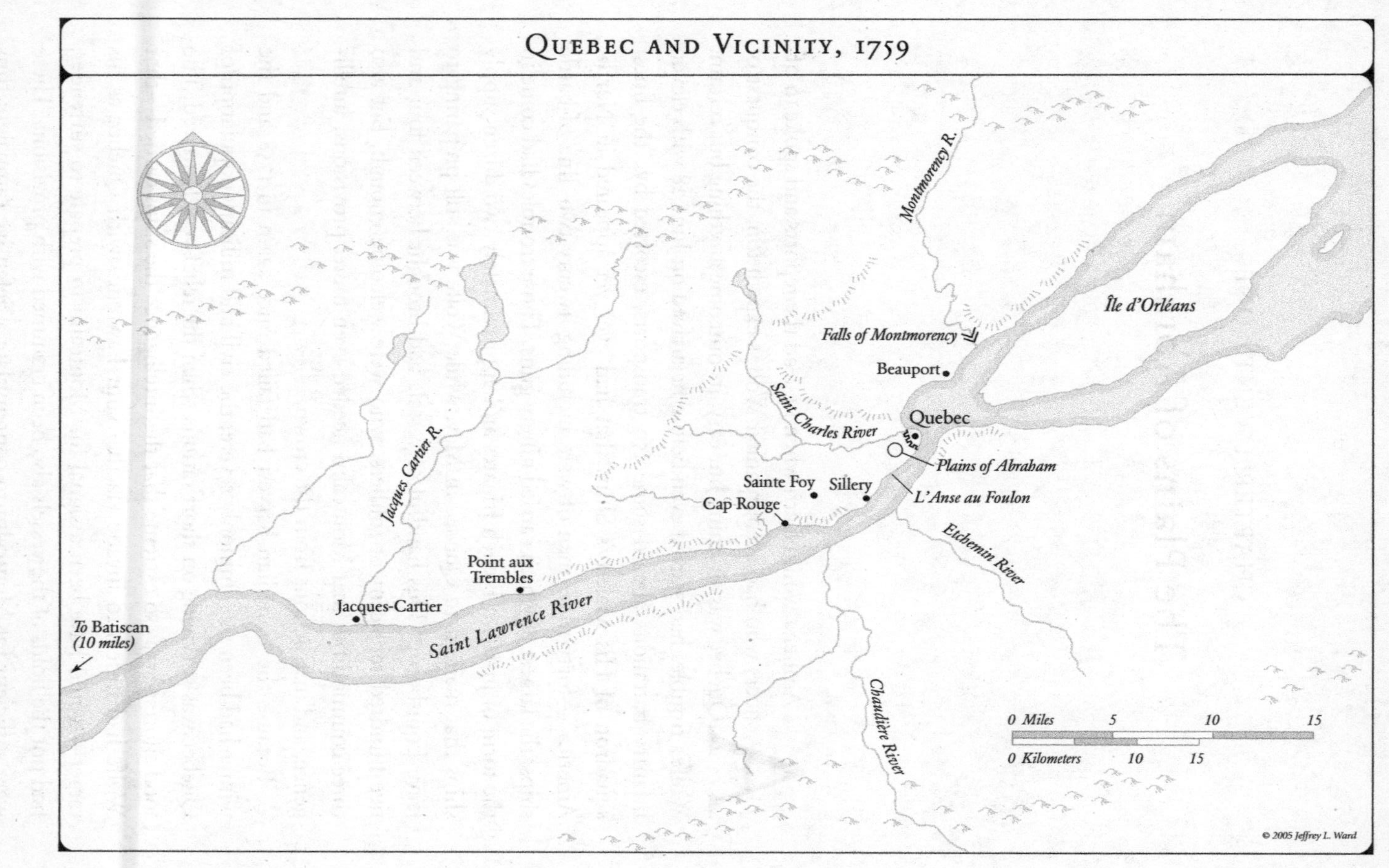
Quebec and Vicinity, 1759
Montmorency R.
Île d'Orléans
Falls of Montmorency
Beauport
Quebec
Saint Charles River
Plains of Abraham
Sainte Foy
Sillery
L'Anse au Foulon
Cap Rouge
Etchemin River
Jacques Cartier R.
Point aux Trembles
Jacques-Cartier
To Batiscan (10 miles)
Saint Lawrence River
Chaudière River
0 Miles 5 10 15
0 Kilometers 10 15
© 2005 Jeffrey L. Ward

he set his men to work to repair and expand Quebec's fortifications and sent the ships fifty miles upriver to Batiscan, creating a supply depot from which he could feed the city's civilians and defenders, and to which (if worse came to worst, and Quebec had to be evacuated) they could retreat. But it was the instructions that arrived in the portfolio of his returning aide, Bougainville, that he relished most. These had been endorsed by the king himself, and they unequivocally transferred supreme authority in all matters relating to Canada's defense to the marquis de Montcalm.

This decision settled his old quarrel with Governor-General Vaudreuil over which strategy—a guerrilla war based on Indian alliances and attacks on the Anglo-American frontiers or a conventional defense relying on professional soldiers and militiamen—would best preserve New France. Because Vaudreuil's military rank had been higher than Montcalm's, his vision of reestablishing the French presence on the Ohio and resuming Indian raids on the Pennsylvania and Virginia frontiers had governed the initial disposition of troops and resources for the campaigns of 1759. This configuration of authority explained the allocation of large numbers of men and Indians to Lignery at Fort Machault (the force he used in trying to relieve Pouchot at Niagara), a strategy that Montcalm thought was folly. Vaudreuil's emphasis on the west and Indian alliances also meant that he had paid little attention to repairing or expanding the fortification system that protected Quebec from a river-borne attack; hence with Wolfe literally at its door, the city's defenses remained remarkably weak.

The new instructions changed everything. They gave Montcalm permission to fight in the conventional, professional mode he knew best, which to him meant implementing a larger version of the hedgehog strategy he had used so effectively at Fort Carillon the previous year. The Indian allies to whom Vaudreuil's agents had appealed with considerable success over the winter and who appeared in surprisingly large numbers in the spring would not, therefore, be put to their traditional use, but instead retained in the vicinity of Quebec to function as irregular auxiliaries, alongside Catholic warriors from the Saint Lawrence *réserves.* Montcalm intended to make Wolfe wear himself out in attacks on entrenched defenses, holding out until winter and the freezing of the river forced his fleet, and his troops, to withdraw. If a peace could be negotiated in Europe (and the severe losses that Frederick the Great had suffered in 1758 gave

Versailles reason to hope that this would happen), Canada might still be saved at the bargaining table.

In the meantime Vaudreuil was helpless to do more than watch and rage as Montcalm ordered General Bourlamaque, commander of the Lake Champlain sector, to withdraw from Forts Carillon and Saint Frédéric, and to take a stand only at Île-aux-Noix. Vaudreuil could only despair when the news of Niagara's surrender arrived in early August, for he had

Marquis de Montcalm, artist unknown. *Louis Joseph de Montcalm, marquis de Montcalm de Saint-Véran (1712–1759), was appointed major general and dispatched to Canada in 1756. Intensely professional in his attitudes, he disdained the irregular warfare practiced by Canadians and American Indians, but nonetheless led mixed forces of French regulars, Canadian militia, and Native American fighters in a series of significant victories, including Oswego (1756), Fort William Henry (1757), and Carillon (1758).* (Library and Archives Canada/C-027665)

no power to stop Montcalm from writing off the western forts, and with them the alliance system they had underpinned for more than a half-century. But, then again, by early August there was little that anyone in New France could do, beyond praying that Montcalm had made the right strategic choice and trusting that the Blessed Virgin, who had protected Quebec for so many years, would not forget the city in the hour of its peril.

For a time it seemed possible that together those protections might suffice. Wolfe had made little headway since he had landed his troops on the Île d'Orléans in the basin below the city, on June 28. Although the total manpower of the British amounted to about twenty-two thousand men as opposed to Montcalm's fifteen thousand regulars and militiamen, only eighty-five hundred of them were redcoats and rangers who could actively participate in siege operations. The normal calculus of success in eighteenth-century siege warfare, which called for the besieging force to outnumber the defenders by no less than two to one, was therefore effectively reversed. Montcalm's engineers had laid out their defensive lines with skill as well as speed, compensating by position and depth for the questionable quality of the Canadian militiamen, untrained in siege defense, who filled the trenches. As Wolfe put it in a letter to his mother, "My antagonist has wisely shut himself up in inaccessible entrenchments, so that I can't get at him without spilling a torrent of blood, and that perhaps to little purpose. The Marquis de Montcalm is at the head of a great number of bad soldiers, and I am at the head of a small number of good ones, that wish for nothing so much as to fight him—but the wary old fellow avoids an action doubtful of the behaviour of his army."

Wolfe had every confidence in his little army, which was in fact superb, but nothing he could do seemed capable of bringing on "an action" in which their superior training and discipline would enable them to prevail. He began on July 12 by shelling Quebec—not the defensive lines before it or the guns on its walls, but the city itself—an act intended to terrorize its civilian population and goad Montcalm into making a sortie against his batteries. The bombardment continued for sixty-eight days, until most of Quebec's buildings were shattered or burned, but no attackers sallied out to avenge the city's suffering. His one attempt to force his way through Montcalm's defenses, a frontal assault on the lines at Beauport near the

Falls of Montmorency on July 31, ended in failure with 210 men dead and 233 wounded. In August, stymied by Montcalm's patience and mastery of defensive operations, Wolfe again tried to make him give battle by attacking the undefended farming settlements below the city, burning churches, houses, barns, and mills, making refugees of the civilian population by allowing his frustrated troops to give rein to their worst impulses.

At the end of a month-long orgy of destruction—what one of Wolfe's brigadiers called a "War of the worst Shape"—an estimated fourteen hundred farmhouses lay in ashes. Alongside a great deal of violence against civilians generally, at least one massacre had occurred, an episode in which a captain of the Forty-third Regiment ordered his men to kill a group of thirty Canadian prisoners and their parish priest. The redcoats scalped the corpses, a practice that Wolfe's prohibition—"The Gen[era]l stricktly forbids the inhuman practice of scalping, except when the enemy are Indians, or Canad[ian]s dressed like Indians"—did nothing to prevent because Indians so often dressed like Canadians and spoke such fluent French. Wolfe's own views of the "Canadian vermin," candidly expressed in a 1758 letter that spoke of the "pleasure" he would take in seeing them "sacked and pillaged and justly repaid for their unheard-of cruelty," suggest that he was not unduly disturbed when his troops failed to make fine-grained distinctions. And yet for all its ferocious brutality, August's campaign of "Skirmishing Cruelty & Devastation" did no more than the shelling of Quebec to lure Montcalm out of his lines.

Enraged at Montcalm's patience and alienated from his own brigadiers, all three of whom loathed him for his willingness to attack defenseless civilians, Wolfe now suffered yet another reverse. In the last half of August, his fragile health collapsed in a prolonged bout of fever. He recovered briefly, only to collapse again on September 4. Rumors flew among the troops that his death was at hand. They had reason to suspect it, and so did Wolfe himself. He had long suffered from "the gravel [kidney stones] & Rheumatism," and through much of the campaign had been compelled to rely on opiates merely to urinate. Yet on September 5 he was up once more—a rapid recovery that suggests it may have been stress and nervous exhaustion that afflicted him, as it had on more than one occasion before—and well enough to order half the units in his army to move upriver.

Five battalions marched up the south shore on September 5 to embark on ships that had previously passed the French guns and anchored near the confluence of the Etchemin River and the Saint Lawrence. Three more battalions made the move aboard more than a score of transports and warships, which rode the flood tide past Quebec's batteries on the seventh. Wolfe's brigadiers—Robert Monckton, Lord George Townshend, and James Murray—had previously urged him to move a force as high as Cap Rouge, nine miles or so above the city, or even Pointe aux Trembles, twenty miles upriver. Their intent was to cut Quebec off from its base of supply, and then to march down against the city. When the squadron anchored off Cap Rouge, they believed he had adopted their plan. But Wolfe had plans of his own.

As the troopships made their way upriver on the seventh, Wolfe was on board the fifty-gun H.M.S. *Sutherland* with Monckton, Townshend, Murray, and Rear Admiral Charles Holmes, intently surveying the north bank through a telescope. He kept his own counsel—at least he said nothing to the brigadiers—but it seems clear that this day of reconnaissance was when he identified a cove on the shore, with a narrow track angling up the face of the 175-foot-tall bluff behind it. At the top of the path stood a small guard encampment, no more than a dozen tents behind a breastwork and an abatis. Behind the camp lay the Plains of Abraham, a plateau less than a mile wide that swept gently upward toward the six-bastioned wall of Quebec, two miles away. The waters of L'Anse au Foulon (the Fuller's Cove) washed up on a hundred-yard-deep shingle, wide enough to handle the deployment of two thousand or more men after debarkation from landing boats. Here Wolfe intended to make his landing, or to die in the attempt.

The troops, in painfully cramped quarters on board the warships and transports anchored off Cap Rouge, waited four days for their orders. All the while they lay under the watchful eye of Bougainville (now a colonel) and more than a thousand infantry and cavalry on shore. Eventually Bougainville's numbers doubled as more soldiers and militiamen arrived to oppose the expected landing.

Wolfe gave no hint of his intentions until eight-thirty on the evening of the twelfth, when he sent his brigadiers a curt message informing them that the boats would not be landing near the anchorage, but rather far downriver at L'Anse au Foulon. Royal Navy crews made ready the boats that Wolfe's men began to board at nine. He would lead the boats downriver on the ebbing tide, with about eighteen hundred troops. Several small vessels carrying ammunition and other supplies would follow in a half-hour's time; a half-hour after that, the brigadiers and the balance of the troops would follow aboard the larger warships.

The moon, in its last quarter, rose a few minutes before ten. By midnight it was high enough to shed a ghostly light over Wolfe's men as they stood or sat silently in the boats, waiting to ride the ebb tide downriver. Finally, at two o'clock a pair of lanterns appeared at the main topmast of the *Sutherland*, the signal to cast off. The moon, now forty degrees above the eastern horizon, cast a glittering light on the water. From his perch in one of the leading boats, Wolfe looked down what would have seemed a pale highway toward the cove, eight and a half miles below, where he would learn the fate of his expedition.

Among the officers of the Royal Navy on the ships at Cap Rouge were several expert hydrographers, including the master of the *Pembroke*, James Cook, who would later explore the South Pacific as captain of the *Endeavour* and the *Resolution*. They understood a great deal about the strength of tidal currents in the river, the times of the moon's rising and setting, and other factors of immense importance to Wolfe, who clearly consulted them in planning this operation. Yet it is almost inconceivable that even these sophisticated officers could have predicted how tide and moonlight would coincide in the early hours of September 13 to make it possible for Wolfe's scheme to succeed. For indeed there was no other night in all of 1759 that could have produced conditions that rendered the boats essentially invisible to observers looking upriver from the French lines along the shore, yet illuminated the river sufficiently for the crews of the boats to steer downstream in safety; no other night when the ebb current would have moved at precisely the speed the British needed to deliver the boats to L'Anse au Foulon at four o'clock, when moonlight streamed across the river from the southeast, allowing the steersmen to pick out the cove and bring the boats to shore without mishap.

The degree to which planning or luck or destiny or sheer coincidence can be credited for allowing Wolfe to arrive at precisely the moment that favored him most, of course, can never be precisely fixed. What is clear, however, is that the British landing party took the small guard at the top of the bluff completely by surprise. By a few minutes after four o'clock a light infantry detachment under Lieutenant Colonel William Howe (the younger brother of Viscount Howe, who had died the year before at Fort Carillon) had killed or captured all but a single member of the French detachment, who ran for the city to give the alarm. Wolfe, who had expected the landing to be opposed, was so surprised by the lack of resistance that he did not at first know what to do, but the numbers of officers and men scrambling up the path soon banished indecision. As they secured an assembly area near the French camp, he moved off with a bodyguard to search for a position nearer the city. Below, in the predawn twilight, the ships from Cap Rouge could be seen dropping downriver. By sunrise they lay anchored off the cove, their masts standing like a small forest above the boats that busily ferried the remainder of Wolfe's force ashore.

Montcalm had not worried about a British landing near the Plains of Abraham, where he expected the cliffs and bluffs of the shore to stand in for the entrenchments that lined the banks below the city. At one point he had dismissed the need for fortifications upriver by observing that "we don't need to believe that the enemy has wings"; at another he maintained that even a hundred "men, well posted, could stop the whole army and give us time to . . . march to . . . that sector." But a wingless enemy had indeed landed, and no army had marched to oppose it because Montcalm had been distracted all night long by an elaborate ruse far downriver, where Admiral Charles Saunders had set boat crews rowing noisily back and forth in front of the Beauport shore, seemingly in preparation for a landing. When word finally reached Montcalm at Beauport around six o'clock, he initially believed the landings upriver were only another diversionary tactic. He issued orders for four battalions to assemble west of the city walls as a precaution, then rode upriver to take a firsthand look at the situation.

What he saw when he reached the Buttes à Neveu, the broken ridge about five hundred yards west of the city walls, left him thunderstruck. Half a mile away, six battalions of men in scarlet coats stood athwart the main road leading to town in a long double line that stretched almost across the Plains of Abraham. Behind them more troops were securing the flanks against the Indian and militia snipers who had begun to fire at them from the cover of trees and cornfields. It was a sight that nothing could have prepared him for, and it left him deeply uncertain about how to proceed.

Slowly absorbing it all, the shocked marquis must have pondered the suddenly tenuous position of the city, where too few provisions were stored to withstand a siege, and where the old western wall was too weak to withstand prolonged bombardment. He could estimate the strength of the British as approximately equal to his own, with about forty-five hundred men on a side. He knew that word had been sent upriver to Bougainville, whose two thousand men included some of the best-trained troops in Canada; but those reinforcements could not arrive in less than three hours. Could he afford to wait that long? By nine-thirty he had concluded he could not, for that was when he ordered his officers to prepare their men to advance against the enemy.

This was the decision that Wolfe had tried for months to provoke, for it played directly to what he knew was his greatest advantage, the superb discipline of the men under his command. Montcalm's force consisted of a mixture of regulars, who knew exactly how to behave in an open-field battle, and militiamen, who did not. Montcalm had used the latter principally as laborers, and had been able to provide little training in marching and maneuver, at which the regulars excelled. Thus while the militiamen understood how to load and fire their muskets and had at least some idea of how to fight from cover, they had no notion at all of how to advance deliberately through a hail of small-arms and cannon fire to a point no more than fifty yards from the enemy line, then halt, deliver close-spaced volleys on command, and finally charge home with the bayonet. Such was the steadiness, precision, and discipline that eighteenth-century armies needed to succeed on the field of battle; without it they could not withstand the extraordinary stresses of combat.

By ten o'clock Montcalm's officers had aligned their men before the Buttes à Neveu. No doubt he cantered the length of the line one last time to check their disposition and hearten them for the fight. Then he gave the order to advance and the ensigns let the regimental colors loose to the breeze. An immense shout went up as the great mass surged—*de bonne grâce,* witnesses said—toward the long double line of British soldiers who had risen to their feet, five hundred yards away, and were steadying themselves to receive the charge.

Wolfe had ordered his men to lie down nearly two hours before. This was not to allow them to rest, though it may have done so to some small degree. Instead Wolfe intended to make them less inviting targets for the enemy snipers who harassed them from the edges of the field, and for the four or five gun crews who had begun firing light cannon from the Buttes à Neveu at about eight o'clock. Now, as they dressed themselves into a double line, the redcoats' steadiness was unmistakable. The men waited stock-still, listening for the order to present arms, make ready, and fire.

There was no such calm in the French troops advancing toward them,

***The Death of General Wolfe*, by Edward Penny, c. 1763–1764.** *The year 1759 became known throughout the British Atlantic world as the* annus mirabilis *(year of miracles) in recognition of British and allied victories in North America, the West Indies, Germany, and India. Wolfe's triumph at Quebec was the most spectacular and emotionally powerful of them all. Writers, artists, sculptors, and tradesmen memorialized his death as the Hero of Quebec in verse, art, and mementos. This painting is one of many versions of the British hero's death.* (Fort Ligonier, Ligonier, Pennsylvania)

whose order began to break down almost immediately after they heard the command to advance. The left lagged, the center pressed ahead of the right wing; the regulars tried to march, as they had been trained to do, but the cheering militiamen lunged toward their foe almost at a run. Their officers managed to halt them at about a "half-musket-shot" (perhaps 125 yards) from the British line, and to deliver their first fire. Then all discernible order broke down. The regulars reloaded standing and advanced on order, as they had been trained to do. The militia threw themselves on the ground and reloaded as if they were in a woodland firefight. Some ran forward again, while others continued firing from their initial positions; still others moved laterally across the field seeking better positions or the safety of cover.

The British stood fast as the French lost coherence, then began firing on order by platoons, reserving their last climactic volleys until their adversaries were within forty yards. A British engineer described the action as clearly as any witness on the field that day:

> The French Line began . . . advancing briskly and for some little time in good order, [but] a part of their Line began to fire too soon, which immediately catch'd throughout the whole, then they began to waver but kept advancing with a scattering Fire.—When they had got within about a hundred yards of us our Line mov[e]d up regularly with a steady Fire, and when within twenty or thirty yards of closing gave a general one; upon which a total route [rout] of the Enemy immediately ensued.

As the last fragments of discipline among the French disintegrated, the British line charged with bayonets fixed, chasing the fleeing men back toward the walls of the city. The whole action had taken fifteen minutes, or even less, to fight. Each side had suffered approximately equal casualties: 58 dead and about 600 wounded for the British, approximately 644 dead and wounded among the French. At the head of the butcher's bill were the two officers who had led the armies.

Wolfe, wounded in the wrist and the chest at the beginning of the battle, bled to death on the edge of the field while his men ran wildly after the defeated enemy. It was an end he had wished for, since he believed his health was irreparably broken, and to fall in battle would secure his reputation for valor in ways nothing else could. And so it did; the British public would embrace Wolfe as the war's greatest hero, enshrining him in a place of honor unrivaled until the next century produced yet another military martyr in Lord Nelson. Coming as it did at the climax of the battle, however, Wolfe's death put his army at great risk, for no one was truly in control of the adrenalized redcoats whose determination to skewer every Frenchman in sight caused an almost complete breakdown in order, even as Bougainville's men approached from the west. Ultimately it was the brigadier who had liked Wolfe least, Lord George Townshend, who rallied two battalions to form and face the French. Had he not done so, Bougainville's two thousand comparatively well-rested professionals would surely have had the capacity to break up the disorganized British force and destroy it piecemeal. As it was, the sight of Townshend's battalions blocking the road made Bougainville hesitate, then break off contact and withdraw to the safety of Sillery Woods while he tried to understand what had taken place. With that, the last French hope of regaining the advantage perished, and with it the prospect of saving Quebec.

Montcalm, too, received a mortal wound in the fighting when a charge of grapeshot from one of the two British six-pound guns on the field tore open his belly and leg. Three men supported him on horseback long enough to reach the city, where he lingered in agony until four the next morning, refusing to give up his command despite the shock and pain that destroyed his capacity for connected thought. On the afternoon of the thirteenth Vaudreuil assumed control and ordered the bulk of the army to evacuate the Beauport lines and the city, skirting north of the British lines and marching upriver to join forces with Montcalm's second-in-command, Brigadier General François-Gaston de Lévis, who was in charge of the Montreal district. Vaudreuil left a skeleton force of militia, sailors, and invalids behind with orders to hold the city as long as possible. Given the extreme shortage of provisions on hand, however, that could at most amount to a matter of days.

The chevalier de Lévis, a bold and active officer, met the refugee army at Jacques-Cartier, about thirty miles upriver from Quebec, on September 17, and immediately set about rallying and reorganizing it in the hope of attacking the British siege lines from the rear, before they could reduce the city to submission. He had already set elements of the force in motion toward Quebec on the eighteenth when word arrived that the city had surrendered the day before. With no artillery at hand to re-besiege the place, Lévis ordered the army back to Jacques-Cartier. There he established a fort to defend the frontier of a New France that had now shrunk to approximately the size of the Montreal district.

Even so, all was not lost, and both Lévis and Vaudreuil busied themselves with preparations for recapturing Quebec. For the first time in years, the harvest in the Montreal district had been bountiful, so provisioning the remainder of the defense force through the winter and spring would be no problem. Between the refugees and the formations that had been stationed in the district, Lévis would have more than seven thousand men (among whom nearly four thousand were regulars) to move against Quebec in the spring. If reinforcements, artillery, and matériel could be sent from France to arrive at the earliest moment after the river thawed, Lévis stood a superb chance of being able to drive the British out. The conquerors of Quebec would have to survive a brutal Canadian winter on the limited stock of salt provisions that the fleet could put ashore before it weighed anchor for Britain in October, and they would have no alternative to living in a town largely ruined by their own merciless bombardment. Such conditions were sure to produce a weakened and vulnerable force by April or May. It was by no means in despair that Lévis and Vaudreuil composed letters describing the events of 1759 and imploring the king to send them aid and men in 1760, while they waited for the British fleet to flee the river, allowing them to run their own ships past the British guns at Quebec, home to France.

CHAPTER TWENTY-TWO

"A Mighty Empire"

The news of the conquest precipitated Britons on both sides of the Atlantic into a delirium of celebration. Bonfires blazed, cannon salutes boomed, church bells rang, skyrockets soared, and rivers of alcohol flowed in honor of what was, by any measure, an exceptionally satisfying victory. New Englanders, so heavily engaged in the war effort and so enthusiastically committed to Protestantism, celebrated in all those ways and with a plentiful helping of sermons, too. Of the many preachers who explicated the providential significance of Wolfe's victory, and extrapolated from it a glorious future for the Protestants of Britain and America alike, none excelled the Reverend Jonathan Mayhew of Boston.

Mayhew's twin discourses, delivered on October 25, 1759, were in many ways the finest and most systematic exposition of the war's meaning to Americans who exulted in their Britishness, and who understood themselves as partners in a great transatlantic political community based on common allegiance, shared religious convictions, and devotion to English laws and liberties. The future of this empire, as Mayhew laid it out, was nothing less than dazzling. Given the general tendency of events, he argued, "Great-Britain must of course, in a little time, be possessed of a territory here in North-America, extending and continued from [Hudson's] Bay . . . as far as Florida to the southward, about two thousand miles; and extending as far back to the westward, almost, as we should desire; reserving always . . . to the savage nations, their just claims, or proper rights."

Those just claims did not necessarily require relinquishing territory to Indian control. The war was likely to conclude not with the annihilation of the French empire but with it being pushed west, beyond the Mississippi; "with a little of our assistance, should the war continue," the British might "make [the natives] glad to confine themselves wholly to the westward of that river." To the east of it, Mayhew foresaw the growth of "a mighty empire (I do not mean an independent one) in numbers little inferior to the greatest in Europe, and in felicity to none." In rhapsodic language he tried to convey not only the importance of that mighty empire, but even how it would look:

> Methinks I see mighty cities rising on every hill, and by the side of every commodious port; mighty fleets alternately sailing out and returning, laden with the produce of this, and every other country under heaven; happy fields and villages wherever I turn my eyes, through a vastly extended territory; there pastures cloathed with flocks, and here the vallies cover'd with corn, while the little hills rejoice on every side!

Lest his audience lose sight of what would be the most important qualities of this new empire, Mayhew pointed out the reason that this land would be such a happy one: religion would be "professed and practiced . . . in far greater purity and perfection, than since the times of the apostles." This realm would have nothing to fear from without or within, for "the Lord [will be] . . . as a wall of fire round about, and the glory in the midst of her! O happy country! happy kingdom!" It was not too much, Mayhew believed, to make direct connections between the impending defeat of the French and the events, prophesied in the Revelation of Saint John, that would "consume and destroy the beast and the false prophet, with their adherents." In the happy fields and villages, the corn-covered valleys and the rejoicing hills, then, Mayhew and many another New Englander glimpsed nothing less than the face of a dawning Millennium.

For Jeffery Amherst and his fellow professional officers, of course, the practical matter of completing the conquest of Canada left little time to contemplate the place of British North America in the New Creation.

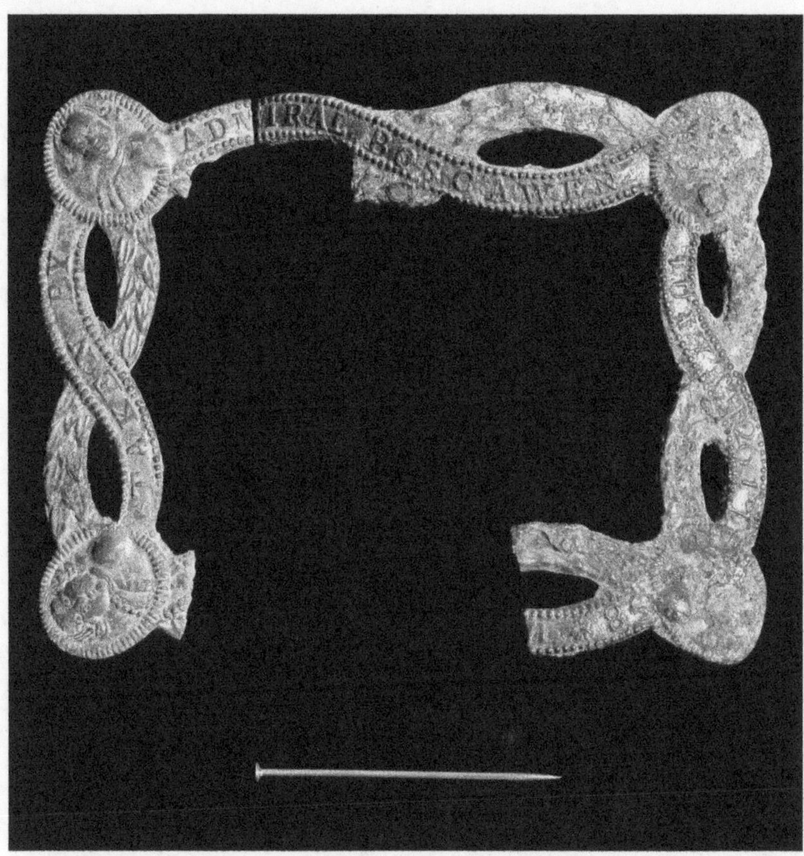

Commemorative shoe buckle, c. 1758–1759. *This artifact, recovered during archeological excavations in Williamsburg, Virginia, commemorates the British admiral Edward Boscawen's role in the 1758 siege and capture of Louisbourg. Americans in every colony reveled in their empire's far-flung victories in the Seven Years' War, celebrating their membership even in such quotidian ways as buckling their shoes with mementos of British military glory.* (Colonial Williamsburg Foundation)

Everything depended on holding Quebec, and on launching what Amherst envisioned as an overwhelming invasion aimed at trapping the remaining defenders of New France at Montreal. In January 1760 Amherst asked the various colonial governments to duplicate the numbers of provincials they had raised in the previous year; the following month he asked Sir William Johnson to procure as many warriors from the Six Nations as possible. To do so would be phenomenally expensive, because provincial volunteers could only be obtained in such numbers by paying wages that exceeded those they could make as civilians, and then adding bounties to raise them yet higher, and finally bidding up the compensation one last time to fill the remaining vacancies in the ranks. On average each provincial soldier who served in 1760 would cost his province approximately £25 in local currency, in wages and bounties alone, and much more when arms and supplies and equipment had been factored in. Each Iroquois warrior would cost virtually the same, once the £17,000 expense of the Indian gifts that Johnson distributed had been computed on a per capita basis.

Vast as these costs were, there was no complaint, no resistance to Amherst's demands, anywhere in the colonies. The economies and systems of public finance in the colonies had been effectively militarized by Pitt's reimbursement policies, which permitted the colonial assemblies to sustain a level of public expenditure inconceivable at any previous time. What one astute observer later said of Massachusetts was true of all the northern colonies: "The generous compensations which had been every year made by parliament, not only alleviated the burden of taxes, which otherwise would have been heavy, but, by the importation of such large sums of specie, increased commerce; and it was the opinion of some, that the war added to the wealth of the province, though the compensation did not amount to one half the charges of government." Important as subsidies and war-driven prosperity were in explaining the willingness of the colonies to undertake such vast exertions, however, ultimately none of it would have been possible without the groundswell of patriotic sentiment everywhere in the British colonies. The successes and shared sacrifices of the war had convinced vast numbers of colonists that they had as much at stake in the empire's present and future glories as any Londoner. The contrast between these attitudes and those that had prevailed in the days of Lord Loudoun could hardly have been more pronounced.

Amherst proposed to put this enthusiasm to use in a three-pronged campaign against the Canadian heartland. As soon as the ice was out of the Saint Lawrence and the winter garrison of Quebec could be reinforced from Louisbourg, warships carrying a force of three thousand or so regulars under Brigadier General James Murray would ascend the great river. A second expedition, made up of about thirty-five hundred regulars and provincials under Brigadier General William Haviland, would advance northward from Crown Point along the Lake Champlain–Richelieu River corridor. A third force, numbering almost eleven thousand, would proceed under Amherst's own command from Oswego down the Saint Lawrence, cutting off all possibility of escape for the French forces, who would presumably be trapped between the three converging armies on the island of Montreal, with no option but to surrender.

It was as ambitious and professionally conceived a campaign as any that would have been conducted in Europe, and in the end it worked out precisely as Amherst had hoped it would, with the three armies converging on Montreal in the first days of September 1760. The commander in chief, who was understandably proud of this achievement and the surrender that followed, ascribed his triumph entirely to military professionalism. Indeed, there was plenty of that: the redcoat soldiers who trapped Lévis's troops in Montreal were as tough and proficient as the best troops of their day, and Amherst was a gifted military administrator. But in fact there was a good deal more to it than military efficiency, competence, and discipline alone.

Three factors key to Amherst's success had nothing to do with the admirable proficiency of his regulars. First, of course, was the sheer mass of incorrigibly *un*professional provincial soldiers who accompanied him, and who served virtually everywhere else in North America during the war. Like most professional officers in America, Amherst scorned them as fabulously expensive for what marginal value they brought to his operations. In a sense he was right: the provincials' short terms of enlistment meant that they were almost never thoroughly trained or disciplined, and their performance in battle, when they had actually fought, had never been of reliably high quality. But for all their unsoldierly qualities, the provincials did one thing of inestimable value for Amherst: they worked. Without their labor, the forts and roads on which Britain slowly built its triumph over New France would simply never have existed. Without their presence in garrisons from Charleston to Louisbourg to Fort Pitt, there would have been no reliable way to assemble the masses of redcoats who fought so well at places like the Plains of Abraham, for they would have been tied down in scattered, tedious, necessary duties that the provincials performed (by no means uncomplainingly) in their stead.

The second factor that allowed Amherst to succeed as spectacularly as he did was the activity and skill of the Royal Navy—particularly as it was engaged in containing French shipping and naval vessels on the other side of the Atlantic. In fact nothing had been permanently decided on the Plains of Abraham; rather it was a naval battle on the French coast, nine weeks after the fall of Quebec, that decided the fate of that critical city. At the Battle of Quiberon Bay on November 25, 1759, a powerful force under Admiral Edward Hawke destroyed the last operational French squadron on the Atlantic, sinking or grounding all but two of the twenty-odd ships of the line that Admiral Herbert de Brienne, comte de Conflans, had commanded. Conflans's task force had threatened an invasion of the British Isles, which had been effectively stripped of land forces and were defended primarily by a not-particularly-effective territorial militia. To prevent that catastrophe from happening, the British navy had stationed the bulk of its warships off western and northern France, keeping up a long, exhausting, and expensive blockade. The destruction of France's last major force on the Atlantic relieved that pressure, and allowed the Royal Navy to concentrate on intercepting French commerce and communications on the Atlantic, and hence to prevent France from resupplying Lévis's army in Canada. For this reason the Royal Navy was able to pick off the Canadian supply convoy that France dispatched from Bordeaux in early April, destroying Lévis's plans to retake Quebec.

In fact, Lévis came remarkably close to doing just that in late April. Just as the river was thawing, he brought down from Montreal eight regular battalions, two battalions of *troupes de la marine,* a battalion of Montreal militiamen, and perhaps three hundred Indians from the Saint Lawrence *réserves,* all of them shepherded by two frigates, *Atalante* and *Pomone*, that had wintered in Canada. It was a formidable and comparatively well-provisioned force of nearly seven thousand soldiers, the greatest shortcoming of which was the small number of cannon (only about a dozen) in its artillery train. Against them Murray could muster only about thirty-eight hundred troops fit enough to fight. The rest of the Quebec garrison had fallen victim to scurvy, intestinal diseases, frostbite, and hy-

Medal commemorating the British victories of 1759 (reverse side). *This medal recalls the British victories of the* annus mirabilis *1759 in North America, Europe, and the West Indies. The obverse features a portrait of George II, while the reverse includes the motto "PERFIDIA EVERSA" ("perfidy overthrown") and "W . PITT . AUSP . GEO . II . PR . MI ." ("William Pitt, Prime Minister, under the auspices of George II").* (© National Maritime Museum, London)

pothermia over the course of the long and bitter winter. Fearing that he would be unable to defend the city from a siege, he marched out to engage the French on the snowy Plains of Abraham on April 28. The resulting Second Battle of Quebec effectively reenacted the First, with far heavier losses. Murray saw 259 of his men killed and 829 wounded, 28 percent of his force; Lévis drove the British from the field, captured all twenty of their field guns, and lost only 12 percent of his men (193 dead and 640 wounded) in doing so. Although the battle had consumed a good deal of Lévis's gunpowder, it left the French in a position to besiege Quebec, and the British barely strong enough to defend it. All Lévis needed to recapture the city were supplies and reinforcements from France.

Thanks to the Battle of Quiberon Bay and the subsequent breakup of the Canada convoy, they never came. When H.M.S. *Lowestoft*, *Vanguard*, and *Diana* appeared at Quebec between May 9 and 15, Lévis had no choice but to retreat to the fort at Jacques-Cartier. He succeeded because the sturdy *Atalante*, under the even sturdier Captain Jean Vauquelin (previously captain of the *Aréthuse*, the only ship to escape from Louisbourg in 1758), maneuvered to block the Saint Lawrence at Pointe aux Trembles and then shot it out with the British ships, sinking the *Lowestoft* before Vauquelin ran out of ammunition and was forced to surrender.

Vauquelin's heroic gesture allowed Lévis to escape and fight another day. But he knew that all he could do was delay the forces that Amherst would send against him. To do that he had to rely on the forts that defended the three routes that his adversaries might take to Montreal. By themselves the forts would pose only temporary impediments, but with sufficient help from Indian warriors he could hope to make the Anglo-American approach a nightmare. This was particularly true of the route of descent from Lake Ontario, via the upper Saint Lawrence. There Captain Pierre Pouchot, back from captivity as an exchanged prisoner of war, built a stout post, Fort Lévis, on an island near the *réserve* of Oswegatchie (near modern Ogdensburg, New York), upriver from a treacherous stretch of rapids. The situation of the island fort made it impossible for Amherst's expedition to pass, and required him to land cannon on shore and nearby islands to batter the fort into submission before facing the challenge of the white water. If the local Indians—Catholic Mohawks—who dominated the shores opposed the British landings, the siege would be protracted. If they joined the French forces in attacking the army as it attempted to pass the rapids, the expedition might well suffer crippling damage, and at the very least be long delayed on its way to Montreal.

When the time came, however, the Indians refused to cooperate as Pouchot and Lévis had hoped they would. Unaided, Pouchot was still able to hold back Amherst's army for a week in late August, and to kill twenty-one of Amherst's troops before he, like Vauquelin, was compelled to strike his colors. But thereafter there would be no further delays. Amherst's force, guided by Indians who knew the local waters well, passed the rapids at the end of August with the loss of only forty-six bateaux, seventeen whaleboats, and a row galley, and a surprisingly small number of men drowned—only eighty-four. Without support from the Mohawks, the four-hundred-man French force that had been positioned to fire on the British as they tried to negotiate the rapids withdrew without firing a shot.

Amherst could descend the Saint Lawrence with such comparative ease because of the Iroquois alliance. The seven hundred or so Six Nations warriors who accompanied his army, along with Sir William Johnson, quite effectively persuaded the formerly French-allied Indians who could have made the British advance a shambles to make peace instead. Iroquois envoys preceded the army at every stage. An Iroquois diplomatic mission to Oswegatchie in advance of Amherst's arrival had induced the Mohawks of the *réserve* to stand neutral during the siege of Fort Lévis, and to aid the army's passage of the rapids on August 31. Something quite similar happened at an Indian settlement outside Montreal the following week, even as the chevalier de Lévis was appealing for aid against the armies now

Montreal medal, 1760. *Jeffery Amherst commissioned 182 silver medals to present to Indian fighters who had remained with his army through the fall of Canada in 1760. The medals bear an image of the city of Montreal, with the nation and name of the warrior to whom they were presented engraved on the back—in this case a Mohican named "Tankalkel."* (Fueter, Daniel Christian/Library and Archives Canada/C-001457 [left], C-014996 [right])

closing in on three sides. On September 4 Lévis was making a speech to the Catholic Mohawks of La Prairie, appealing for warriors to join him against Amherst, when a native messenger stepped into the council circle. He informed the assembled chiefs that the villages upriver had made their peace with Amherst, who could be expected to arrive in a day or two. That ended the conference, and Lévis's last hope. As he described the incident in his journal, "In a moment [the chiefs] dispersed leaving M. le Chevalier de Lévis with the officers [who had accompanied him] quite alone." With grim resignation, Lévis "thereupon resolved to have all the troops on the south shore fall back to Montreal, a movement that was executed in good order the next morning."

That was where Amherst found them on September 7, 1760, within the walls of an indefensible town, helpless to resist the closing ring of British and Anglo-American troops. It was Vaudreuil who worked out the capitulation that could no longer be delayed. He asked that the inhabitants of the colony might be guaranteed their property and the right to practice their Catholic faith without molestation, and that the forces of His Most Christian Majesty be allowed to surrender with the honors of war, which would have allowed them to return to France and continue to serve their king. Amherst agreed to all provisions dealing with the Canadian civil population, but to none of the ones that would soften the blow of defeat for Lévis and his men. The French troops, he said, "must lay down their arms, and shall not serve during the present war." They would be transported to Europe as prisoners of war and exchanged for British prisoners there, provided that they gave their word not to serve again in the course of the war. The officers could retain their personal possessions, but would be required to surrender their colors.

Lévis and his fellow officers understood this as the humiliation and calculated insult that Amherst intended, and insisted that Vaudreuil break off negotiations so they could take their stand on the nearby Île Sainte-Hélène and die without dishonor. Vaudreuil refused, allowing them only the time it took to burn their regimental flags in secret. Thereafter the surrender of New France proceeded without incident. On the morning of September 9 the remnants of the last ten French battalions in North America lay down their arms, explaining that they had no colors to surrender because *(hélas!)* those had all been so badly damaged in six years of campaigning that they had been forced to destroy them. Amherst, who knew perfectly well that it was a lie, looked the other way and spared Lévis further humiliation. In the end the flags of ten beaten regiments were of little consequence in comparison with the conquest of half a continent. He had done what he had come to do.

CHAPTER TWENTY-THREE

The Spanish Gambit

Immense waves of celebration swept over the English-speaking world after the conquest of Canada. But for all the bells rung and loyal healths drunk, the war was still far from over. Europe, the principal theater of conflict, remained locked in bloody indecision. In the west, neither France's many mediocre marshals (Soubise, Contades, Clermont, Richelieu) nor its most able (de Broglie) could translate their vast numerical superiority into a lasting advantage over Prince Ferdinand of Brunswick, who commanded the mixed German-British force that opposed them in western Germany. Ferdinand's virtuoso maneuvering skills, however, could do little more than keep France from regaining control of Hanover, which alone could have brought Britain to negotiate a peace. Farther east, in Prussia, Saxony, Silesia, Moravia, and Austria, the war dragged on in a way that was even more dangerous to Britain's interests. Frederick the Great, Britain's principal ally on the Continent, was undeniably a brilliant general, but not an invariably successful one. His early triumphs at the battles of Rossbach and Leuthen (1757) had given way to victories like Zorndorf (1758) that were almost too costly to bear, and then to defeats at Hochkirch (1758) and Kunersdorf (1759) that bled his armies white. Although his principal opponents—the able but cautious Austrian field marshal Leopold von Daun and Russia's best field general, Piotr Semenovich Saltykov—repeatedly failed to deal Prussia a deathblow, by 1760

Robert Clive and Mir Jaffier After the Battle of Plassey, **by Francis Hayman, 1757.** *The British artist Francis Hayman produced this study for one of four monumental history paintings commemorating his nation's victories in the Seven Years' War. Completed in 1762, the image depicts the British commander Robert Clive after his victory over French and native East Indian forces at the 1757 Battle of Plassey, in Bengal.* (National Portrait Gallery, London)

Frederick seemed to be using his last reserves of genius merely to skirt, by ever narrower margins, the precipice of disaster.

The European stalemate encouraged Pitt, whose successes in America meant that he faced no effective political opposition, to continue seeking a decisive outcome in attacks against French imperial interests, while keeping Britian's allies afloat in Europe by sending subsidies to Frederick and troops to Ferdinand. Thanks largely to the success of the Royal Navy in defeating its French counterpart and asserting control over commercial shipping on the Indian Ocean, in India events now heavily favored Britain. Beginning in 1757 with the Battle of Plassey, native troops of the East India Company under the remarkable clerk-turned-commander

Robert Clive, together with smaller numbers of regulars under Colonel Eyre Coote, had won impressive victories over the French in Bengal and on the subcontinent's east coast, south of Madras. The climactic moment came early in 1761 with the surrender of Pondicherry, France's last great stronghold on the Coromandel Coast. Although the news would not reach England for another half-year, this victory effectively terminated the influence of France in India, just four months after Vaudreuil's capitulation had accomplished the same result in Canada.

Pitt understood these nearly simultaneous successes in South Asia and North America as functions of the Royal Navy's ability to cooperate with British regulars and other forces on land. This could be an indirect complementarity, as in the case of Quiberon Bay and the conquest of Canada, or a direct one, as in the amphibious operations at Louisbourg and Quebec. A textbook case of the latter could be found in Britain's taking of Guadeloupe and its small neighbor, Marie-Galante, in the spring of 1759. The war's disruption of trade with France had left the planters of Guadeloupe (and indeed of the whole French West Indies) sitting on a mountain of worthless sugar, in a sea of unmerchantable molasses, with no supply of the imports—slaves, manufactured goods, livestock, barrel staves, and provisions—that they needed to keep the local economy running. Conquest, paradoxically, solved the planters' problems. After less than a year of British occupation, Guadeloupe's economy was booming as planters shipped ten thousand tons of sugar to London merchants and bought thousands of slaves (imported from French West African slaving stations that the Royal Navy had seized in 1758–1759) and vast quantities of manufactured goods from British suppliers in return. That Guadeloupe offered a formula for translating military victory into commercial profits—hence securing support for the war among Britain's powerful merchant class—was not lost on Pitt as he contemplated the operations that were to follow the surrender of Canada.

So well did the dismemberment of the French empire seem to be going in late 1760 that the greatest threat to Pitt's continued success seemed to come less from his enemies than from the court of Saint James's itself. The heart attack that killed King George II on October 25, a little less than three weeks after the news arrived of Canada's capitulation, brought his twenty-two-year-old grandson to the throne as George III. The new king's father (Frederick Lewis, Prince of Wales) had died nine years before, as deeply alienated from George II as Hanoverian heirs typically were from their fathers. This meant that as he grew up the new monarch had formed his closest political and emotional ties with courtiers and politicians who despised George II and all the political corruption and devotion to Hanover that he stood for. George's mother, Augusta, and his tutor, the earl of Bute, had encouraged him to see himself as a "patriot king," who would rise above the petty factions of parliamentary politics and provide his nation with the kind of disinterested, virtuous leadership it needed to realize its destiny in the world. In 1760, to the new king this meant, above all, ending a war he saw as needless and destructive. To do so he needed to replace Pitt, whom he hated, with Bute, whom he loved.

Pitt, confident that he could handle this challenge, continued to pursue the policies that had made him the greatest war leader in his nation's history. He remained successful and popular—except of course with the king and his circle—until mid-1761, when Spain's intervention in the war became a live possibility. At the outset of the war King Ferdinand VI and his advisers had been equally wary of France and Britain, fearing that both had designs on the Pacific, and had therefore elected to remain neutral and allow the two crowns to fight it out between themselves. Ferdinand's death in August 1759 brought a more dynamic figure, Charles III, to the throne, a man deeply concerned about the future of his empire. The Battle of Quebec, coming soon after his accession, opened his reign in an atmosphere of heightened anxiety about Spain's position in the Americas and the Pacific if the British succeeded in conquering New France. The first manifestation of Charles's concern was an offer to act as mediator in arranging a diplomatic settlement of the war—in effect, a separate peace between Britain and France that would preserve the balance of power in North America.

Pitt, of course, had no interest in any such agreement either before or after conquering New France, and the attempted mediation went nowhere. With the news of each British victory Charles grew more and more concerned. Finally in the spring of 1761 he authorized negotiations with France to reestablish the "Family Compact," an old agreement by the Spanish branch of the Bourbon royal family to coordinate its diplomatic interests with those of its French Bourbon cousins. The compact was formally concluded on August 15, 1761. What was not made public was a secret annex to the compact by which Spain promised to enter the war as France's ally on May 1, 1762, if the war had not been concluded before that date.

Pitt knew of the secret protocol by mid-September 1761 because British intelligence agents intercepted a diplomatic dispatch that Spain's ambassador to France had sent to his counterpart in London. Accordingly Pitt pressed for a preemptive declaration of war on Spain. This was unacceptable to the new king, who refused to countenance anything that would expand the conflict. A brief crisis ensued as Pitt tried to force the issue by threatening resignation, not fully realizing that his fellow cabinet ministers had no intention of backing him to the point of offering resignations of their own. When the Great Commoner tendered his resignation on October 5, George accepted it with barely concealed delight, for he eagerly anticipated appointing the earl of Bute as Pitt's replacement, and bringing the war to a quick, negotiated end.

Circumstances soon dashed the young king's hopes. The cabinet ministers who had declined the opportunity to resign with Pitt did not favor making a separate peace with France, for such a move would entail the abandonment of Britain's allies in the Germanies. To avoid a crisis in government that would compel the king to recall Pitt, George and Bute found it necessary to take a hard line with Spain, issuing a formal demand that Madrid declare its intentions toward Britain as peaceful ones or suffer the consequences. When Spain did not reply, Britain's ambassador to Madrid issued an ultimatum on November 19: if the Spanish government did not unequivocally renounce any belligerent intent, Britain would regard its silence as tantamount to "an absolute Declaration of War." Madrid did not reply. On January 4, 1762, Britain declared war on Spain; two weeks later the Spanish reciprocated.

The result, for Spain, was sheer disaster. Charles III and his advisers had gambled that throwing Spain's weight into the balance alongside France would induce Britain to make peace. Instead they found they had placed their nation and its empire squarely in Britain's sights. A fully mobilized British war machine, having had two months to prepare for hostilities, quickly added an expedition against Spain's most important colony in the

Caribbean, Cuba, to the agenda of campaigns against the French sugar islands already under way. A half-year before, in June 1761, British forces had scooped up the French island of Dominique (Dominica), just south of Guadeloupe. Prior to his resignation, Pitt had ordered Amherst to launch an expedition against the next island to the south, Martinique. That venture had begun at the end of the hurricane season, and continued irrespective of Pitt's departure from power with landings in January; the island capitulated on February 16, 1762. Thereafter the rest of the French Antilles collapsed like a house of cards. By mid-March British forces had seized Saint Lucia, Grenada, the Grenadines, and Saint Vincent. Then, not missing so much as a beat in the tempo of conquest, Britain's navy and army turned their attention toward the greatest prize of all: Cuba.

Havana, the jewel of the West Indies, was the point at which all the trade of the Spanish Caribbean gathered in preparation for the annual sailing of the treasure fleet to Spain. It was also the chief naval base for the Spanish navy in the New World. British battalions landed six miles from Havana on June 7, even as Royal Navy warships blockaded the harbor, sealing the entire Caribbean squadron—one-quarter of the Spanish navy—inside. The formal siege of the city and its outlying fortifications commenced the next day.

The siege of Havana lasted until August 13. It was the longest, costliest, most brutal enterprise of the war for Britain and its colonies, and not only because Havana was strongly fortified. Rather it was the heat of summer and the ferocious disease environment of northwestern Cuba that made the siege of Havana into a particularly vivid representation of hell. The total number of British and provincial soldiers and sailors killed in battle amounted to 766; by the end of the summer, malaria, yellow fever, and the usual array of diseases that accompanied eighteenth-century military campaigns (in particular typhus, typhoid, and dysentery) had killed over 6,000 more—in all, half of all British and colonial troops engaged.

But the prize, however dearly bought, was immense. As in the case of conquests of the French islands, the planters proved delighted to trade with their conquerors, and within the next eleven months of occupation literally hundreds of British vessels arrived to exchange manufactures and

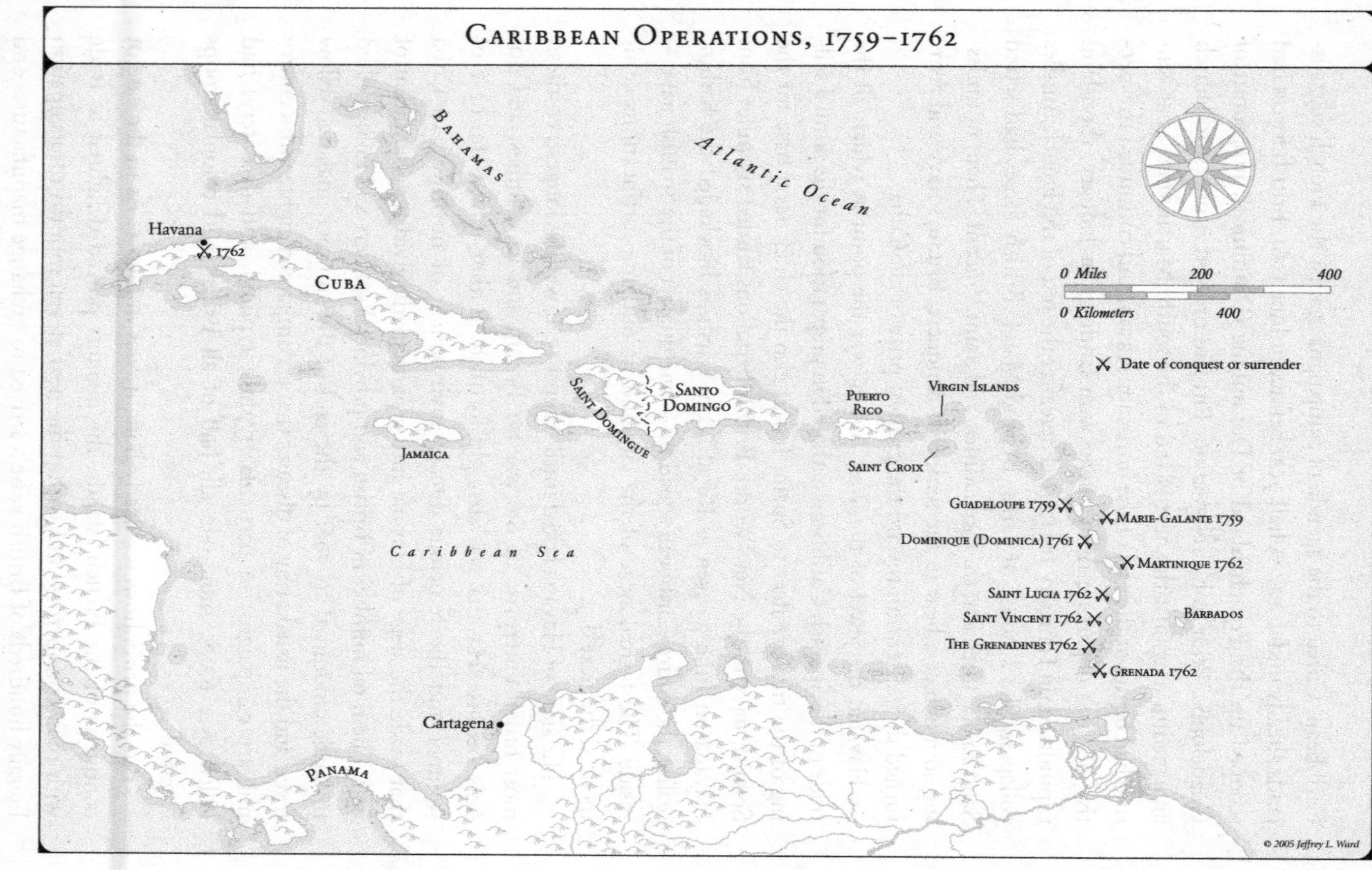
Caribbean Operations, 1759–1762
Bahamas
Atlantic Ocean
Havana
1762
Cuba
Santo Domingo
Saint Domingue
Jamaica
Puerto Rico
Virgin Islands
Saint Croix
Caribbean Sea
Guadeloupe 1759
Marie-Galante 1759
Dominique (Dominica) 1761
Martinique 1762
Saint Lucia 1762
Saint Vincent 1762
The Grenadines 1762
Grenada 1762
Barbados
Cartagena
Panama
0 Miles 200 400
0 Kilometers 400
Date of conquest or surrender
© 2005 Jeffrey L. Ward

slaves for the vast stores of cattle hides, sugar, tobacco, and other tropical products in the city's warehouses. Yet it was not only commercial wealth the British gained, but also £3,000,000 in silver bullion that had been consigned to the treasure fleet of 1762—a fleet that would never sail.

Roughly a month after Havana surrendered, British forces on the far side of the world embarked on the last great enterprise of the war: the seizure of Manila. Lieutenant Colonel William Draper of the Seventy-ninth Regiment was home from India on leave at the time the crown declared war on Spain, and left soon thereafter with orders authorizing him to raise men in India for an expedition against the city—a place that was arguably even more critical for Spain's Pacific empire than Havana was for the Caribbean. When Havana fell, Draper's motley force—made up of his own Seventy-ninth Foot, one artillery company, two companies of French deserters, and several hundred Asian recruits—was halfway from Madras to the Philippines. Draper hoped that his small flotilla of warships and transports would be able to pass the harbor's formidable defenses before anyone in Manila knew that Britain and Spain were enemies. That was precisely what happened on September 22. Immediately thereafter, Draper's oddly assorted force ("such a Banditti," he quipped, had "never assembled since the time of Spartacus") established batteries before the walls of Manila, and in just under two weeks' time succeeded in making a breach large enough to rush through and take the city by storm. Not including the plunder individually appropriated by the soldiers and sailors, the value of booty seized at Manila exceeded £1,300,000 sterling.

Diplomatically, the conquest of Manila counted for nothing, for by the time the news reached London six months later, the war had ended. The news itself, however, counted for a great deal, for it convinced the British public that their military was indeed invincible, and their empire the greatest since Rome's. What the exuberant Britons did not know about the Philippine adventure, however, was in some ways the most important of all.

Unlike the planters of Guadeloupe, Cuba, and the other islands Britain had seized in the West Indies, the people of the Philippines did not respond to conquest by cooperating with their conquerors, but by mounting

The Triumph of Britannia, by Simon François Ravenet (1706–1774), after Francis Hayman (1708–1776), c. 1765. *This engraving reveals the design of one of Hayman's monumental history paintings celebrating the success of British arms; the allegorical elements in this treatment differ strikingly from his more literal portrayal of Robert Clive in India. Here, portrait medallions of British admirals surround Neptune, who drives a seaborne chariot bearing the figure of Britannia to symbolize dominion over the seas.* (Engraving, 15 x 20½ in [38.1 x 52.1 cm], Yale Center for British Art, Paul Mellon Collection, B1977.14.11723)

an insurrection that effectively confined the British to Manila and its immediate surroundings. By the time Britain finally returned the capital to Spanish sovereignty on May 31, 1764, the East India Company had spent hundreds of thousands of pounds beyond what it had initially realized in plunder, in trying to hold on to a colony whose inhabitants preferred killing their occupiers to trading with them. The lesson of Manila was a simple and powerful one, but a British public transfixed by the glories of imperial victory did not grasp its significance. Armed force could conquer lands and peoples, but only voluntary cooperation could maintain imperial control. Wherever the conquered withheld their consent, the empire's sway could not exceed the range of its guns.

CHAPTER TWENTY-FOUR

Peace

It was fortunate for the earl of Bute, who was now Britain's de facto prime minister, that the news of Manila's fall took so long to reach London, for had the victory been widely known, he would have found it impossible to offer peace in open negotiations with France and Spain. The conquest of Havana made it hard enough, for it ultimately required a reshuffling of the cabinet to remove ministers who could see no reason to end a war that was increasing British imperial power by the month, and which might produce yet further gains for British interests in Europe. That, of course, was what Bute and the king feared most, for it would inevitably lead to an unstable peace. As their political ally the duke of Bedford had explained more than a year earlier, to grasp at supremacy "would be as dangerous for us . . . as it was for Louis XIV, when he aspired to be the arbiter of Europe, and might be likely to produce a grand alliance against us."

In the end the Definitive Treaty of Peace, negotiated by Bedford, signed on November 3, 1762, at Paris, and finally ratified on February 10, 1763, could only be implemented at considerable political cost to the king and Bute. Favorable as its terms were to Britain—and it sealed the most unequivocal victory in British military history with the greatest gains in the history of British diplomacy—the Peace of Paris became a lightning rod for the London mob as well as for opposition members of Parliament, whose emotional loyalty to Pitt only grew stronger with his absence from power. Within two months of the ratification, Bute was driven from office, and the king found himself compelled to accept a new ministry headed by a politician he neither liked nor trusted, in order to regain domestic stability and deal with urgent problems of finance and control that were cropping up everywhere from Kent to Canada.

Unlike the nearly simultaneous Treaty of Hubertusburg, which ended the war in Europe between the exhausted states of Prussia, Austria, and Russia by restoring the *status quo ante bellum,* the Peace of Paris transferred vast territories from French and Spanish to British control. With a few strokes of the pen, Britain acquired all France's North American possessions east of the Mississippi River (save New Orleans), as well as Spanish Florida, consisting of the peninsula and the Gulf Coast as far west as the Mississippi. The French received back all their conquered sugar islands except Grenada and the Grenadines, while Havana was restored to Spanish sovereignty as an "equivalent" for Florida. Britain granted French fishermen the right to take cod from the Grand Banks and dry them on two small islands (Miquelon and Saint Pierre) that France was allowed to retain in the Gulf of Saint Lawrence; otherwise, France retained neither territory nor commercial rights north of the Caribbean. The French returned Minorca to British control, disarmed their fortifications at Dunkirk, and handed back what scraps of territory they still held in Hanover, Hesse, Brunswick, and Westphalia to the princes of those states. All remaining prisoners of war would be repatriated. Outstanding commercial claims (mainly dealing with merchant vessels that had been taken by privateers) would be settled by arbitration.

With that, Europe settled once more (with, one imagines, a vast and weary sigh) into a state of peace. In Britain the bells of victory rang out again in celebration—albeit one tempered by the intensified political conflict and mobbish unrest that would soon drive Bute from office. At Whitehall and in Westminster public officials were soberly aware that the debts Pitt's policies had run up would somehow have to be repaid, and the vast new territories and non-English-speaking peoples that were now part of the empire would need to be mastered. On those great tasks the future of the empire depended, and with it the regeneration of British public life that the earnest young king yearned to accomplish: the nurturing of a true, self-abnegating patriotism that alone could overcome the self-interest and factionalism that had dominated Parliament and soiled the politics of the realm.

Yet even as the new administration of George Grenville, Bute's successor, was laying plans for the fiscally prudent and administratively coherent imperial order that would sustain Britain's position of supremacy in a new age of peace, events in North America were rushing once more toward chaos. Early British efforts at retrenchment and a misguided desire to reform Indian relations had convinced those native peoples who had lately fought alongside the French that the British had no proper conception of the obligations that allies owed one another. Having concluded that, like dimwitted pupils, the British needed to have these issues explained in no uncertain terms, the Indians prepared to give them a thrashing they would never forget.

CHAPTER TWENTY-FIVE

Insurrection

The great Indian war that erupted at Fort Detroit on May 9, 1763, utterly surprised the man who did more than anyone else to provoke it, General Sir Jeffery Amherst.* The surrender of Canada had left him with an immense set of problems to solve, beginning with the administration of territories that (in theory, at least) extended from Labrador to the Mississippi to the Gulf of Mexico, and which included more than eighty thousand French Catholics and an unknowable number of Indians. To garrison and supply Britain's forts from Louisbourg, on Cape Breton Island, to Fort Loudoun, in what is now Tennessee—a distance equal to that from Paris to Moscow—*and* to occupy the enemy posts that had come into his control as well was simply beyond his capability. He had no choice but to continue to call on the provincial governments for men to garrison Britain's forts and money to pay and supply them, and even to rely on the French officers in command of the more remote interior forts to retain control of them and the surrounding regions.

As Amherst's administrative responsibilities exponentially increased, his financial and manpower resources withered. The conquest of the French West Indian islands and Cuba required him to provide large numbers of redcoats from what had come to be known as "the American Army." Half of them never returned. Among those who did, large numbers

*In 1761 he had been made a knight of the Bath in recognition of his exemplary services.

Portrait of Colonel Theodore Atkinson, **by Joseph Blackburn, 1760.** *Theodore Atkinson (1697–1779) served as provincial secretary of New Hampshire through the French and Indian War. One of the papers arranged beneath his right hand reads "Enlistmts returnd/for 1760"—a reference to the province's heavy contributions of manpower to the final campaign against New France.* (Worcester Art Museum, Worcester, Massachusetts, museum purchase)

came back crippled by wounds or debilitated by tropical disease. Meanwhile the enormous financial demands that came with carrying out naval operations on the Atlantic and in the Indian Ocean and campaigning in

Europe, the Caribbean, and India caused the War Office to make deep cuts in Amherst's budget. There had been little enough money in it in the first place—Amherst had on several occasions been forced to ask the New York assembly for loans to tide him over between shipments of specie—and there were few places where he could cut expenses. The one that he concentrated on, the Indian department, proved to be the worst of all possible choices.

In the fall of 1761 Amherst suspended the practice of distributing gifts to Indian allies, including the customary provision of ammunition. The trading relations that had been established with local peoples at the various posts, he believed, sufficed to fulfill the promises made at Easton and by other treaties. If Indians were not being continually "bribed" with handouts, he thought, they could not indulge their proclivity for idleness. As he explained to an incredulous Sir William Johnson, the cessation of regular gift-giving "will oblige them to Supply themselves by barter, & of course keep them more Constantly Employed by means of which they will have less time to concert, or Carry in to Execution any Schemes prejudicial to His Majesty's Interests." It would be particularly wise, he thought, to keep "them scarce of Ammunition . . . since nothing can be so impolitick as to furnish them with the means of accomplishing the Evil which is so much Dreaded." Finally, having observed the vastly destructive influence of alcohol on native communities, he also forbade all further trade in rum and other liquors, which had become a mainstay of the Indian trade because they were consumable items that fed an essentially bottomless demand. To prohibit access to alcohol, Amherst believed, would not only increase the ability of Indians to be productive hunters, but reduce the violence that plagued their villages and improve their character in general.

What made matters even worse in the view of the western Indians was that the British had failed to establish trading posts in the interior and then withdraw their troops from the region, as they had promised. Rather they had continued to maintain garrisons there, in imposing posts that suggested nothing so much as permanent occupation. (Surely it was impossible for the Ohio Indians to draw any other inference from Fort Pitt, ten times the size of Fort Duquesne and built to house a thousand men.) Permanence seemed all the more likely insofar as the British commandants had encouraged white farmers to take up residence near their

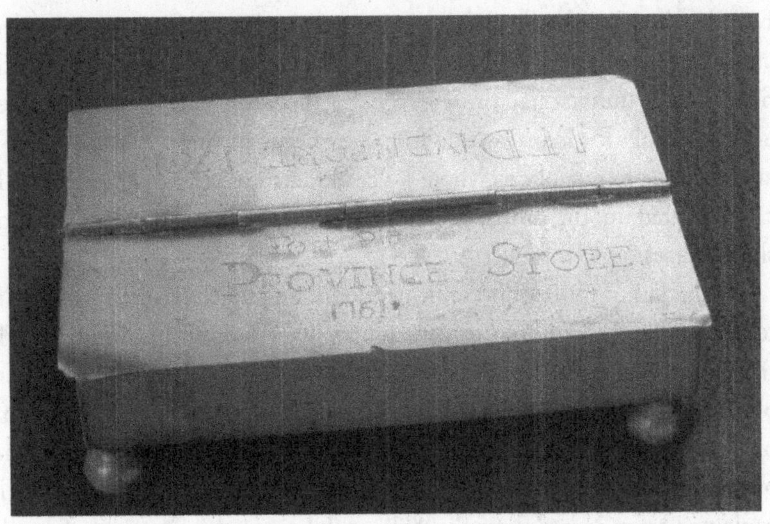

Writing stand, c. 1760. *Pennsylvania's provincial assembly opened several trading posts in 1758–1759 in an effort to correct abuses in the Indian trade that had alienated the Delawares and other Indian nations. The former provincial officer Josiah Franklin Davenport (b. 1727), Benjamin Franklin's nephew, managed the "province store" at Pittsburgh from 1761 to 1765. Josiah led a company of volunteer militia in the defense of Fort Pitt during the summer of 1763.* (Courtesy of the Historical Society of Western Pennsylvania)

forts. In fact, the commanders had little choice but to welcome these settlers, for they had access to neither the money nor the means of transportation to feed the garrisons otherwise. Although these settlements were arguably only temporary expedients to be removed at the end of the war when the garrisons could safely be withdrawn, in fact they formed only the most visible components of a fast-spreading white settler population in the Transappalachian region. And those thousands of farmers and hunters were in turn attracting the attention of land speculators on both sides of the Atlantic—powerful men who sensed vast potential profits in the sale of western lands. Their ability to influence government policies toward the interior so far exceeded that of native groups that the Indians' capacity to defend their interests dwindled to a single, terrible option: war.

To the Indians these policies and the broken promises they bespoke were nothing short of betrayals, and a fundamental threat to their ability to carry on with the way of life they knew. Gift-giving and trade on generous terms had been integral to alliances between European and native peoples for more than a century and a half. To suspend the one and to restrict the other, and then to tolerate (and even invite) settlement on Indian lands, could only be understood as hostile acts. When British local commanders proved unwilling—because, in fact, they were unable—to respond to native protests, Indian leaders concluded that they would have to teach the British how to behave with proper respect for their allies and hosts. Of all the major nations in the northeast and the Great Lakes Basin, only the Iroquois held back, and even they were not unanimous in doing so. Despite Sir William Johnson's influence with the League Council, the Seneca—historically the Iroquois nation most favorably disposed toward the French—showed a strong preference for joining the growing resistance movement.

In advocating war as a remedy for Britain's affronts, native leaders were doing nothing new. Indian groups had always used force when necessary to bring erring partners to their senses, and to force them to reinstitute proper, respectful, and mutually beneficial trading relationships. One thing, however, had changed. In previous decades the French alliance had provided the framework for cooperation among most of the groups that found themselves distressed by Britain's seeming arrogance and ill conduct.

Now that the French were no longer able to function as a coordinating diplomatic influence, native groups used Neolin's nativist prophecies to create an alliance system that was animated not by any human Father but by the Master of Life himself.

The Ottawa war chief Pontiac, an early and persuasive advocate of military action against the British, explicitly appealed to Neolin's teachings in late April and early May 1763 when he convinced the leaders of the Potawatomi and Wyandot bands who lived near Fort Detroit to join him in attacking the British garrison there, but to spare the French farmers who lived outside the fort. Over the next weeks, as word spread of the attack on Detroit, similar councils took place near every British-held fort throughout the *pays d'en haut.* The resulting surprise attacks, conducted in rapid succession across a vast geographical range with such great effectiveness, stunned British commanders at all levels. They could only conclude that renegade French officers and missionaries were behind the rebellion. Nothing of the sort was true. Rather, the war that they mislabeled "Pontiac's Rebellion" was a true pan-Indian movement, the first successful one (with the arguable exception of the 1680 Pueblo Revolt) in North American history.

Originating in the common grievances that Amherst's policies had created among native peoples, the great Indian insurrection was a coordinated uprising in only the most general sense. Yet by any military measure it achieved extraordinary success from the very beginning. In less than two months from Pontiac's May 9 attack on Detroit the western Indians had taken all but three British interior forts: Detroit, Pitt, and Niagara. The rest had been seized by force or guile, their garrisons annihilated or taken captive. Indian warriors then launched raids on the vulnerable frontiers of Pennsylvania, Maryland, and Virginia, throwing settler populations into panic just as they had in 1755–1758. In desperation during June and July 1763, Sir Jeffery Amherst scraped together expeditionary forces from the remains of regiments that had been shattered by West Indian campaigning and tried to reinforce the garrison at Detroit, which was barely holding on, and to resupply Niagara and Fort Pitt, which were in better, but still perilous, condition. He instructed his field commanders to employ measures of extreme ruthlessness, including the killing of Indian prisoners. "We must," he wrote, "Use Every Stratagem in our power to reduce them," "their extirpation being the only security for our future safety." Such was Amherst's mood when, infamously, he approved the desperate measure that Fort Pitt's commandant, Captain Simeon Ecuyer, had tried on June 24: taking advantage of a truce, Ecuyer had given the local chiefs a diplomatic present that included blankets and handkerchiefs that had recently been used by smallpox patients in the fort's hospital.

There is no evidence that Amherst's genocidal intentions and Ecuyer's abominable act actually succeeded in spreading smallpox among the Shawnees and Delawares who besieged Fort Pitt, for smallpox was already

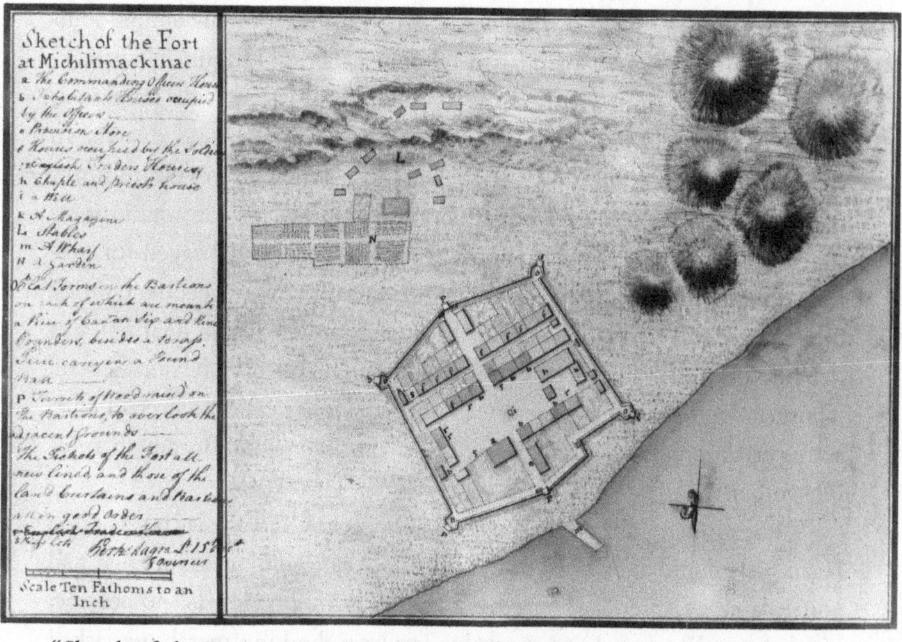

"Sketch of the Fort at Michilimackinac," 1766. *British forces occupied the stockaded French mission and village at Michilimackinac in 1761, following the fall of New France. Two years later a large group of Ojibwa and Sauk warriors, inspired by Pontiac's attack on Detroit, used an ingenious stratagem to seize the fort. Playing an extended game of lacrosse outside the walls on the morning of June 2, 1763, the warriors chased a ball thrown into the fort's interior through the open gate, taking weapons as they ran from women spectators who had hidden them beneath their blankets. Within minutes they killed or captured the garrison, taking control not only of the fort but also a large quantity of supplies, arms, and ammunition, without the loss of a single warrior.* (William L. Clements Library, University of Michigan)

endemic in both groups at the time. The intent, however, is more important than the result, for it indicates the extent to which native peoples had been dehumanized in the minds of Amherst and his beleaguered fellow officers. This level of Indian-hating can only be ascribed to what was now nearly a decade of intermittent warfare, and it was surely no more pronounced among the commanders of the British forces in America than in the white population of the colonies generally. Particularly in the frontier districts of Pennsylvania and Virginia most exposed to raids, the renewal of captive-taking and terror attacks only deepened the conviction, born of war, that the only good Indian was a dead one.

Once his initial, hysterical reaction to the Indian rebellion had passed, Amherst's strategy for restoring order settled on the brutally simple solution of waiting for the warriors to run out of ammunition, then attacking their communities to destroy food supplies. Faced with starvation, the Indians would make peace on terms the empire would dictate. In the end, however, this was not to be, for the new Grenville ministry decided to recall Amherst from America, ostensibly for consultations on the state of the colonies. Sir Jeffery, who had previously begged for permission to return home to deal with pressing personal concerns (among others, his estate had fallen into disrepair and his wife had gone mad), was delighted to turn the office of commander in chief over to Major General Thomas Gage, the long-experienced, unimaginative officer who had been acting as military governor of Montreal. He sailed for Britain in mid-November 1763.

What Amherst did not know until he had arrived was that it was not a hero's welcome that awaited him, but serious questioning about what had gone wrong in America. There would be no princely reward—no peerage, much less a Blenheim—to mark his services; the king merely remarked that while Sir Jeffery's accomplishments were no doubt impressive, they "would not be lessened if he left the appreciating [of] them to others." Amherst's most important patrons could do nothing to help him: Pitt was in opposition with no real hope of returning to power, and the king's uncle the duke of Cumberland, once captain-general of the British army, had suffered an incapacitating stroke. Sir William Johnson's powerful friends and associates, on the other hand, had done their well-connected best to ensure that Amherst would be blamed for an insurrection in which at least

General Thomas Gage, by John Singleton Copley (1738–1815), c. 1768. *Thomas Gage (c. 1719–1787) commanded the British advance guard at the Battle of the Monongahela, and served throughout the French and Indian War. He raised a regiment of light infantry trained in irregular tactics and married the New Jersey native Margaret Kemble in 1758. When Jeffery Amherst was recalled to England in 1763, Gage succeeded him as commander in chief of His Majesty's forces in North America, a position he held until 1775.* (Oil on canvas mounted on masonite, 50 x 39¾ in [127.0 x 101.0 cm], Yale Center for British Art, Paul Mellon Collection, B1977.14.45)

four hundred regulars and two thousand colonists had been killed or taken captive, with no end in sight.

Back in America, Gage did his best to fulfill Amherst's plans to end the insurrection in 1764. Militarily, the results were uneven, but in the end that did not matter, for it was not force but negotiation and concession that brought peace once more to the frontiers. In October 1763 the king issued a royal proclamation reaffirming the promises that had been made at the Treaty of Easton by formally prohibiting white settlement beyond the crest of the Appalachian Mountains. Those who still lived there were instructed "forthwith to remove themselves," leaving the interior of the continent as a vast, unorganized Indian reservation, in which the sole representatives of royal authority would be the commandants of British forts. At a series of treaty talks begun in 1764, Sir William Johnson and his representatives built on the Proclamation of 1763 by offering to reinstitute the giving of diplomatic gifts and to permit an essentially unrestricted trade in ammunition and rum. Johnson asked that various Indian groups, in return, agree to return the captives they had taken. Given the role captives served in Indian families and communities, this was no small concession, and it took a great deal of time and negotiation to secure it. Ultimately, however, most native groups agreed, and rested content in the knowledge that the British, if arrogant and not particularly bright, were at least educable in the realities of power.

By late 1765 the empire's relations with the Indians had at last stabilized. From Whitehall's perspective, this resolution came not a moment too soon. Even as imperial authority had once more been established in the interior of North America, it was coming under even more severe challenges in the colonies along the eastern seaboard. From New Hampshire to Georgia, colonists who had recently exulted in their empire's victory over France suddenly, inexplicably, seemed willing to launch an insurrection of their own. It would prove to be a rebellion of such scope and potential destructiveness that Pontiac's War seemed in comparison but a minor bump in the road.

By the KING,

A PROCLAMATION.

GEORGE R.

WHEREAS We have taken into Our Royal Conſideration the extenſive and valuable Acquiſitions in *America*, ſecured to Our Crown by the late Definitive Treaty of Peace, concluded at *Paris* the Tenth Day of *February* laſt; and being deſirous, that all Our loving Subjects, as well of Our Kingdoms as of Our Colonies in *America*, may avail themſelves, with all convenient Speed, of the great Benefits and Advantages which muſt accrue therefrom to their Commerce, Manufactures, and Navigation; We have thought fit, with the Advice of Our Privy Council, to iſſue this Our Royal Proclamation, hereby to publiſh and declare to all Our loving Subjects, that We have, with the Advice of Our ſaid Privy Council, granted Our Letters Patent under Our Great Seal of *Great Britain*, to erect within the Countries and Iſlands ceded and confirmed to Us by the ſaid Treaty, Four diſtinct and ſeparate Governments, ſtiled and called by the Names of *Quebec*, *Eaſt Florida*, *Weſt Florida*, and *Grenada*, and limited and bounded as follows; *viz.*

Firſt. The Government of *Quebec*, bounded on the *Labrador* Coaſt by the River *St. John*, and from thence by a Line drawn from the Head of that River through the Lake *St. John* to the South End of the Lake nigh *Piſſin*; from whence the ſaid Line croſſing the River *St. Lawrence* and the Lake *Champlain* in Forty five Degrees of North Latitude, paſſes along the High Lands which divide the Rivers that empty themſelves into the ſaid River *St. Lawrence*, from thoſe which fall into the Sea; and alſo along the North Coaſt of the *Baye des Chaleurs*, and the Coaſt of the Gulph of *St. Lawrence* to Cape *Roſieres*, and from thence croſſing the Mouth of the River *St. Lawrence* by the Weſt End of the Iſland of *Anticoſti*, terminates at the aforeſaid River of *St. John*.

Secondly. The Government of *Eaſt Florida*, bounded to the Weſtward by the Gulph of *Mexico*, and the *Apalachicola* River; to the Northward, by a Line drawn from that Part of the ſaid River where the *Catahouchee* and *Flint* Rivers meet, to the Source of *St. Mary's* River, and by the Courſe of the ſaid River to the *Atlantick* Ocean; and to the Eaſtward and Southward, by the *Atlantick* Ocean, and the Gulph of *Florida*, including all Iſlands within Six Leagues of the Sea Coaſt.

Thirdly. The Government of *Weſt Florida*, bounded to the Southward by the Gulph of *Mexico*, including all Iſlands within Six Leagues of the Coaſt from the River *Apalachicola* to Lake *Pontchartrain*; to the Weſtward by the ſaid Lake, the Lake *Maurepas*, and the River *Miſſiſippi*; to the Northward, by a Line drawn due Eaſt from that Part of the River *Miſſiſippi* which lies in Thirty one Degrees North Latitude, to the River *Apalachicola* or *Chatahouchee*; and to the Eaſtward by the ſaid River.

Fourthly. The Government of *Grenada*, comprehending the Iſland of that Name, together with the *Grenadines*, and the Iſlands of *Dominico*, *St. Vincents*, and *Tobago*.

And, to the End that the open and free Fiſhery of Our Subjects may be extended to and carried on upon the Coaſt of *Labrador* and the adjacent Iſlands, We have thought fit, with the Advice of Our ſaid Privy Council, to put all that Coaſt, from the River *St. John's* to *Hudſon's Streights*, together with the Iſlands of *Anticoſti* and *Madelaine*, and all other ſmaller Iſlands lying upon the ſaid Coaſt, under the Care and Inſpection of Our Governor of *Newfoundland*.

We have alſo, with the Advice of Our Privy Council, thought fit to annex the Iſlands of *St. John's*, and *Cape Breton* or *Iſle Royale*, with the leſſer Iſlands adjacent thereto, to Our Government of *Nova Scotia*.

We have alſo, with the Advice of Our Privy Council aforeſaid, annexed to Our Province of *Georgia* all the Lands lying between the Rivers *Altamaha* and *St. Mary's*.

And whereas it will greatly contribute to the ſpeedy ſettling Our ſaid new Governments, that Our loving Subjects ſhould be informed of Our Paternal Care for the Security of the Liberties and Properties of thoſe who are and ſhall become Inhabitants thereof; We have thought fit to publiſh and declare, by this Our Proclamation, that We have, in the Letters Patent under Our Great Seal of *Great Britain*, by which the ſaid Governments are conſtituted, given expreſs Power and Direction to Our Governors of Our ſaid Colonies reſpectively, that ſo ſoon as the State and Circumſtances of the ſaid Colonies will admit thereof, they ſhall, with the Advice and Conſent of the Members of Our Council, ſummon and call General Aſſemblies within the ſaid Governments reſpectively, in ſuch Manner and Form as is uſed and directed in thoſe Colonies and Provinces in *America*, which are under Our immediate Government; and We have alſo given Power to the ſaid Governors, with the Conſent of Our ſaid Councils, and the Repreſentatives of the People, ſo to be ſummoned as aforeſaid, to make, conſtitute, and ordain Laws, Statutes, and Ordinances for the Publick Peace, Welfare, and Good Government of Our ſaid Colonies, and of the People and Inhabitants thereof, as near as may be agreeable to the Laws of *England*, and under ſuch Regulations and Reſtrictions as are uſed in other Colonies: And in the mean Time, and until ſuch Aſſemblies can be called as aforeſaid, all Perſons inhabiting in, or reſorting to Our ſaid Colonies, may confide in Our Royal Protection for the Enjoyment of the Benefit of the Laws of Our Realm of *England*; for which Purpoſe, We have given Power under Our Great Seal to the Governors of Our ſaid Colonies reſpectively, to erect and conſtitute, with the Advice of Our ſaid Councils reſpectively, Courts of Judicature and Publick Juſtice, within Our ſaid Colonies, for the hearing and determining all Cauſes, as well Criminal as Civil, according to Law and Equity, and as near as may be agreeable to the Laws of *England*, with Liberty to all Perſons who may think themſelves aggrieved by the Sentences of ſuch Courts, in all Civil Caſes, to appeal, under the uſual Limitations and Reſtrictions, to Us in Our Privy Council.

We have alſo thought fit, with the Advice of Our Privy Council as aforeſaid, to give unto the Governors and Councils of Our ſaid Three New Colonies upon the Continent, full Power and Authority to ſettle and agree with the Inhabitants of Our ſaid New Colonies, or with any other Perſons who ſhall reſort thereto, for ſuch Lands, Tenements, and Hereditaments, as are now, or hereafter ſhall be in Our Power to diſpoſe of, and them to grant to any ſuch Perſon or Perſons, upon ſuch Terms, and under ſuch moderate Quit-Rents, Services, and Acknowledgements as have been appointed and ſettled in Our other Colonies, and under ſuch other Conditions as ſhall appear to Us to be neceſſary and expedient for the Advantage of the Grantees, and the Improvement and Settlement of Our ſaid Colonies.

And whereas We are deſirous, upon all Occaſions, to teſtify Our Royal Senſe and Approbation of the Conduct and Bravery of the Officers and Soldiers of Our Armies, and to reward the ſame, We do hereby command and impower Our Governors of Our ſaid Three New Colonies, and all other Our Governors of Our ſeveral Provinces on the Continent of *North America*, to grant, without Fee or Reward, to ſuch Reduced Officers as have ſerved in *North America* during the late War, and to ſuch Private Soldiers as have been or ſhall be diſbanded in *America*, and are actually reſiding there, and ſhall perſonally apply for the ſame, the following Quantities of Lands, ſubject at the Expiration of Ten Years to the ſame Quit-Rents as other Lands are ſubject to in the Province within which they are granted, as alſo ſubject to the ſame Conditions of Cultivation and Improvement; *viz.*

To every Perſon having the Rank of a Field Officer, Five thouſand Acres.—To every Captain, Three thouſand Acres.—To every Subaltern or Staff Officer, Two thouſand Acres.—To every Non-Commiſſion Officer, Two hundred Acres.—To every Private Man, Fifty Acres.

We do likewiſe authorize and require the Governors and Commanders in Chief of all Our ſaid Colonies upon the Continent of *North America*, to grant the like Quantities of Land, and upon the ſame Conditions, to ſuch Reduced Officers of Our Navy, of like Rank, as ſerved on Board Our Ships of War in *North America* at the Times of the Reduction of *Louiſbourg* and *Quebec* in the late War, and who ſhall perſonally apply to Our reſpective Governors for ſuch Grants.

And whereas it is juſt and reaſonable, and eſſential to Our Intereſt and the Security of Our Colonies, that the ſeveral Nations or Tribes of *Indians*, with whom We are connected, and who live under Our Protection, ſhould not be moleſted or diſturbed in the Poſſeſſion of ſuch Parts of Our Dominions and Territories as, not having been ceded to, or purchaſed by Us, are reſerved to them, or any of them, as their Hunting Grounds; We do therefore, with the Advice of Our Privy Council, declare it to be Our Royal Will and Pleaſure, that no Governor or Commander in Chief in any of Our Colonies of *Quebec*, *Eaſt Florida*, or *Weſt Florida*, do preſume, upon any Pretence whatever, to grant Warrants of Survey, or paſs any Patents for Lands beyond the Bounds of their reſpective Governments, as deſcribed in their Commiſſions; as alſo, that no Governor or Commander in Chief in any of Our other Colonies or Plantations in *America*, do preſume, for the preſent, and until Our further Pleaſure be known, to grant Warrants of Survey, or paſs Patents for any Lands beyond the Heads or Sources of any of the Rivers which fall into the *Atlantick* Ocean from the Weſt and North Weſt, or upon any Lands whatever, which, not having been ceded to, or purchaſed by Us as aforeſaid, are reſerved to the ſaid *Indians*, or any of them.

And We do further declare it to be Our Royal Will and Pleaſure, for the preſent as aforeſaid, to reſerve under Our Sovereignty, Protection, and Dominion, for the Uſe of the ſaid *Indians*, all the Lands and Territories not included within the Limits of Our ſaid Three New Governments, or within the Limits of the Territory granted to the *Hudſon's Bay* Company, as alſo all the Lands and Territories lying to the Weſtward of the Sources of the Rivers which fall into the Sea from the Weſt and North Weſt, as aforeſaid; and We do hereby ſtrictly forbid, on Pain of Our Diſpleaſure, all Our loving Subjects from making any Purchaſes or Settlements whatever, or taking Poſſeſſion of any of the Lands above reſerved, without Our eſpecial Leave and Licence for that Purpoſe firſt obtained.

And We do further ſtrictly enjoin and require all Perſons whatever, who have either wilfully or inadvertently ſeated themſelves upon any Lands within the Countries above deſcribed, or upon any other Lands, which, not having been ceded to, or purchaſed by Us, are ſtill reſerved to the ſaid *Indians* as aforeſaid, forthwith to remove themſelves from ſuch Settlements.

And whereas great Frauds and Abuſes have been committed in the purchaſing Lands of the *Indians*, to the great Prejudice of Our Intereſts, and to the great Diſſatisfaction of the ſaid *Indians*; in order therefore to prevent ſuch Irregularities for the future, and to the End that the *Indians* may be convinced of Our Juſtice, and determined Reſolution to remove all reaſonable Cauſe of Diſcontent, We do, with the Advice of Our Privy Council, ſtrictly enjoin and require, that no private Perſon do preſume to make any Purchaſe from the ſaid *Indians* of any Lands reſerved to the ſaid *Indians*, within thoſe Parts of Our Colonies where We have thought proper to allow Settlement; but that if, at any Time, any of the ſaid *Indians* ſhould be inclined to diſpoſe of the ſaid Lands, the ſame ſhall be purchaſed only for Us, in Our Name, at ſome Publick Meeting or Aſſembly of the ſaid *Indians* to be held for that Purpoſe by the Governor or Commander in Chief of Our Colonies reſpectively, within which they ſhall lie; and in caſe they ſhall lie within the Limits of any Proprietary Government, they ſhall be purchaſed only for the Uſe and in the Name of ſuch Proprietaries, conformable to ſuch Directions and Inſtructions as We or they ſhall think proper to give for that Purpoſe: And We do, by the Advice of Our Privy Council, declare and enjoin, that the Trade with the ſaid *Indians* ſhall be free and open to all Our Subjects whatever; provided that every Perſon, who may incline to trade with the ſaid *Indians*, do take out a Licence for carrying on ſuch Trade from the Governor or Commander in Chief of any of Our Colonies reſpectively, where ſuch Perſon ſhall reſide; and alſo give Security to obſerve ſuch Regulations as We ſhall at any Time think fit, by Ourſelves or by Our Commiſſaries to be appointed for this Purpoſe, to direct and appoint for the Benefit of the ſaid Trade; and We do hereby authorize, enjoin, and require the Governors and Commanders in Chief of all Our Colonies reſpectively, as well Thoſe under Our immediate Government as Thoſe under the Government and Direction of Proprietaries, to grant ſuch Licences without Fee or Reward, taking eſpecial Care to inſert therein a Condition, that ſuch Licence ſhall be void, and the Security forfeited, in caſe the Perſon, to whom the ſame is granted, ſhall refuſe or neglect to obſerve ſuch Regulations as We ſhall think proper to preſcribe as aforeſaid.

And We do further expreſly enjoin and require all Officers whatever, as well Military as Thoſe employed in the Management and Direction of *Indian* Affairs within the Territories reſerved as aforeſaid for the Uſe of the ſaid *Indians*, to ſeize and apprehend all Perſons whatever, who, ſtanding charged with Treaſons, Miſpriſions of Treaſon, Murders, or other Felonies or Miſdemeanors, ſhall fly from Juſtice, and take Refuge in the ſaid Territory, and to ſend them under a proper Guard to the Colony where the Crime was committed of which they ſtand accuſed, in order to take their Tryal for the ſame.

Given at Our Court at *Saint James's*, the Seventh Day of *October*, One thouſand ſeven hundred and ſixty three, in the Third Year of Our Reign.

GOD ſave the KING.

LONDON:

Printed by *Mark Baskett*, Printer to the King's moſt Excellent Majeſty; and by the Aſſigns of *Robert Baskett*. 1763.

The Proclamation of 1763. *Issued on October 7, 1763, this royal proclamation asserted British imperial control over newly won territories in North America even as it sought to reduce tensions with the Native Americans by prohibiting all white settlement beyond the Appalachian ridge and promising to open a regulated Indian trade in the interior. These measures effectively restated promises made in the 1758 Treaty of Easton; as before, they were essentially unenforceable, and widely ignored.* (William L. Clements Library, University of Michigan)

CHAPTER TWENTY-SIX

Crisis and Resolution

The issues that brought Britain and its American colonies repeatedly to blows between 1765 and 1775 were old ones, arising from the attempts of colonial leaders to defend local privileges against the power of imperial authorities trying to impose order on a region they were supposed to govern. The Seven Years' War and the subsequent Indian rebellion had strained the system of public finance to the breaking point, making British leaders all the more desperate to impose order on a vastly enlarged, disorderly imperial periphery. In effect the war's extraordinary outcome meant that familiar tensions within the empire could no longer be handled in the traditional way, by merely ignoring them and allowing events to take their own course.

As in Pontiac's War, the Stamp Act crisis of 1765–1766 erupted when governmental practices that had come to be understood as rights were abruptly challenged by reforms imposed from above, in the name of British sovereignty. In neither case was the violence of those who resisted revolutionary in character. Far from being aimed at the destruction of imperial authority, Indian rebellion and colonial resistance alike reflected a desire to readjust imperial relationships, and make the empire function in a way that those who lived on its margins could recognize as both legitimate and tolerable.

Pitt's policies, which depended on subsidizing German allies and British colonies as well as on direct military expenditures, had been phenomenally expensive. In 1755 the British national debt had stood at what was then regarded as a very high level, £72,000,000 sterling; in 1763 George Grenville as first lord of the treasury estimated that the war had doubled the debt, to a staggering £146,000,000. Taxes on land and manufactured products that the war had pushed to the limit of British subjects' ability to pay were yielding annual receipts, by 1763, of approximately £10,000,000. Half of that went to pay interest on the debt; the other half was consumed with fixed costs of government and defense. Nothing could have been clearer to Grenville, the best fiscal technician of his day, than that the money to administer and defend the expanded empire had to come from other pockets than those of taxpayers in the British Isles.

Grenville and his fellow ministers thought it self-evident that the colonies, which had gained so much in security and prosperity from the war, should shoulder the costs of their own defense as a first step toward assuming the larger costs of imperial administration. Never in the past had the metropolis tried to impose these burdens on the colonies. Instead of spending metropolitan money to govern the colonies, the crown had allowed the colonial assemblies to set tax rates and collect revenues sufficient to govern and defend their provinces. This policy, which the opposition politician and writer Edmund Burke called "salutary neglect," had encouraged legislators in every colony to imagine that they were somehow equal to members of Parliament in taxing authority. The members of colonial assemblies believed that inasmuch as the power to tax arose from the consent of the governed, only they, as duly elected representatives, had the right to impose taxes on their constituents.

But what seemed patently obvious to colonial leaders seemed obviously absurd to George Grenville, and indeed to anyone who understood the British constitution in the technical and sophisticated way His Majesty's attorney general and solicitor general did. The colonial assemblies existed by virtue of royal charter and hence had no higher legal standing than the aldermen's corporation in any English borough, or indeed a joint-stock business enterprise. For the colonists to claim that such bodies exercised a taxing authority in their own right was ridiculous. The power to tax, British legal authorities agreed, inhered in the sovereign authority of the state, which by definition possessed the power to appropriate property (in taxation) and take life (in justice and in defense). This all-encompassing, indivisible power belonged solely to the tripartite entity constitutionally vested with sovereign authority: the king, the House of Lords, and the House of Commons "in Parliament assembled." Together these three possessed all legitimate authority to pass laws and enforce them. Of the three only the House of Commons could originate tax legislation—its most important, and jealously guarded, power. To argue that sovereign authority could be shared between mere chartered corporations and the king-in-Parliament was an insidious, as well as a legally groundless, position. British jurists universally held that to divide sovereignty was to create a state within a state *(imperium in imperio),* and hence to invite anarchy, and civil war.

To colonists who understood the right to consent to taxation as fundamental to all English liberty, arguments based on sovereignty alone were fraught with peril. Colonists and their assemblies therefore objected to Parliament's assumption that it had the right to impose even the lightest of taxes upon them. The fact that the stamp tax that Grenville proposed in 1764 and Parliament passed in 1765 was an exceptionally light duty on legal, commercial, and public documents (deeds, wills, shipping manifests, newspapers, diplomas, and other items) only alarmed them more, for it seemed so clearly to be a vehicle to establish a precedent by which Parliament could in the future levy universal, direct taxes on the colonists. Grenville's assurances that revenues from the stamp duty would remain in the colonies and pay for the redcoat soldiers who would be permanently stationed there to defend them did nothing to assuage colonial fears. The French empire was gone forever. The Spanish were weak and distant, their control confined to lands west of the Mississippi. Where, then, was an aggressor to threaten the colonies? Only the Indians remained a potential enemy, and against them the regulars had lately proven to be of little, if any, use.

A permanent royal garrison, the colonists concluded, could only be intended to act as a constabulary that would enforce the dictates of a sovereign king-in-Parliament. That was what made the prospect of taxation without representation intensely worrying for the colonists. They believed that if a penny could be extracted from their purses without their consent, shillings and pounds might follow willy-nilly until their whole estates

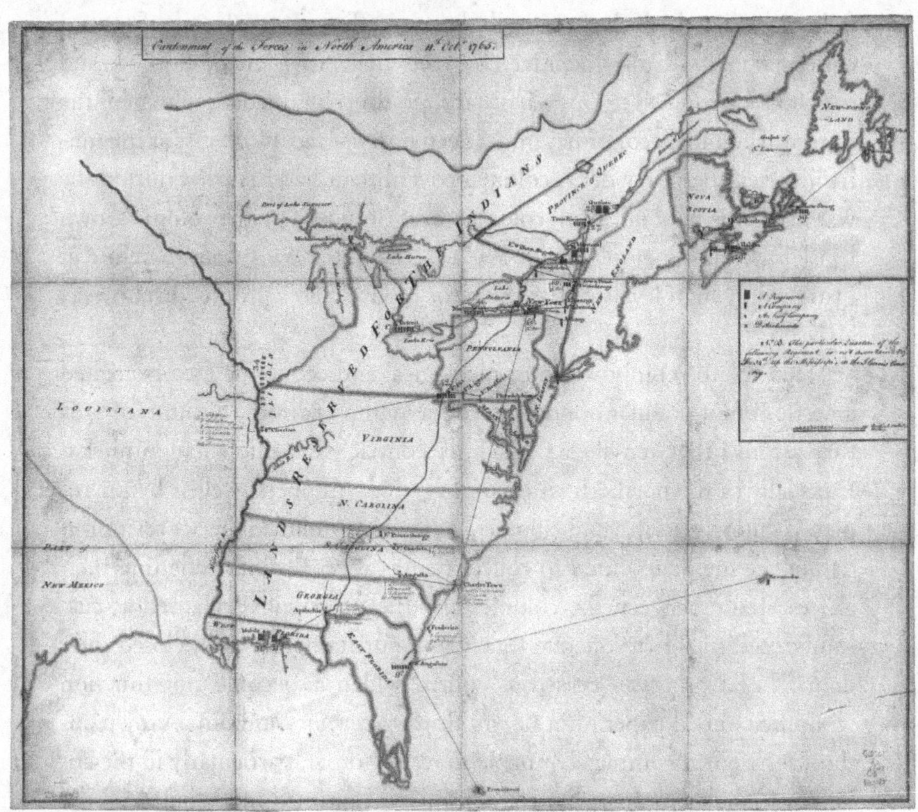

Cantonment of the British forces in North America, October 11, 1765. *This map records the location of British forces in North America at the time of the Stamp Act, a tax levied by Parliament to raise funds for the defense of its newly expanded American empire. It shows a virtually complete absence of royal troops from the port cities—Boston, Newport, New York, Philadelphia, and Charleston—where opposition to the act resulted in mob violence, the destruction of property, and the intimidation of crown officers.* (Library of Congress, Geography and Map Division)

had been confiscated. Then, having been reduced to husks of men with neither property nor rights—that is, to slaves—they would be powerless to resist the arbitrary rule of governors backed by the bayonets of royal troops.

The current state of the colonial economies gave additional cause for alarm. With the return of peace, the transfer payments that had made it possible for the colonies to sustain the very high levels of taxation and participation that had characterized the war effort in 1758 and afterward ended, along with the lucrative contracts that provisioned, clothed, and supplied provincial troops. This abrupt drop in income plunged the northern colonial economies into a deep postwar recession, just at the moment when the heavy debts colonial government had incurred during the war had to be paid off. Both colonial taxes (imposed by the colonists' own legislators) and unemployment levels in the port towns were therefore at distressingly high levels just as the news of Grenville's proposed stamp tax arrived.

This volatile combination of ideological and economic factors created an eruption of popular opposition to the stamp tax in the autumn of 1765 that astonished Grenville as much as Pontiac's Rebellion had Amherst. Especially in the northern cities, mobs—their numbers swelled by unemployed sailors, artisans, and laborers—effectively nullified the act by intimidating the men appointed to collect the tax revenues into resigning their offices. Trade between the colonies and the metropolis collapsed as customhouses, unable to operate legally without stamped paper, closed their doors. Legal processes ceased as courts, which also could not function without stamped paper, shut down. Royal governors and other crown authorities seemed completely unable to restore order, particularly in the absence of regular troops, who were primarily cantoned in Canada and the newly reoccupied western posts.

Chaos in the colonies was red meat to opposition politicians in Parliament, and Pitt's followers in particular made the most of it with calls for Grenville's resignation. Even more significantly, the disorders mobilized British merchants whose livelihoods depended on trade with America and the collection of debts from their colonial correspondents. They lost no time in organizing to pressure the ministry to repeal a law that was clearly a fiasco. At first Grenville seemed determined to enforce the act, but in July 1765 he found himself forced from office by an unrelated matter (the king, who was devoted to his mother, concluded that Grenville had behaved disrespectfully toward her). A new ministry, headed by the marquis of Rockingham, sympathized with the merchants and groped its way toward a resolution of the crisis over the next half-year, striving to find some basis for repeal that would not seem to bow to the pressure of mob violence or grant the validity of the colonists' arguments, or (worst of all) undermine Britain's claims to unlimited sovereignty over the colonies. Finally, in March 1766, the Rockingham ministry found the formula it needed, repealing the law on the indisputable grounds that it was unenforceable and simultaneously passing a Declaratory Act that asserted that Parliament "had, hath, and of a right ought to have, full power and authority to make laws and statutes of sufficient force and validity to bind the colonies and people of America in all cases whatsoever."

The colonists scarcely noticed the Declaratory Act as they celebrated the repeal of the stamp tax. A level of public rejoicing unseen since the fall of Canada indicated that the colonists wanted nothing more than to return to business-as-usual in the empire. Americans still regarded themselves as true Britons in 1766, and indeed the great majority would

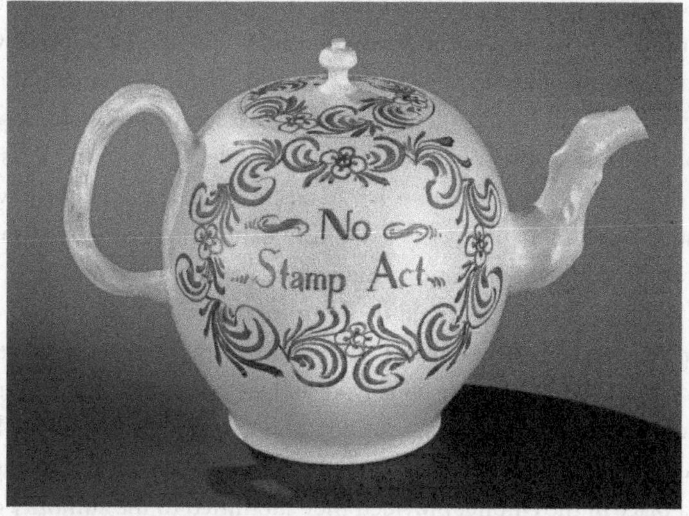

"No Stamp Act" teapot. *Although the anticipated cost to colonists was slight, many colonial leaders considered the Stamp Act duties to be extremely dangerous to their political liberties, because for American colonists to submit to taxation without representation was to accept an essentially limitless British authority over their lives and estates. This ceramic teapot protesting the Stamp Act was produced in England for American customers—a testimony to both the vital economic life of the transatlantic empire and to the integration of the colonies in British political culture.* (Colonial Williamsburg Foundation)

continue to do so until the mid-1770s. The repeal of the Stamp Act, they believed, affirmed that they were in fact what the glorious years 1758–1760 had suggested: partners in empire. Their very devotion to the empire, indeed, was what made the second and third postwar convulsions, the Townshend Acts controversy of 1767–1770 and the Tea Crisis of 1773–1774, so traumatic. Far from being foreshadowings of independence, these were passionate debates over what the empire should be, and what membership in it would mean for Britons on both sides of the Atlantic. Only the outbreak of civil war in Massachusetts in the spring of 1775 finally made it clear to colonial leaders that their hope for reconciliation might be an illusion. Even then it took more than a year of bloodshed to convince the members of the Continental Congress that they had no alternative left but to declare independence.

With the unmistakable clarity of a lightning flash, the Stamp Act crisis revealed that two quite different ideas of the empire, and how it should function, had emerged in the postwar empire. One was an imperial vision of unity and integration, in which a sovereign king-in-Parliament directed the energies of all British subjects toward a common end by the wise, benevolent exercise of supreme power. Such a model began with the assumption that the purpose of empire was to create order, applying the power of the state to promote prosperity and create harmony (or at least to prevent destructive competition) among the various groups that constituted it. In such an imperium there would be room for a broad, diverse range of inherently *un*equal subjects, all of them living together under the protection of a crown to which all were equally loyal. Heathen Indians in the interior, Francophone Catholics in Canada and Louisiana, German Pietists in Pennsylvania, English and Scots and Scotch-Irish Protestants, even Africans, all had a place in the empire, provided they submitted to the authority of the king and his representatives. This was an empire based on the assumptions of subordination that had brought Scotland into union with England and Wales to create the United Kingdom, in 1707—a union enforced by British military power in the suppression of the Scottish rebellions of 1715 and 1745. This was an empire as General Braddock and Lord Loudoun had construed it, and the colonists cared no more for it in the postwar era than they had in 1755–1757.

As opposed to this unitary conception, the second model assumed that the empire was in essence a great community of white, Protestant, English-speaking subjects who shared the same rights and avowed a common allegiance, no matter whether they lived in the Shenandoah Valley or the Vale of Kent. Because their rights as subjects came first, the power of the British state over its colonies was contingent upon their consent, expressed through the acts and deliberations of elected representatives, irrespective of whether they sat in Westminster as members of Parliament or in Williamsburg as burgesses. Because common allegiance to the king and a common Protestant identity bound them together, constitutional arguments based on the dangers of divided sovereignty made no emotional sense to the colonists; it was their own freely offered consent, not some legal technicality, that made their assemblies equal to the House of Commons in privileges and authority.

This conception of empire mirrored the assumptions that connected England and Ireland, in which a royally appointed lord lieutenant represented the king to a colony whose Parliament represented the interests of its freeholders. It was an empire that amounted to a confederation of colonies, where English-speaking Protestants composed a transnational political community that ruled over local minorities just as in Ireland the English-speaking Protestant Ascendancy (backed, as needed, by royal troops) ruled over the never-to-be-enfranchised Irish Catholics. This vision of empire had been effectively realized in 1758–1760, when Pitt treated Americans as allies and asked for their support rather than seeking to compel it. The Reverend Jonathan Mayhew had painted the future glories of an empire conceived on such terms in the most vivid possible way when he preached his sermons on the conquest of Quebec in 1759.

Whether the empire was unitary or confederated; whether its basis lay in the indivisible sovereignty of king-in-Parliament or the universal exercise of Englishmen's rights; whether what held it together was state power or voluntary affiliation; whether its fundamental goal was the creation of order or the enjoyment of liberty: these were the issues at stake as American and metropolitan Britons debated the nature of the imperial community in the Stamp Act crisis and the decade of on-and-off crises that followed it. What ultimately drove these debates from disagreements expressed in words and pamphlets to sterner disputes conducted with powder and ball were concerns for the future. What made them irreconcilable, in the end, was the knowledge that the empire's future would be worked out in the interior of the continent, on lands freed from the grip of the tyrant king of France in the most successful war Britain had ever fought.

CHAPTER TWENTY-SEVEN

A Patriot's Progress

Believing that their sacrifices of blood and treasure entitled them to share in the fruits of victory, the colonists of British North America assumed that they had a stake in the empire's future. Few of them felt that conviction more keenly than Colonel George Washington of Virginia. His postwar career illuminates how, in the aftermath of Britain's greatest victory, men who regarded themselves as committed British patriots would defend their vision of the empire, and their understanding of their rights within it, with such fervor as to bring about a Revolution.

So far as the twenty-seven-year-old colonel was concerned, retirement from command of the Virginia Regiment at the end of 1758 marked the end of military ambition. He hoped, as he wrote to a British merchant the following year, "to find more happiness in retirement than I ever experienced amidst a wide and bustling World." By "retirement," of course, he merely meant living on his plantation and minding his own business, not withdrawing from the world; for in fact Washington's goal remained what it had always been, to become a leading member of his colony's ruling elite. The important role he had played in the war had established his reputation for the public-spiritedness that Virginia's leaders were supposed to demonstrate, but in the end there was no real power in Virginia without a great fortune to sustain it. With marriage to Martha Dandridge Custis he made rapid progress on that front in early 1759. Over the following decade he used Martha's wealth to expand his Tidewater properties from about five thousand acres to more than twelve thousand, and to double his holding of slaves.

Washington proved less successful in growing tobacco that could command a premium price in London, however, and found his debts with British merchants mounting even as he expanded his estates. Reluctantly he shifted from planting tobacco to growing wheat in 1767, but the effect proved less dramatic than he wished. Even when he supplemented farming with flour-milling, textile-weaving, shad-fishing, and brandy-distilling, his profits remained slender, his debts stubbornly substantial. In response he pitched ever-greater hopes on land speculation, an enterprise he had engaged in since his late teenage years, but which he now practiced with ever-increasing enthusiasm.

His most secure basis for speculation lay in the colony's promise to grant 200,000 acres in the Ohio Valley to men who served under him in 1754. As colonel, Washington had personal rights to twenty thousand of those acres. He spent the decade after the war buying warrants—certificates that entitled each captain to nine thousand acres, and individual privates to four hundred acres apiece—from his former subordinates. Eventually he accumulated rights to an additional twenty-five thousand acres. By 1767 he thought it prudent to engage an old comrade, Captain William Crawford, to identify and survey prime parcels that he could claim along the south bank of the river. That the Proclamation of 1763 forbade white settlement west of the Appalachian crest did not concern him. As he explained to Crawford, the Proclamation was but "a temporary expedient to quiet the Minds of the Indians" that "must fall of course in a few years." When it did, he intended to be in a position to profit from the immense westward surge of settlers that was sure to follow. With this in mind, he visited the Ohio Valley himself in the fall of 1770, carefully examining lands from Pittsburgh to the mouth of the Great Kanawha, two hundred miles downstream.

Washington's acquisition of lands on the Ohio had its counterpart in his ambitious plan to improve transportation links between the Potomac (on which Mount Vernon and his primary Tidewater holdings were located) and the Ohio country. Key to this scheme was the formation of a canal company to make the Potomac "the Channel of conveyance of the

Virginia, ſſ.

By the Hon. *ROBERT DINWIDDIE*, Eſq; His Majeſty's Lieutenant-Governor, and Commander in Chief of this Dominion.

A PROCLAMATION,

For Encouraging MEN to enliſt in his Majeſty's Service for the Defence and Security of this Colony.

WHEREAS it is determined that a Fort be immediately built on the River *Ohio*, at the Fork of *Monongahela*, to oppoſe any further Encroachments, or hoſtile Attempts of the *French*, and the *Indians* in their Intereſt, and for the Security and Protection of his Majeſty's Subjects in this Colony; and as it is abſolutely neceſſary that a ſufficient Force ſhould be raiſed to erect and ſupport the ſame: For an Encouragement to all who ſhall voluntarily enter into the ſaid Service, I do hereby notify and promiſe, by and with the Advice and Conſent of his Majeſty's Council of this Colony, that over and above their Pay, Two Hundred Thouſand Acres, of his Majeſty the King of *Great-Britain*'s Lands, on the Eaſt Side of the River *Ohio*, within this Dominion, (One Hundred Thouſand Acres whereof to be contiguous to the ſaid Fort, and the other Hundred Thouſand Acres to be on, or near the River *Ohio*) ſhall be laid off and granted to ſuch Perſons, who by their voluntary Engagement, and good Behaviour in the ſaid Service, ſhall deſerve the ſame. And I further promiſe, that the ſaid Lands ſhall be divided amongſt them immediately after the Performance of the ſaid Service, in a Proportion due to their reſpective Merit, as ſhall be repreſented to me by their Officers, and held and enjoyed by them without paying any Rights, and alſo free from the Payment of Quit-rents, for the Term of Fifteen Years. And I do appoint this Proclamation to be read and publiſhed at the Court-Houſes, Churches and Chapels in each County within this Colony, and that the Sheriffs take Care the ſame be done accordingly.

Given at the Council-Chamber in *Williamsburg*, on the 19th Day of *February*, in the 27th Year of his Majeſty's Reign, *Annoque Domini* 1754.

ROBERT DINWIDDIE.

GOD Save the KING.

Robert Dinwiddie, "A PROCLAMATION, For Encouraging MEN to enlist in his Majesty's Service . . . February 19, 1754." *Virginia offered shares in 200,000 acres of land near the Forks of the Ohio as an inducement to enlist in the 1754 campaign. Following the fall of Canada, Washington began purchasing fellow veterans' certificates, amassing claims to 45,000 acres of western land. His ability to secure possession of this vast estate depended on the impermanence of the 1763 Proclamation Line and the cooperation of imperial officials.* (This item is reproduced by permission of *The Huntington Library, San Marino, California*)

extensive & valuable Trade of a rising Empire" in the West, connected to the Ohio by Braddock's Road and the Youghiogheny and Monongahela rivers. That this rising empire would be British went without saying. A pair of agreements negotiated between the crown and major Indian groups in 1768 seemed to suggest that it was only a matter of time before the Proclamation would be rescinded. The Treaty of Hard Labor and the Treaty of Fort Stanwix both grew out of attempts to define a secure boundary between Indian and white settlement in the aftermath of Pontiac's War. By the former the Cherokees, and by the latter the Six Nations ceded their claims to certain lands south of the Ohio to the crown in return for large diplomatic gifts. Since neither group exercised any real control over the Ohio—the Delawares, Shawnees, Mingo Seneca, and others who lived there remained stubbornly unwilling to forgo their own claims to independence, and to the land—these treaties marked only a partial advance toward stabilizing Indian relations in the interior. Nonetheless, to Washington and other speculators, they seemed to herald an era in which the Ohio country would be opened to white settlement. Washington accordingly devoted immense attention to positioning himself to take advantage of his claims when the longed-for day finally dawned.

Washington's future-oriented thinking disposed him to political moderation when Parliament once again tried its hand at reforming imperial governance in the Townshend Acts, and triggered a second postwar crisis in colonial-metropolitan relations. Washington helped draw up the covenant of the Virginia Non-Importation Association in 1769 and joined in boycotting trade with Britain as a means of protesting the Townshend duties, but this still indicated no revolutionary sentiments. He objected not to the empire but rather to the way it was currently being run. Meanwhile the trade boycott gave him and his fellow gentlemen a chance to reduce their consumption of the manufactures that were running them ever more deeply into debt. When a new ministry headed by Frederick, Lord North, repealed all of the duties except a symbolic tax on tea imports to the colonies in 1770, Washington gratefully joined with other moderates in relaxing the nonimportation agreements. As business-as-usual resumed within the empire and the long postwar recession seemed finally to be at an end, support for nonimportation declined. By mid-1771 the boycotts had collapsed altogether and colonists resumed their habit of consuming vast quantities of affordable, high-quality British manufactures.

The arrival that autumn of John Murray, Lord Dunmore, as Virginia's new governor offered cause for further optimism about the future. Dunmore had an intense interest in developing the Ohio country, and no excessively scrupulous view of the Proclamation of 1763. Over the next year and a half Washington and Dunmore built a cordial relationship around their common goals in the West—so much so that Washington offered to act as the governor's personal guide on a tour of the Ohio Valley in the summer of 1773.

A family emergency—the sudden death of Martha's daughter Patsy—kept Washington from making good on that offer, and in the end Dunmore went west himself. What the governor saw in the vicinity of Pittsburgh—by his estimate, at least ten thousand white settlers illegally inhabiting lands that were supposed to be reserved for Indians—made him determined to extend Virginia's jurisdiction over the region by expanding the bounds of Augusta County to the north and west. The Penn family, who as proprietors of Pennsylvania had as plausible a claim to the region as Virginia, did not relish the thought of another colony's government issuing patents to legalize the holdings of the local settlers and thus depriving them of the opportunity to sell the land and diminishing the tax base of Pennsylvania as well. The Penns therefore moved to organize the area around Pittsburgh as Westmoreland County, appointing magistrates to counter those of Virginia. By the spring of 1774 competition between the two colonies over control of the area had grown so intense as to suggest that civil war might break out between pro-Pennsylvania and pro-Virginia settlers.

Meanwhile the empire had entered a third phase of crisis with Parliament's passage of the Tea Act. Lord North's administration had intended this measure to bail out the British East India Company, which had sustained such expenses as a result of the Seven Years' War that by 1773 it was in immediate danger of going bankrupt. His Majesty's government lacked surplus funds to offer as a direct subsidy, and the company had no assets to liquidate, apart from the 17,000,000 pounds of tea that lay in its English warehouses—an amount so vast that to sell it would have glutted the British market, rendering the tea worthless. The Tea Act was brilliant insofar as granting the company a monopoly on tea sales in the colonies could be expected to transmute those 17,000,000 pounds of otherwise unmerchantable leaves into the money it desperately needed. Yet inasmuch as the one duty that remained unrepealed from the Townshend Acts was a tax on tea imports, the Tea Act was a fiasco. Protests erupted everywhere in the colonies over what the colonists (their ideological sensitivity raised by the two previous crises of empire) understood as a subtle and devious parliamentary effort to tax them without their consent. The protests largely remained contained, except in Boston, where, for a variety of local reasons, things got out of hand. On the night of December 16, 1773, radical protesters disguised as Mohawk Indians destroyed tea worth £11,000 sterling by dumping it over the gunwales of East India Company vessels, into Boston Harbor. It was a provocation too extreme for His Majesty's government to ignore. For the good of the empire as a whole, Lord North and his fellow ministers agreed, Boston had to be chastised, and shown the error of its ways.

The example Britain made of Boston taught a very clear lesson indeed, but not one that wiser heads might have chosen, for it demonstrated above all the extent of Britain's sovereign power over the colonies—precisely the sort of unlimited power that colonial radicals had warned against since 1765. In swift sequence North's ministry closed the port of Boston, rewrote the Massachusetts charter to reduce the extent of representative government, limited the authority of Massachusetts's courts to prosecute royal officers accused of crimes, assigned more than four thousand soldiers to occupy the town, and appointed the American commander in chief, Lieutenant General Thomas Gage, as the governor of the province.

Everywhere protests blossomed in support of Boston. In Virginia even moderate politicians (including Colonel Washington) joined in passing a resolution in the House of Burgesses on May 24, 1774, calling for a day of prayer and fasting in solidarity with the suffering Bostonians. Governor Dunmore, furious at what he regarded as an offense against the king's majesty, summarily dissolved the House. Washington joined his fellow burgesses in adjourning to a nearby tavern. There they reconstituted themselves as a Convention and voted to invite Virginia's "Sister Colonies" to meet with it in a Continental Congress, so that they could jointly consider "such Measures as shall be judged most effectual for the Common Rights and Liberty of British America."

It was in this context of political unrest that Dunmore, thinking he could defuse opposition to the crown and Parliament, ordered the militia regiments of western Virginia to stand ready to defend the frontier against Indian attacks and called for twenty-four hundred volunteers to undertake a campaign against the Shawnee Indians in the Ohio Valley. The occasion for this expedition, and what came to be called Lord Dunmore's War, was entirely trumped up. Disorganized violence between natives and whites was endemic on the Ohio, so the killing of three traders by Cherokee warriors in April had been far from an unusual event. But Lord Dunmore's supporters in Pittsburgh quite calculatedly chose to blame the murders on the Shawnees who lived north of the Ohio in the Scioto Valley and claimed lands on the opposite bank as their hunting grounds, because the Shawnees had taken no part in the Treaty of Hard Labor or the Treaty of Fort Stanwix. Not participating in those agreements had made the Shawnees the last plausible Indian claimants to the lands immediately south of the Ohio; because they actually used the region for their livelihood (unlike the Cherokees and the Iroquois), they were unlikely to surrender their rights to it. It therefore made enormous sense to Dunmore and his supporters at Pittsburgh to force a war against them, no matter how specious the grounds were, so that Virginia could claim the area by right of conquest. To do so would clear the way, once the Proclamation of 1763 was revoked, for Virginia to extend its jurisdiction over the whole southern half of the Ohio Valley.

This titanic landgrab was precisely what Dunmore had in mind when he ordered the raising of more troops than Virginia had ever fielded to defend its frontier during the last war; but more than mere conquest was on Dunmore's mind as he led the troops west to attack the Shawnees in September and October 1774. It was at that same moment exactly that the delegates of the First Continental Congress, George Washington among them, were meeting in Philadelphia. What Dunmore intended was to join the interest of the land-speculating gentry in acquiring Ohio lands with the impassioned Indian-hating of white Virginians generally, in order to divert attention from the Continental Congress's protests and build support for himself and the empire.

Lord Dunmore knew that the irritation of the Virginians with Parliament had at least as much to do with restrictions on western settlement as it did with the occupation of Boston and the summary remodeling of Massachusetts's governmental institutions. He was gambling that a successful strike at the Shawnees would make him a hero and yield such a fund of goodwill for the empire that Virginia's leaders would back off from their support of the Bostonians and let matters take their course. Once that wretched city had been taught its lesson and Britain's sovereign authority had been firmly reestablished, both he and the power of the crown would be in a stronger position than they had ever been in Virginia. It was true, of course, that Dunmore was launching an utterly unauthorized war of conquest to attain these ends. It was also true that the stakes were high enough that he was prepared to risk censure or dismissal in order to attain the rewards, for the empire and himself alike, that a successful campaign might bring.

Dunmore very nearly succeeded; indeed, had success not tempted him to overplay his hand, he might well have done so. A battle between Shawnee warriors and half of the Virginia forces at a bend in the river called Point Pleasant, on October 10, 1774, enabled him to claim a victory. The subsequent decision by peace-minded Shawnee chiefs to accept an armistice, temporarily suspend hunting south of the Ohio, and attend a peace conference the next spring created an illusion of conquest sufficiently strong that upon his return Dunmore found himself lionized among the gentry. When a new Virginia Convention assembled in March 1775 to choose delegates to the Second Continental Congress, the members issued a formal resolution that praised Dunmore "for his truly noble, wise and spirited Conduct on the late Expedition against our Indian Enemy." Colonel Washington, whom the Convention chose as a delegate to the Congress precisely because his views were so temperate, joined in the applause. He continued to nurture the hope that the divisions within the empire could be amicably resolved and that settlement in the interior might at last proceed in the way he had longed to see.

Three occurrences following closely upon one another in April destroyed Washington's faith that all might yet be well. The first was personal. On April 18 Governor Dunmore, believing himself in a strong position, declared his intent to invalidate, on purely technical grounds, Washington's title to the forty-five thousand acres of Ohio land he had patented within the Virginia Regiment's claim. It seems clear that Dunmore had thought that doing so would force Washington to reconsider his connection to the intercolonial protest movement, and perhaps to absent himself from the upcoming Congress. Washington, astonished and outraged, was still trying to understand the meaning of the governor's act when Dunmore struck again. On April 21, in an evident attempt to bring the population of Virginia's capital to its knees, he ordered Williamsburg's

***John Murray, Fourth Earl of Dunmore,* by Sir Joshua Reynolds, 1765.** *The Scottish Lord Dunmore (1732–1809) found common cause with George Washington in asserting Virginia's control of lands in the Ohio Valley. Dunmore's 1774 campaign against the Shawnee Indians in the Ohio country, which opened the prospect of seizing lands between the Appalachian Mountains and the Ohio River, boosted the governor's popularity with the Virginia gentry.* (Scottish National Portrait Gallery, Edinburgh)

entire stock of gunpowder to be secretly removed from the town's magazine and taken on board the Royal Navy's station ship, H.M.S. *Fowey.* This was ostensibly to protect the powder supply, but it happened when rumors of a slave conspiracy were flying up and down the James River Valley, and it set not only the capital but the province in an uproar. Virginia's leaders were still attempting by pleas and threats to make Dunmore return the powder when news arrived on April 28 that formations of Massachusetts militia had clashed with His Majesty's troops outside Boston nine days before. The disorderly day-long Battle of Lexington and Concord had left seventy-three regulars and forty-nine militiamen dead, and hundreds more wounded. Reports that followed in rapid succession revealed that thousands of militiamen from all four New England colonies had massed outside Boston, laying siege to the city and effectively trapping General Gage and his soldiers inside.

All three events, occurring within ten days' time, help explain Washington's decision to attend the meetings of the Second Continental Congress wearing the blue-and-buff uniform of the Fairfax Independent militia company. At every level he could understand—as a speculator, as a Virginian, as an American colonist—these events had shown the abusive exercise of power that such radicals as Thomas Jefferson and John Adams had warned against. Unlike those men, Washington was not a particularly sophisticated political thinker. But he was a matchlessly astute judge of men and events, and what he had seen told him that arguments alone would no longer protect his and other colonists' rights. It was now clear that the empire he and other Americans had dreamed of since the war—the transatlantic partnership of Britons who would carry English institutions and laws into the heart of the conquests they had won together—had no place in the thinking of the men who made imperial policy at Whitehall and Westminster.

The master of Mount Vernon had seen enough of human bondage to understand that what distinguished free men from slaves were the rights that protected individuals from those who wished to exercise absolute power over them. He had seen enough of war to know that once men had shed each other's blood in a dispute over fundamental principles, they were unlikely to stop until one side had bent the other to its will, or both sides had reached exhaustion. The hard schooling he had undergone between 1754 and 1758 had taught him that wars could best be won by those who fought by the disciplined codes of European regular officers, and indeed that military professionalism was perhaps the only way to limit the destructiveness of armed conflict.

Washington knew war too well to welcome it in 1775, but when his fellow delegates at the Congress offered him the command of the provincial troops besieging Boston, he accepted with little hesitation. Better perhaps than any other delegate present at Philadelphia on June 16, 1775, the day he formally took up his commission, he understood what suffering and sacrifice lay ahead. Because he understood so much, he doubted that his experiences and training had adequately prepared him for what he called "the Command I am honoured with." Yet because his honor was at stake and his countrymen's rights and the future for which he had striven were at risk, he could not decline.

And there was another factor in his decision as well. He hinted at it on June 18 when he wrote to tell Martha that he would not be coming home as planned, but leaving for Massachusetts and the provincial forces who had just been designated as the Continental Army. "I shall rely . . . confidently," he wrote, "on that Providence which has heretofore preserv[e]d, & been bountiful to me, not doubting that I shall return safe to you in the fall—I shall feel no pain from the Toil, or the danger of the Campaign—My unhappiness will [only] flow, from the uneasiness I know you will feel at being left alone." Washington was not a particularly religious man in conventional terms: he attended Anglican services dutifully enough, but consistently left church before communion, rarely spoke of Christ, gave little credence to miracles, and seemed lukewarm even in his affiliation with the Freemasons. Nonetheless, he deeply felt that the power he called Providence (or, on other occasions, the Author of the Universe, the Great Ruler of Events, the Supreme Being, God) ordered the world and its events. He knew that in the late war his life had been spared on several occasions. He did not understand why, but trusted that there must have been some reason behind his survival, some purpose he had yet to serve. God knew what purpose that might be; he did not. But that did not make him believe in it less.

A year later, when the siege of Boston had been carried to its successful end and Washington had moved his headquarters to New York to oppose the coming British invasion, it would at least have been clear to him that his role in an unfolding drama of revolutionary war was no incidental one. Nor, obviously, was it to be any easier than the difficult part he had played in the war for empire. That was why, on July 9, 1776—the same day he ordered his men to assemble on parade to hear the Declaration of Independence read out by their battalion officers—he paused to make a "grateful remembrance" of his "escape . . . on the Banks of Monongahela," twenty-one years before. This was why he hoped, as he wrote to the old comrade who had shared in that adventure, that "the same Provedence that protected us" then, would "continue his Mercies, and make us happy Instruments in restoring Peace & liberty to this once favour'd, but now distressed Country."

Great as the perils that faced him in 1776 were, and as long as the odds against success seemed as twenty-five thousand redcoats backed by the most powerful fleet on earth prepared to attack his much smaller army, there is no indication that Washington worried much about what, precisely,

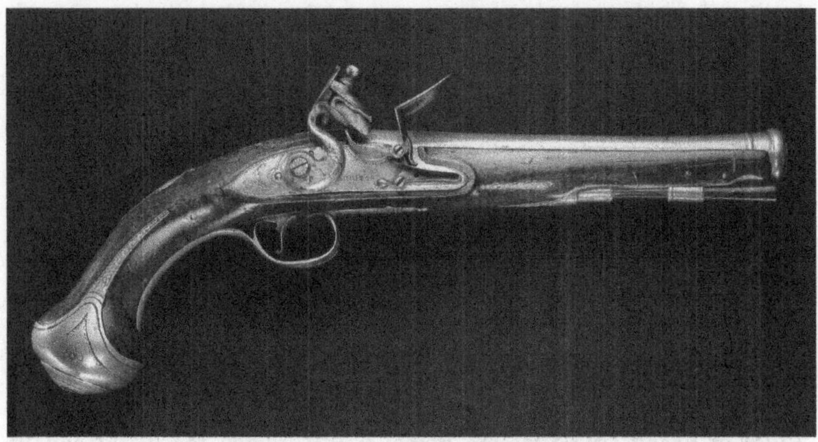

Holster pistol, c. 1750. *The British general Edward Braddock gave this pistol to his young aide George Washington during the 1755 campaign against Fort Duquesne. In 1777 Washington (or one of his servants) temporarily misplaced it, revealing his sentimental attachment to the piece. "His Excellency is much exercised over the loss of this pistol," an associate noted, "it being given to him by Gen. Braddock, and having since been with him through several campaigns, and he therefore values it highly."* (Smithsonian Institution)

his destiny might be. There would have been little point in doing so, for as he explained much later, "the great ruler of events" alone knew the purpose of whatever happened on earth. Therefore, he believed, "we may safely trust the issue to him, without perplexing ourselves to seek for that, which is beyond human ken; only taking care to perform the parts assigned us, in a way that reason and our own conscience approve of."

It was an austere faith, but a real one. His duty lay before him. That was enough.

Epilogue: Legacies

Twenty years later, in the summer of 1796, President George Washington found himself contemplating how best to announce to his fellow Americans that he would return to private life. After seven years as chief executive he had grown weary of public office, and felt that he might not have long to live. What time remained he intended to spend at Mount Vernon, under (as he put it) his own "vine and fig tree," far from the bitter partisan wrangling that had overtaken the United States during his second term of office. Yet as much as his quarrelsome countrymen had disappointed him, he had not yet given up on them, and was determined to leave them with a Farewell Address pointing out how they might still preserve the values of the Revolution and fulfill its liberating potential. Above all, he cautioned, Americans must "guard against the Intreigues of *any* and *every* foreign Nation," avoiding all entanglements with European powers while concentrating on developing the interior of the continent. If the United States could avoid war for even a generation and build unity through strength at home, it would become truly independent: a nation able "to bid defiance, in a just cause, to any earthly power whatsoever."

It was a fundamentally imperial prescription for the future of the Republic, and so far as Washington was concerned, there was nothing ironic in that at all. His whole adult life, in one way or another, had tended toward opening the interior of North America to orderly colonization. In 1754 he had first tried to impose British imperial order on the Ohio country—and failed, triggering the war that changed the landscape of power in America forever. Forty years later, in 1794, he had overseen two military campaigns that subordinated that region and its peoples to the authority of the United States. With the suppression of the Whiskey Rebellion at Pittsburgh and the defeat of the Ohio Valley Indian peoples at the Battle of Fallen Timbers, the United States had succeeded where Britain failed, proving itself capable of projecting military power west of the Appalachians, and thus of exercising dominion as far as the Mississippi. What remained now was for the citizens of the Republic to occupy, settle, and civilize that vast realm in a way consistent with the liberties that the Revolution had secured. To do less would be to betray its promise.

By the time Washington died, in 1799, white American citizens were marshaling their strength to conquer the continent, and their first staging ground for that long campaign would be Pittsburgh. They would not do it in the systematic way that Washington had intended, but in a democratic and disorderly fashion that nevertheless proved highly effective. Before another half-century had passed, these triumphant, populist empire-builders would come to believe that the existence of their nation and its expansion across North America had somehow been inevitable all along, and that Washington's role in starting it had been divinely ordained. They did not understand how the barely remembered imperial war that began Washington's military career had created the conditions that made it possible for the America they knew—the spread-eagle, expansionist republic of Andrew Jackson and James Knox Polk—to extend its sway across ever-greater territories until it spanned the continent.

Yet it had been the French and Indian War that removed the French imperial presence from America and deprived the Indians of the ally they needed to arm them against the Anglo-American settlers who lusted after their lands. It had been Britain's unexampled victory in that war that tempted the men who governed the British empire to imagine that their military and naval supremacy was such that they could solve the massive problems of the postwar era by exercising power over the American colonists without restraint. It had been that war that inspired the colonists to conceive of themselves as equal partners in the empire, ultimately enabling them to rebel against Britain's sovereign power in the name of liberty. Finally, by encouraging the Americans to see Indians as enemies to be hated without reserve or distinction, that war had encouraged them, in the midst of Revolution and afterward, to see native peoples as impediments to the expansion of freedom in North America, who could justly be attacked and rightly be subdued. In all these ways the French and Indian War opened the door to Revolution and to the destruction or subjugation of native societies west of the Appalachian Mountains.

When a desperate Indian chief murdered a French ensign before a young Virginian's horrified eyes in 1754, then, an old world—one in which native peoples played determining roles in diplomacy and war—began to pass away. Within a half-century it was gone forever. Today its traces linger mainly in the names—Allegheny, Youghiogheny, Monongahela, Ohio—that forgotten peoples gave to places that we now claim as our own. That we remember so little of this earlier world—and understand so little of its peoples and their ways—bears witness to the evanescence of all historical worlds, including the one that we ourselves inhabit. In that sense, to grasp the story of the great transformation that the French and Indian War began is above all to understand it as a cautionary tale: one that demonstrates the unpredictability and irony that always attend the pursuit of power, reminding us that even the most complete victories can sow the seeds of reversal and defeat for victors too dazzled by success to remember that they are, in fact, only human.

Bibliographic Note

It is a truth universally acknowledged, that a historian who possesses the hope of reaching a wide audience must be eager to flee from footnotes.

Well, perhaps not universally acknowledged, but a common enough assumption, and not really true at all. What *would* be universally acknowledged among historians is that writing without footnotes, whether in textbooks or in popular histories, makes us uneasy. Notes give us a sense of security, in the knowledge that our peers will find us honest in our use of their work and that of other scholars. Writing without them, on the other hand, creates unfamiliar anxieties, particularly the fear of inadvertent plagiarism. I hope that I have not been guilty of this, but as the sentence above will attest, memorable phrases are apt to stick in my brain. Thus when I tipped my hat to *Pride and Prejudice* just now, I did so not only to make my own prose seem a little less gray, but also to pay a small tribute to a writer whose wit and style I greatly admire. When it comes to the writings of my fellow historians, on the other hand, I have done my best to paraphrase only, recounting their interpretations at what I hope is at least a good arm's length from their own words. Should any author find that I have failed in this, I can only apologize in the hope she or he can somehow understand it as an unintended example of the kind of homage I more consciously wanted to pay Austen. For I am in fact deeply grateful to many historians, living and dead, without whose work I could never have written this book.

Most of those secondary sources on which I have drawn can be found cited in the notes of a longer book I wrote several years ago, *Crucible of War: The Seven Years' War and the Fate of Empire in British North America, 1754–1766* (New York: Alfred A. Knopf, 2000), and in the relevant sections of a work that Andrew Cayton and I published more recently, *The Dominion of War: Empire and Liberty in North America, 1500–2000* (New York: Viking, 2005); see especially pages 85–206. This essay, therefore, is less an attempt to be exhaustive than an effort to point out books and articles that are of particular value, and to identify important works that have appeared since *Crucible of War*, or of which I was unaware when I wrote.

The starting point in the historiography of the Seven Years' War in America is of course Francis Parkman's masterpiece, *Montcalm and Wolfe*, 2 vols. (Boston: Little, Brown & Company, 1884)—a work that reflects the racial and religious attitudes of patrician Americans in the late nineteenth century, but which continues to delight readers with the sheer force and vigor of its narrative. All American histories of the war, this one included, are in some measure commentaries on Parkman. This is also true of those written from a Canadian perspective, beginning with Abbé H. R. Casgrain's *Wolfe and Montcalm* (Toronto: Morang & Company, 1905; reprinted by the University of Toronto Press, 1964). For more up-to-date Canadian histories of the war see especially Guy Frégault, *Canada: The War of the Conquest* (Toronto: Oxford University Press, 1969); George F. G. Stanley, *New France: The Last Phase, 1744–1760* (Toronto: McClelland and Stewart, 1968); several pungent essays by W. J. Eccles (notably "The History of New France According to Francis Parkman," "New France and the Western Frontier," "The Social, Economic, and Political Significance of the Military Establishment in New France," "The Battle of Quebec: A Reappraisal," and "Sovereignty Association 1500–1783"), all of which have been collected in his *Essays on New France* (Toronto: Oxford University Press, 1987); and the last two chapters of Eccles's synthesis, *France in America* (East Lansing, Mich.: Michigan State University Press, 1990).

The Seven Years' War was of course a worldwide conflict, and the historiography of its European and other aspects grows from concerns and traditions that have little to do with Parkman, except insofar as authors have habitually mined his work for background material on the American war. The most nearly comprehensive work dealing with Britain's military, naval, and diplomatic history in the conflict remains Julian S. Corbett, *England in the Seven Years' War: A Study in Combined Strategy*, 2 vols. (London: Longmans, Green & Company, 1907), while for France it is Richard Waddington, *La guerre de sept ans: histoire diplomatique et militaire*, 5 vols. (Paris: Firmin-Didot et Cie., 1899–1914). For the German war in the east, see the relevant portions of Dennis Showalter, *The Wars of Frederick the Great* (New York: Longman, 1996); in the west, Reginald Savory, *His Britannic Majesty's Army in Germany during the Seven Years' War* (Oxford: Oxford University Press, 1966); and, generally, Russell Weigley, *The Age of Battles: The Quest for Decisive Warfare from Breitenfeld to Waterloo* (Bloomington: Indiana University Press, 1991). A forthcoming work by Paul W. Mapp will illuminate the diplomacy of the war's origins and progress as no other book has; until it is published, readers should consult his Ph.D. dissertation, "European Geographic Ignorance and North American Imperial Rivalry: The Role of the Uncharted American West in International Affairs, 1713–1763" (Harvard University, 2001; available from ProQuest/University Microfilms International, Ann Arbor, Michigan, publication No. AAT 3011433, ISBN 0493214216).

No history has yet encompassed the entire war. The one that comes closest is Lawrence Henry Gipson, *The British Empire Before the American Revolution*, 15 vols.

(Caldwell, Idaho, and New York: Caxton Printers and Alfred A. Knopf, 1936–1970). The three central volumes of this magnum opus deal directly with the Seven Years' War, forming a subseries entitled *The Great War for the Empire.* That title, as well as those of volumes 6, 7, and 8—*The Years of Defeat, The Victorious Years,* and *The Culmination*—bears witness to the fundamental Anglocentrism of Gipson's account. Nevertheless, this great work remains a landmark of twentieth-century historical scholarship and a monument to Gipson's industry, integrity, and erudition. Several general narratives have appeared in recent years. Among these, see especially William M. Fowler Jr.'s excellent and highly readable *Empires at War: The French and Indian War and the Struggle for North America* (New York: Walker & Company, 2004); the three volumes by William R. Nester, *The Great Frontier War: Britain, France, and the Imperial Struggle for North America, 1607–1755* (Westport, Conn.: Praeger, 2000), *The First World War: Britain, France, and the Fate of North America, 1756–1775* (2001), and *"Haughty Conquerors": Amherst and the Great Indian Uprising of 1763* (2000); and Frank W. Brecher, *Losing a Continent: France's North American Policy, 1753–1763* (Westport, Conn.: Greenwood, 1998). Given the severe limitations on length imposed by the publisher, two slender illustrated volumes by Daniel Marston do a remarkably good job of narrating the major campaigns: *The Seven Years' War* (Oxford: Osprey, 2001) and *The French-Indian War, 1754–1760* (Oxford: Osprey, 2002). Seymour I. Schwartz, *The French and Indian War, 1754–1763: The Imperial Struggle for North America* (New York: Simon & Schuster, 1994; reprinted Edison, N.J.: Castle Books, 2000), supports a splendid set of reproduced period maps, portraits, and views with a concise narrative of the campaigns.

Francis Jennings, who dedicated his scholarly career to counteracting what he saw as Parkman's distortions and misrepresentations, produced a body of work essential to modern understandings of the French and Indian War. *The Ambiguous Iroquois Empire: The Covenant Chain Confederation of Indian Tribes with English Colonies from Its Beginnings to the Lancaster Treaty of 1744* (New York: W. W. Norton, 1984) and *Empire of Fortune: Crowns, Colonies, and Tribes in the Seven Years War in America* (New York: W. W. Norton, 1988) are sometimes intemperate but always important in placing Indians at the center of the war's events. *The Creation of America: Through Revolution to Empire* (New York: Cambridge University Press, 2000) was his heroic attempt, at the very end of his life, to work out the implications for the Revolutionary and early national periods of the story he had begun in those earlier volumes.

Other scholars of the native experience have extended our understanding of the era of the Seven Years' War beyond Jennings's work. Notable among those later contributions are Daniel K. Richter's masterful synthesis, *Facing East from Indian Country: A Native History of Early America* (Cambridge, Mass.: Harvard University Press, 2001); Richard White, *The Middle Ground: Indians, Republics, and Empires in the Great Lakes Region, 1650–1815* (New York: Cambridge University Press, 1991), a seminal work in the field; James H. Merrell, *Into the American Woods: Negotiators on the Pennsylvania Frontier* (New York: Norton, 1999), an eloquent and moving examination of the limits of accommodation; Michael N. McConnell, *A Country Between: The Upper*

Ohio Valley and Its Peoples, 1724–1774 (Lincoln: University of Nebraska Press, 1992); Colin G. Calloway, *The Western Abenakis of Vermont, 1600–1800: War, Migration, and Survival* (Norman: University of Oklahoma Press, 1990); Gregory Evans Dowd, *A Spirited Resistance: The North American Indian Struggle for Unity, 1745–1815* (Baltimore, Md.: Johns Hopkins University Press, 1992) and *War Under Heaven: Pontiac, the Indian Nations and the British Empire* (Baltimore, Md.: Johns Hopkins University Press, 2002); D. Peter MacLeod, *The Canadian Iroquois and the Seven Years War* (Toronto: Dundurn Press, 1996); Richard Aquila, *The Iroquois Restoration: Iroquois Diplomacy on the Colonial Frontier, 1701–1754* (Detroit : Wayne State University Press, 1983); Jane Merritt, *At the Crossroads: Indians and Empires on a Mid-Atlantic Frontier, 1700–1763* (Chapel Hill: University of North Carolina Press, 2003); and Tom Hatley, *The Dividing Paths: Cherokees and South Carolinians through the Era of Revolution* (New York: Oxford University Press, 1993).

Works on empire and its shaping influence on North American (and, more broadly, Atlantic) history have lately regained interest and influence, and complement the new scholarship on Indians. Some older works retain great value. In addition to Gipson's fifteen volumes, cited above, see especially Stanley M. Pargellis, *Lord Loudoun in North America* (New Haven, Conn.: Yale University Press, 1933; reprinted New York: Archon, 1968); Richard Pares, *War and Trade in the West Indies, 1739–1763* (Oxford: Oxford University Press, 1936); and Clarence W. Alvord, *The Mississippi Valley in British Politics: A Study of Trade, Land Speculation, and Experiments in Imperialism Culminating in the American Revolution*, 2 vols. (Cleveland, Ohio.: Arthur H. Clark Company, 1917), a remarkable work updated and extended by Jack M. Sosin in *Whitehall and the Wilderness: The Middle West in British Colonial Policy, 1760–1775* (Lincoln: University of Nebraska Press, 1961).

Several newer works on empire stand out for the creative and powerful ways in which they have built on this older scholarship. The articles in *The Oxford History of the British Empire*, vol. 2: *The Eighteenth Century*, ed. P. J. Marshall (New York: Oxford University Press, 1998), offer excellent summaries of recent developments. Alison Gilbert Olson takes a transatlantic perspective in *Making the Empire Work: London and American Interest Groups, 1690–1790* (Cambridge, Mass.: Harvard University Press, 1992). Eric Hinderaker, *Elusive Empires: Constructing Colonialism in the Ohio Valley, 1673–1800* (New York: Cambridge University Press, 1997), brilliantly treats empire on the ground level as a set of negotiated cultural relations, a conceptualization that Timothy J. Shannon develops with great success in *Indians and Colonists at the Crossroads of Empire* (Ithaca, N.Y.: Cornell University Press, 2002). A somewhat older work, Alan Rogers's *Empire and Liberty: American Resistance to British Authority, 1755–1763* (Berkeley: University of California Press, 1975), examines the strains that the war imposed on Britain's transatlantic political community.

Several important books examine the British empire and its politics principally from the metropolitan perspective. In this connection, see especially Eliga H. Gould, *The Persistence of Empire: British Political Culture in the Age of the American Revolution* (Chapel Hill: University of North Carolina Press for the Omohundro Institute of

Early American History and Culture, 2000); John Brewer, *The Sinews of Power: War, Money and the English State, 1688–1783* (New York: Alfred A. Knopf, 1989); Richard Middleton, *The Bells of Victory: The Pitt-Newcastle Ministry and the Conduct of the Seven Years' War, 1757–1762* (Cambridge: Cambridge University Press, 1985); David Armitage, *The Ideological Origins of the British Empire* (New York: Cambridge University Press, 2000); and Linda Colley, *Britons: Forging the Nation, 1707–1837* (New Haven: Yale University Press, 1992) and *Captives* (New York: Pantheon, 2002). The latter, addressing the general experience and significance of those members of the imperial community taken prisoner by unsubjugated peoples on the periphery, has a more closely focused American counterpart in June Namias, *White Captives: Gender and Ethnicity on the American Frontier* (Chapel Hill: University of North Carolina Press, 1993). For an illuminating comparison between the major European imperialisms, see Anthony Pagden, *Lords of All the World: Ideologies of Empire in Spain, Britain, and France, c.1500–c.1800* (New Haven, Conn.: Yale University Press, 1998). Pagden takes an even broader view in *Peoples and Empires: A Short History of European Migration, Exploration, and Conquest, from Greece to the Present* (New York: Modern Library, 2001).

War, of course, was one of the principal engines by which imperial identities and structures of governance took shape. General works dealing with the projection of military power, its consequences, limits, and ironies include John Shy's classic account, *Toward Lexington: The British Army and the Coming of the American Revolution* (Princeton: Princeton University Press, 1965). A recent book by Stephen Brumwell, *Redcoats: The British Soldier and War in the Americas, 1755–1763* (New York: Cambridge University Press, 2002), complements it nicely with a greater emphasis on social history. Two fine books by Douglas Edward Leach, *Arms for Empire: A Military History of the British Colonies in North America, 1607–1763* (New York: Macmillan, 1973) and *Roots of Conflict: British Armed Forces and Colonial Americans, 1677–1763* (Chapel Hill: University of North Carolina Press, 1986), narrate and analyze eighteenth-century war and empire within an essentially North American frame of reference. The standard narrative account of colonial warfare is Ian K. Steele, *Warpaths: Invasions of America* (New York: Oxford University Press, 1994). A provocative, brief, and brilliant analysis of the topic can be found in John Grenier, *The First Way of War: American War Making on the Frontier, 1607–1814* (New York: Cambridge University Press, 2005).

Several local studies, dealing with colonies or regions and their societies, treat the war's impact from a variety of perspectives. These include Fred Anderson, *A People's Army: Massachusetts Soldiers and Society in the Seven Years' War* (Chapel Hill: University of North Carolina Press for the Institute of Early American History and Culture, 1984); Kerry A. Trask, *In Pursuit of Shadows: Massachusetts Millennialism and the Seven Years' War* (New York: Garland, 1989); William Pencak, *War, Politics and Revolution in Provincial Massachusetts* (Boston: Northeastern University Press, 1981); Harold E. Selesky, *War and Society in Colonial Connecticut* (New Haven, Conn.: Yale University Press, 1990); James Titus, *The Old Dominion at War: Society, Politics, and Warfare in Late Colonial Virginia* (Columbia, S.C.: University of South Carolina Press, 1991);

Matthew Ward, *Breaking the Backcountry: The Seven Years' War in Virginia and Pennsylvania* (Pittsburgh, Pa.: University of Pittsburgh Press, 2004); Stephen F. Auth, *The Ten Years' War: Indian-White Relations in Pennsylvania, 1755–1765* (New York: Garland, 1989); Geoffrey Plank, *An Unsettled Conquest: The British Campaign Against the Peoples of Acadia* (Philadelphia: University of Pennsylvania Press, 2001); and John Mack Faragher, *A Great and Noble Scheme: The Tragic Story of the Expulsion of the French Acadians from their American Homeland* (New York: W. W. Norton, 2005). A forthcoming work by Jay Cassel will treat the colony regular troops of New France in greater depth than any previous account; until it appears, consult his Ph.D. dissertation, "The *Troupes de La Marine* in Canada, 1683–1760: Men and Matériel" (University of Toronto, 1988; ProQuest/University Microfilms Publication No. AAT NL43490, ISBN: 0315434902).

Studies of battles, campaigns, and even an individual year of the Seven Years' War add considerable depth to the broader narratives of the conflict. On Braddock's defeat, see Paul Kopperman, *Braddock at the Monongahela* (Pittsburgh, Pa.: University of Pittsburgh Press, 1977; reprinted, 2003). The siege of Fort William Henry and its tragic aftermath receive definitive treatment in Ian Steele's *Betrayals: Fort William Henry and the "Massacre"* (New York: Oxford University Press, 1990). Brian Leigh Dunnigan, *Siege—1759: The Campaign Against Niagara* (Youngstown, N.Y.: Old Fort Niagara Association, 1996), provides a similarly comprehensive view of that critical event. C. P. Stacey's *Quebec, 1759: The Siege and the Battle* (Toronto: Macmillan, 1959) is the classic account of the Battle of the Plains and its contexts. Donald E. Graves has recently updated and expanded it in a new edition (Toronto: Robin Brass Studio, 2002). Even this version of events at Quebec, however, is incomplete without reference to a remarkable analysis of astronomical and hydrographical information by Donald W. Olson, William D. Liddle, et al., "Perfect Tide, Ideal Moon: An Unappreciated Aspect of Wolfe's Generalship at Quebec, 1759," *William and Mary Quarterly*, 3rd ser., 59 (2002): 957–74. Frank McLynn paints the largest context for understanding Britain's *annus mirabilis* in a popular history, *1759: The Year Britain Became Master of the World* (New York: Atlantic Monthly Press, 2004).

Studies of individuals can allow an even closer approach to events than the examination of localities, groups, or even individual episodes. For Washington there are many; among the best for understanding this period in his life are Thomas A. Lewis, *For King and Country: George Washington, the Early Years* (New York: John Wiley and Sons, 1993); Don Higginbotham, *George Washington and the American Military Tradition* (Athens: University of Georgia Press, 1985); and Joseph Ellis, *His Excellency: George Washington* (New York: Alfred A. Knopf, 2004). Investigations of other significant or emblematic actors include Stephen Brumwell's finely nuanced study of Major Robert Rogers in the context of his Rangers' raid on the *réserve* of Saint Francis, *White Devil: A True Story of War, Savagery, and Vengeance in Colonial America* (Cambridge, Mass.: Da Capo Press, 2005); Nicholas B. Wainwright, *George Croghan: Wilderness Diplomat* (Chapel Hill: University of North Carolina Press for the Institute of Early American History and Culture, 1959); William G. Godfrey, *Pursuit of Profit and Preferment in Colonial North America: John Bradstreet's Quest* (Waterloo, Ontario: Wilfrid Laurier University Press, 1982); Milton W. Hamilton, *Sir William Johnson: Colo-*

nial American, 1715–1763 (Port Washington, N.Y.: Kennikat Press, 1976); Robert C. Alberts, *The Most Extraordinary Adventures of Major Robert Stobo* (Boston: Houghton Mifflin, 1965); Anthony F. C. Wallace, *King of the Delawares: Teedyuscung, 1700–1763* (Syracuse: Syracuse University Press, 1949; reprinted, 1990); Lee McCardell, *Ill-Starred General: Braddock of the Coldstream Guards* (Pittsburgh, Pa.: University of Pittsburgh Press, 1958; reprinted 1986); J. C. Long, *Lord Jeffery Amherst: A Soldier of the King* (New York: Macmillan, 1933); Stuart Reid, *Wolfe: The Career of General James Wolfe from Culloden to Quebec* (Rockville Center, N.Y.: Sarpedon Publishers, 2000); Jeremy Black, *The Elder Pitt* (New York: Cambridge University Press, 1992). Meriwether Liston Lewis, *Montcalm, the Marvelous Marquis* (New York: Vantage, 1961), is unfortunately the nearest approximation of a biography in English; nevertheless, the portrait of Montcalm by his chief aide in Edward P. Hamilton, ed., *Adventure in the Wilderness: The American Journals of Louis Antoine de Bougainville, 1756–60* (Norman, Okla.: University of Oklahoma Press, 1964), gives a keen notion of his qualities and character. Other memoirs and personal writings similarly animate the experience of war. See especially Andrew Gallup, ed., *Memoir of a French and Indian War Soldier: "Jolicoeur" Charles Bonin* (Westminster, Md.: Heritage Books, 1993); Christian Frederick Post, *Journey on the Forbidden Path: Chronicles of a Diplomatic Mission to the Allegheny Country* (Philadelphia: American Philosophical Society, 1999); Pierre Pouchot, *Memoirs of the Late War in North America Between France and England*, ed. Brian Leigh Dunnigan (Youngstown, N.Y.: Old Fort Niagara Association, 1994); Robert Kirkwood, *Through So Many Dangers: The Memoirs and Adventures of Robert Kirk, Late of the Royal Highland Regiment*, ed. Ian McCulloch and Timothy Todish (Fleischmanns, N.Y.: Purple Mountain Press, 2004); James E. Seaver, *A Narrative of the Life of Mrs. Mary Jemison*, ed. June Namias (Norman, Okla.: University of Oklahoma Press, 1992); Colin Calloway, ed., *North Country Captives: Selected Narratives of Indian Captivity from Vermont and New Hampshire* (Hanover, N.H.: University Press of New England, 1992); Robert Eastburn, *A Narrative of the Dangers and Sufferings of Robert Eastburn during His Captivity in the Years 1756–1757* (Fairfield, Wash.: Galleon Press, 1996); and Frederick Drimmer, ed., *Captured by Indians: Fifteen Firsthand Accounts, 1750–1870* (New York: Dover, 1985 [contains the memoirs of James Smith, Thomas Brown, and Alexander Henry]). The writings of George Washington can be found in an excellent edition by W. W. Abbot et al., eds., *The Papers of George Washington, Colonial Series*, 10 vols. (Charlottesville: University Press of Virginia, 1983–1995). Richard Middleton's expert selection and annotation make his edition of Amherst's papers, *Amherst and the Conquest of Canada* (London: Army Records Society, 2003), particularly valuable. Other worthwhile collections include Alexander C. Flick et al., eds., *The Papers of Sir William Johnson*, 14 vols. (Albany: University of the State of New York, 1921–1965); Charles Henry Lincoln, ed., *Correspondence of William Shirley, Governor of Massachusetts and Military Commander in North America, 1731–1760*, 2 vols. (New York: Macmillan, 1912); Gertrude Selwyn Kimball, ed., *Correspondence of William Pitt when Secretary of State with Colonial Governors and Military and Naval Commissioners in America*, 2 vols. (New York: Macmillan, 1906; reprinted New York: Kraus Reprints, 1969); Stanley M. Pargellis, ed., *Military Affairs in North America, 1748–1765* (London: Appleton-Century Company, 1936; reprinted Hamden, Conn.: Archon, 1969); Robert

Rogers, *The Annotated and Illustrated Journals of Major Robert Rogers*, ed. Timothy J. Todish (Fleischmanns, N.Y.: Purple Mountain Press, 2002); and E. B. O'Callaghan et al., eds., *Documents Relative to the Colonial History of the State of New York*, 15 vols. (Albany: Weed & Parsons, 1853–1887; reprinted New York: AMS, 1969).

Several scholarly articles in addition to those cited above help illuminate aspects of the Seven Years' War and its significance. Undoubtedly the most provocative and important of all is John M. Murrin, "The French and Indian War, the American Revolution, and the Counterfactual Hypothesis: Reflections on Lawrence Henry Gipson and John Shy," *Reviews in American History*, 1 (1973): 307–18; it should be read together with John Shy, "The Empire Remembered: Lawrence Henry Gipson, Historian," in Shy, *A People Numerous and Armed: Reflections on the Military Struggle for American Independence* (New York: Oxford University Press, 1976), 109–131, and Jack P. Greene, "The Seven Years' War and the American Revolution:The Causal Relationship Reconsidered," in Peter Marshall and Glyn Williams, eds., *The British Atlantic Empire before the American Revolution* (London: Frank Cass, 1980). Among the rest (and there are hundreds) the following are particularly useful. On disease and its impact, see D. Peter MacLeod, "Microbes and Muskets: Smallpox and the Participation of the Amerindian Allies of New France in the Seven Years' War," *Ethnohistory*, 39 (1992): 42–64; Bernhard Knollenberg, "General Amherst and Germ Warfare," *Mississippi Valley Historical Review*, 41 (1954): 489–95; and Elizabeth Fenn, "Biological Warfare in Eighteenth-Century North America: Beyond Jeffery Amherst," *Journal of American History*, 86 (2000): 1552–80. Canada's food shortages and their impact are admirably explicated in Jean Elizabeth Lunn, "Agriculture and War in Canada, 1740–1760," *Canadian Historical Review*, 16 (1935): 123–36. Various aspects of military tactics and logistics are treated in J. M. Hitsman and C. L. J. Bond, "The Assault Landing at Louisbourg, 1758," *Canadian Historical Review*, 35 (1954): 314–30; Peter Russell, "Redcoats in the Wilderness: British Officers and Irregular Warfare in Europe and America, 1740–1760," *William and Mary Quarterly*, 3rd ser., 35 (1978): 629–52; Leroy V. Eid, " 'A Kind of Running Fight': Indian Battlefield Tactics in the Late Eighteenth Century," *Western Pennsylvania Historical Magazine*, 71 (1988): 147–71; and Theodore Thayer, "The Army Contractors for the Niagara Campaign, 1755–1756," *William and Mary Quarterly*, 3rd ser., 14 (1957): 31–46. John R. Maass, " 'All This Poor Province Could Do': North Carolina and the Seven Years' War, 1757–1762," *North Carolina Historical Review*, 79 (2002), 50–89, scrupulously reconstructs the impact of the war on the politics of public finance in British North America's poorest colony.

Finally, in addition to the works by Daniel Marston and Seymour Schwartz cited above, numerous works splendidly illustrate the look of contemporary forts, people, clothing, and equipment. Among these the most notable are R. Scott Stephenson, *Clash of Empires: The British, French, and Indian War* (Pittsburgh: Historical Society of Western Pennsylvania, 2005); Charles Morse Stotz, *Outposts of the War for Empire: The French and English in Western Pennsylvania . . . 1749–1764* (Pittsburgh, Pa.: University of Pittsburgh Press, 1985; reprinted 2005); René Chartrand, *Colonial American Troops, 1610–1774*, 3 vols. (Oxford: Osprey, 2002), *Monongahela, 1754–1755: Washington's Defeat, Braddock's Disaster* (Oxford: Osprey, 2004), *Quebec 1759* (Oxford: Osprey, 1999), and *French Fortresses in North America, 1535–1763: Quebec, Montreal, Louisbourg, and*

New Orleans (Oxford: Osprey, 2005); Gary Zaboly, *American Colonial Ranger: The Northern Colonies, 1724–1764* (Oxford: Osprey, 2004); Timothy J. Todish, *America's First World War: The French and Indian War, 1754–1763* (Fleischmanns, N.Y.: Purple Mountain Press, 2002). Illustrated books shade over into books for children; among these, see especially Christopher Collier and James Lincoln Collier, *The French and Indian Wars, 1660–1763* (New York: Benchmark Books, 1998); Joy Hakim, *From Colonies to Country* (New York: Oxford University Press, 1993); Betsy Maestro and Giulio Maestro, *Struggle for a Continent: The French and Indian Wars, 1689–1763* (New York: HarperCollins, 2000).

Acknowledgments

Like all writers of historical syntheses, my greatest debt is to the other historians who have written on my topic. I have identified as many as possible in the bibliographic essay, but there are at least as many more whose work in related fields I have admired and whose scholarship and insights have influenced my approach. There is no graceful way to list them here, but I would be unforgivably remiss if I failed to acknowledge the most important one of all, Virginia DeJohn Anderson. No words can explain how much I have gained as a scholar from a quarter-century of intellectual companionship and conversation about every aspect of the practice of history. Nor can anything I might say adequately express my gratitude for the patience she has shown, and the emotional support and love she has unfailingly given, to a husband who is all too prone to self-absorption, and far too apt to become preoccupied with his work.

There are four people without whom this project could not have begun, much less reached fruition. Laura Smith Fisher, senior vice president of the Allegheny Conference on Community Development, director of French and Indian War 250, Inc., and co-executive producer of the documentary series *The War That Made America*, first urged me to write a companion volume, then saw to it that I made good on my promise to do so. Laura has been a tireless advocate, cheerleader, and friend to book and author alike, and for all those things I am truly grateful. Scott Stephenson freely lent his scholarly counsel, as well as his remarkable knowledge of art and artifacts, to this project. His hand is evident throughout, and the appearance of his name on the title page represents at best an inadequate acknowledgment of the contribution he has made. For years now Lisa Adams of the Garamond Agency has looked after my interests and preserved my sanity by her expert parsing of contracts, negotiation of schedules, and performance of every manner of technical task related to publishing. Most of all, however, whenever I have needed the counsel of a calm, wise, and thoroughly knowledgeable friend, she has been there to provide it. Finally, while Drew Cayton would doubtless be the last to admit it, he too had a crucial role. As sounding board, literary consultant, amateur headshrinker, sometime ghostwriter, and steadfast friend he has no peer, and in all those capacities he has helped me make an end of this book.

Consulting in the writing of a television documentary was an endlessly illuminating experience for me, and contributed greatly to the shaping of this narrative. George Miles, president and chief executive officer of WQED Multimedia, was an enthusiastic supporter of the film project from its inception more than five years ago. The advocacy and support of Mike Watson, vice president and director of the Richard King Mellon Foundation, and the enormous personal commitment of Dick and Prosser Mellon were crucial to the making of the series. Crucial in another way were the many consultants who offered advice and support: Darren Bonaparte, Jay Cassel, Michael Galban, and Scott Stephenson, who participated directly in the filming and offered expert advice on scripts; and Drew Cayton, Dave Edmunds, Bill Hart, Holly Mayer, John Murrin, Dan Richter, John Shy, and Ian Steele, who like me had never laid eyes on a set but whose astute criticism of treatments and scripts was fundamental to maintaining the quality of the film's historical interpretations. Working with the filmmakers themselves—co-executive producer Deb Acklin; project director Geoff Miller; Ben Loeterman and Eric Stange, the writer-directors; Kerry Falvey, the staff researcher and production assistant, and Didier Fontaine and Jamie Pennisi—was always a pleasure, and taught me that books are only one way to communicate the drama and character of past events to general audiences. I have learned an enormous amount from my association with them; I hope they gained something more than frustration in return.

At Viking, this book and its author benefited from the ministrations of three editorial guardian angels—Brett Kelly, Jane von Mehren, and Wendy Wolf—as well as the indefatigable attention of Beth Greenfeld as copy editor, Nancy Resnick as designer, Barbara Campo as production editor, and Laura Ogar as indexer. No author could have had better treatment, more timely encouragement, or more welcome aid than I did, and for all of those gifts I am deeply grateful.

Several institutions have contributed to this project as well. Six years ago the Allegheny Conference on Community Development first sponsored an effort to use French and Indian War–era historic sites in the Pittsburgh area as foci for commemorating the 250th anniversary of the conflict. Since then, the commemoration has spawned a not-for-profit corporation, French and Indian War 250, Inc., which fosters educational and other programs in twenty-six states. Both organizations have provided generous support for the film and this book. The University of Colorado at Boulder, my academic home, has also sustained the project by releasing me from teaching responsibilities in the spring term of 2004 so I could read and write without interruption. I am deeply grateful to Provost (now Chancellor) Phil DiStefano, Dean Todd Gleeson, and the director of the Center of Humanities and Arts, Jeff Cox, for this support.

Colleagues and friends at the University of Colorado and elsewhere have continued to sustain me as they have for years. Peter Boag, Susan Buckley, Ira Chernus, Brian DeLay, Robert Ferry, Randy Fertel, Matthew Gerber, Julie Greene, John Grenier, Martha Hanna, Robert Hanna, Eric Hinderaker, Warren Hofstra, Susan Kent, Thea Lindquist, Eric Love, Gloria Main, Mark Pittenger, Lynne Squilla, and Dennis Van Gerven have contributed more than they realize to this book, by making it possible to live and write within a community of scholarly endeavor and personal friendship. Similarly (and much more directly) by his careful proofreading of the manuscript when the final deadline loomed, Samuel DeJohn Anderson also played a large and helpful role. I doubt that any writer ever had a better proofreader; I know that no father ever had a better son.

Finally, the gaffers of Fort Collins know full well who they are and why they are of such singular importance to me. The debts that I owe them are ones I can never repay. Nothing could give me greater pleasure than dedicating this volume to them, with an admiration and affection that has only grown with the passage of the decades since they changed my life forever.

Index

Page numbers in *italics* refer to illustrations.

AVAILABLE FROM PENGUIN BOOKS

The Dominion of War

Empire and Liberty in North America, 1500–2000

Fred Anderson and Andrew Cayton

Americans often think of their nation's history as a movement toward ever-greater democracy, equality, and freedom. Wars in this story are understood both as necessary to defend those values and as exceptions to the rule of peaceful progress. In *The Dominion of War,* historians Fred Anderson and Andrew Cayton boldly reinterpret the development of the United States, arguing instead that war has played a leading role in shaping North America from the sixteenth century to the present.

HB 10.27.2023 0613